On Becoming

MW01283701

Advances in Consciousness Research

Advances in Consciousness Research provides a forum for scholars from different scientific disciplines and fields of knowledge who study consciousness in its multifaceted aspects. Thus the Series will include (but not be limited to) the various areas of cognitive science, including cognitive psychology, linguistics, brain science and philosophy. The orientation of the Series is toward developing new interdisciplinary and integrative approaches for the investigation, description and theory of consciousness, as well as the practical consequences of this research for the individual and society.

Series B: Research in progress. Experimental, descriptive and clinical research in consciousness.

Editor

Maxim I. Stamenov
Bulgarian Academy of Sciences

Editorial Board

David Chalmers, *University of Arizona*
Gordon G. Globus, *University of California at Irvine*
Ray Jackendoff, *Brandeis University*
Christof Koch, *California Institute of Technology*
Stephen Kosslyn, *Harvard University*
Earl Mac Cormac, *Duke University*
George Mandler, *University of California at San Diego*
John R. Searle, *University of California at Berkeley*
Petra Stoerig, *Universität Düsseldorf*
† Francisco Varela, *C.R.E.A., Ecole Polytechnique, Paris*

Volume 43

On Becoming Aware: A pragmatics of experiencing
Edited by Natalie Depraz, Francisco J. Varela and Pierre Vermersch

On Becoming Aware
A pragmatics of experiencing

Natalie Depraz
Université de la Sorbonne (Paris IV)

Francisco J. Varela
LENA, CNRS & CREA, Paris

Pierre Vermersch
CNRS, Paris

John Benjamins Publishing Company
Amsterdam / Philadelphia

TM The paper used in this publication meets the minimum requirements of American National Standard for Information Sciences – Permanence of Paper for Printed Library Materials, ANSI z39.48-1984.

Library of Congress Cataloging-in-Publication Data

On Becoming Aware : A pragmatics of experiencing / edited by Natalie Depraz, Francisco J. Varela and Pierre Vermersch.
    p. cm. (Advances in Consciousness Research, ISSN 1381–589X ; v. 43)
    Includes bibliographical references and indexes.
    1. Experience. 2. Awareness. I. Depraz, Natalie. II. Varela, Francisco J., 1946- III. Vermersch, Pierre. IV. Series.

    B105.E9 O5 2002
128´.4-dc21   2002074567
ISBN 90 272 5167 3 (Eur.) / 1 58811 243 8 (US) (Hb; alk. paper)
ISBN 90 272 5163 0 (Eur.) / 1 58811 216 0 (US) (Pb; alk. paper)

© 2003 – John Benjamins B.V.
No part of this book may be reproduced in any form, by print, photoprint, microfilm, or any other means, without written permission from the publisher.

John Benjamins Publishing Co. · P.O. Box 36224 · 1020 ME Amsterdam · The Netherlands
John Benjamins North America · P.O. Box 27519 · Philadelphia PA 19118-0519 · USA

Table of contents

Introduction
A guide for the perplexed

What are we up to?

In this book we seek *the sources and means for a disciplined practical approach to exploring human experience.* Since that's already quite a program, please be patient while we explain what we mean.

A practical approach to human experience

The spirit of this book is entirely *pragmatic*, for at least two related reasons. First of all, because of our *approach*: we will have to discover what pertains to our question as we go along; we will have to learn on the job, rather than give you ready-made results. *Une dynamique d'amorçage* in the french original. The verb *amorcer* means to bait, to entice, to start or begin, to prime. The intended meaning here is to help something get going by giving it a little help, like pushing a car to jump-start it, running some fluid through a pump in order to let it begin working on its own, or picking up some tricks of the trade from your elders while an apprentice. We will use "jump-start," "learning as we go along," or "learning on the job," and so on to translate *une dynamique d'amorçage*. In other words, we must keep things open in our exploration of this new field, a *terra incognita* of which we know almost nothing. We proceed armed only with a sketchy map and some surveyor's tools, and so the progressive unfolding of the book follows the very emergence of conscious activity as it happens.

Secondly, because of our *theme*: since we are not trying to set forth *a priori* a new theory of experience as the neo-Kantians might have done, but instead want to describe an activity, a concrete *praxis*, we investigate conscious activity in so far as it perceives itself unfolding in an operative and immanent mode, at once habitual and pre-reflective.

What is at stake in becoming aware?

Briefly put, we wish to understand how we come to examine what we live through. That is, we wish to understand that most peculiar of human acts: becoming aware of our own mental life. Now the range of experience of which we can become aware is vast. It includes not only all the ordinary dimensions of human life, (perception, motion, memory, imagination, speech, everyday social interactions), as well as cognitive events that can be precisely defined as tasks in laboratory experiments, (for example, a protocol for visual attention), but also manifestations of mental life more fraught with meaning, (dreaming, intense emotions, social tensions, altered states of consciousness). Among all these acts of consciousness which remain in a condition of immanence, there lives, unperceived, a form of pre-reflexivity on the basis of which consciousness is able to perceive its very self at work.

Hence our central assertion in this work is that this immanent ability or capacity is habitually ignored or at best practiced unsystematically, that is to say, blindly, and that exploring human experience amounts to developing and cultivating this basic ability. What type of "reflexivity" is proper for exploring without disembodying this unreflected level of our life, traversed as it is by habitual patterns and sedimented experiences? In other words, how do we gain access to this pre-reflective and pre-given zone of our subjectivity in making it conscious? Other than what is merely on the fringe of consciousness, are there other levels of pre-noetic experience that become available when rigorously explored? These are open questions. Only a hands-on, non-dogmatic attitude can lead to progress, and that is what animates this book.

What do we mean by experience?

We mean the lived, *first-hand* acquaintance with, and account of, the entire span of our minds and actions, with the emphasis not on the context of the action but on the immediate and embodied, and thus inextricably personal, nature of the content of the action. Experience is always that which a *singular* subject is subjected to *at any given time and place*, that to which s/he has access "in the first person."

The experience of a given subject is at once precise, concrete, and individuated. It is centered on particular spatio-temporal parameters, and is thus new and different each time: at the same time it covers the whole of the already lived and sedimented life of the experiencing subject. That is why it is very difficult to speak of subjective experience without being equally interested in the full range of lived conscious activity, a life that is lived both innerly and in relationship with the outside world (in phenomenological terms: immanently *and* intentionally), that is, a life related to itself *and* related to objects, be they perceptive, affective or indeed for that matter, apperceptive, self-reflective.

We will thus speak, in the terms of various disciplines, of "first-hand accounts", "first-person access", "introspection", "phenomenal data", or "lived experiences (*vécus, Erlebnisse*)", but we will also – acknowledging the realm of embodied habits which the process of becoming aware is to reveal – speak of the unconscious, the preconscious, the pre-reflective, the self-present, the pre-noetic, the pre-predicative, or of one's sedimented habitual life or *habitus*. As the book unfolds we hope the differences and articulations of these various terms will become apparent.

To whom are we talking?

It should not be surprising that the aim of this book raises many questions. Our purpose, as we said, is not to form a theory, system, or unifying philosophy of experience and consciousness. Rather, we seek the explicit characterization of a very specific human *ability:* becoming aware as *coming to know in the first person.* We want to find the commonalities and isomorphisms between the practices found in different domains for different reasons. Specifically, we are referring to the need for first-person data in the cognitive neurosciences, the need for reduction as a concrete and embodied *praxis* in phenomenology, the need for introspection in cognitive psychology, the need for various know-hows in a wide range of psychotherapies, and the needs of various spiritual practices which highlight the "examination of consciousness" and the "practice of effortless effort". We take a long-range view of these various resources in working toward finding a common pattern. Impossible, you say? Perhaps, but we firmly believe we are on to something of value, which we hope those readers who make it past the Introduction will see for themselves!

The results presented here will thus stand or fall only in so far as they can provide the means for reaching, *via a disciplined practice*, the experience characteristic of all the domains we mention above. In the contemporary context, given the way this book integrates the typically disjointed discourses of the cognitive sciences, applied psychology, philosophy, and spiritual traditions, it has no direct antecedents. Perhaps our closest ancestor in the English-speaking world is the pioneering work of Gendlin (1962/1997). As far as continental philosophy is concerned, Ricoeur (1950/1988) is the only one, as far as we know, to have broached this issue in his description of numerous "practical acts of consciousness (attention, emotion, effort, habit)". This was written before he abandoned his project in favor of hermeneutics. In fact, the description of the passage from involuntary to voluntary is another possible formulation, no doubt the most classical, of what we attempt in this work.

Because of this lack of precedents we are in trouble, since we have no clearly defined audience. Our hunch is that we are addressing ourselves primarily to those people *within* each of the domains we mention above who have become sensitive to the need for further work on the method of exploring experience. If you are a cognitive scientist who just can't stand the very idea of working with first-person data, then you might as well just put this book down right now. Likewise if you are a philosopher who doesn't find the phenomenological reduction and the *epoche* to be the crucial truly operative method of phenomenology. And so on.

Are you still there? Good. This probably means that, being familiar with one of our domains, you are already sensitized to some of their internal shortcomings. In other words, you the reader might be able to identify with one or another of the following scenarios:

1. You are a research neuroscientist and it is beginning to dawn on you that first-person accounts are becoming more and more important for exploiting the latest tools of the trade, such as brain imaging.
2. You are a philosopher whose heightened sensitivity to phenomenology extends to actually engaging in new, fresh examinations and descriptions of experience, as opposed to the study of texts in the phenomenological tradition.
3. You are a research psychologist dissatisfied with the current tools for accessing subjective contents.
4. You are involved in one of the many professions dealing with human transformation, such as education, remedial therapies, knowledge management, and so on, and you know how difficult it is to have adequate guides for what clients have to do in their daily therapeutic work.
5. You are personally interested in a spiritual tradition that engages in self-analysis and a close examination of the sources of experience, and you are finding it necessary to connect your particular spiritual tradition with a broader, secular perspective.

If any of these scenarios, or ones similar to them, pop up in your life, then this book will help you by providing a sketch of the very act of becoming aware, the common ground of all these domains. You are not alone in your concerns, and there's a lot to gain by having a look around!

More trouble: Three heads, six hands, one book

Given the scope and ambition of our book it would be silly to imagine that any one person could pull it off. It is no surprise then that this is a collective effort, but this poses many problems, including finding a single voice. To achieve such unity would have taken many more years of work, though, so rather than putting up with such a delay we have gone ahead with what we have. We will just have to ask our readers to forgive the occasional infelicities.

Since our own individual areas of work motivated this pragmatic inquiry, let us now speak about them. Depraz is a philosopher who has worked for many years in contemporary Husserlian phenomenology. Varela is a cognitive neuroscientist who works both in the laboratory and in theoretical biology. Vermersch is a research psychologist who has become interested in the development of methods of making knowledge explicit. Beyond these professional backgrounds each one of us has an interest in one or several spiritual traditions dealing with human transformation. *Caveat lector*: these inspirational sources are not to be simply assigned to the author of the essays, but rather to a complex network of concerns shared by the three of us, albeit with different degrees of emphasis and expertise.

How did such a joint work come about?

The history of this book is worth telling at this point. The authors met in december 1994 in Vermersch's Seminar on "Psychologie et Phénoménologie." We each gave a presentation and immediately found a resonance between our texts, leading to intense discussions through the summer, when we decided to bring our work together. The unifying spark was introduced by Vermersch's piece, which went far beyond his original presentation, and was to provide a context for our discussions. That tentative, open-ended and incomplete manuscript was the seed for this book.

Between then and now every line of the book has been reworked, with several new chapters added and some older ones deleted. In fact it was *the very process of writing* that led us to our core results, since we had not foreseen many of them when we started, and they did not fully come together until the summer of 1997. On a pleasant country retreat during that time we produced a version close to the present one. On the whole, we would say that this book is the record of a discovery voyage rather than a report of pre-established findings. This also means that throughout all the writing stages we have become immersed in each other's language, ideas and styles to the extent that what we say here we say with a collective voice. Thus in this six-handed performance we have equally shared responsibilities; in particular, we would like to stress that the order of authors' names is strictly alphabetical.

So what's the bottom line?

You will find the core of the book in Part I. There we set forth a methodical and practical description, the dynamic of becoming aware. We distinguish five principal steps.

Step 1: the movement of *epoche* as an initial suspension, repeated at each step.
Step 2: the recognition of intuitive evidence as the criterion of truth internal to each act.
Step 3: the expression of the content of each act.
Step 4: the intersubjective validation of findings from Step 3.
Step 5: the becoming aware of the multi-layered temporality of each act.

The first two steps form, strictly speaking, the kernel of each act of becoming aware (what we call the Basic Cycle); the two following steps inscribe the act in its communicability and objectification; the final, transversal, step reveals the unique temporal dynamic of each act. Obviously this thumbnail sketch remains mysterious and silent before it is fleshed out. But we set it forth here so you might see both the nature and limits of the research we are offering.

Our main contribution is the formulation of a research program:
A common ground for a multiplicity of approaches to becoming aware

In other words, this is not a fully articulated book. It is more like a Progress Report: sufficiently detailed to be communicated and shared, but not yet mature enough to warrant a "definitive" presentation. In fact, all three of us took off from the writing of this book in our own different directions, without spending too much time on the subtleties of its expression. Writing this book opened our eyes; in that spirit we share it with you the reader.

Why isn't this just psychology?

One might think that studying becoming aware, the very structure of reflective activity, should legitimately be the concern of a psychology research program. But that's easy to say! As if it were only a matter of studying this structure from an experimental point of view, that is to say from a first-person (and, as we will see, a second-person) point of view. But this is precisely what most of scientific psychology has spent a century rejecting, disqualifying and ignoring. We acknowledge that after the downfall of behaviorism, experimental psychology and cognitive science have opened themselves up to considering mental contents and verbal reports. But these are merely the tip of the iceberg of the full range of a person's lived experience.

This paradox can only be solved if psychology reinvests introspection while modernizing it, perfecting its technique and refreshing it with a practical knowledge at once direct and formalized. However, such a conversion does not only imply a renewed and rigorous methodology, but also precise descriptions of subjective experience. Now the prolonged absence of psychology from these grounds means that one has only a few psychological materials at one's disposal. Hence the necessity of turning to both the immanent mode of categorization of practitioners (teachers, psychotherapists, coaches, trainers) and to the remarkable source of *psychological* inspiration contained in the descriptive work of Husserl. If our work is going to take its rightful place in a psychology research program, it's only going to happen via an opening up to a "psycho-phenomenology." In this sense our book can be seen as a re-awakening of introspective psychology.

Isn't this book just more phenomenology?

Of course, beyond the practical ontology of this book, another important common denominator is the phenomenological *approach* we adopt here even as we re-appropriate and renew it. But, from the outset, we should clear up a certain number of misunderstandings that are attached to the term "phenomenology." Among philosophers, it mostly refers to the tradition founded by Husserl and pursued by (among the most well-known) Heidegger, Merleau-Ponty, Sartre, and then reinvigorated by Levinas and Michel Henry. Among psychologists and sociologists along the lines of Schütz and Garfinkel it refers to an interest in describing and categorizing concrete experience. Among cognitive scientists it has yet another usage, referring to the still controversial possibility of a first-person access to data which are scientifically credible, that is, objective.

There are thus several usages of this term, more or less restricted, which range from 1) traditional texts to 2) an interest in returning to first person concrete experience. Hence a certain conceptual hesitation, indeed a terminological blurriness, surrounds the contemporary use of this term. We ourselves insist on experience in a wide sense, yet 1) centered on its concrete singularity, and with reference to 2) its effective workings, its *praxis*, and 3) to its procedural description. With this range of meaning, the "phenomenology" we invoke evidently borrows from the sense of the term current in the human and cognitive sciences – hence the search for a methodology oriented to gaining access to such singular experience – all the while calling upon the resources of meaning and rigor inherent in a still-lively phenomenological philosophy.

Don't you know that contemporary philosophers have shown that experience is not something that can be "explored"?

We acknowledge that our pragmatic orientation is likely to leave some readers a bit cold. The skeptical reader will no doubt want to raise perhaps the most fundamental objection to our inquiry, namely: "How do you know that by exploring experience with a method you are not, in fact, deforming or even creating what you claim to 'experience'? Experience being what it is, what is the possible meaning of your so-called 'examination' of it?"

We can call this the "excavation fallacy," or in philosophical terms, the *hermeneutical* objection (inspired as it is by a Heideggerian move). In still another formulation, this is the *deconstructive* objection, based on post-modern philosophical analysis (mostly derived from Derrida). All these objections go to the heart of our project here. They all emphasize the claim that there is no such thing as a "deep" pre-linguistic layer of experience, since any account is "always already" enfolded in language. Hence any new account will be only an inflection of linguistic practices that "go all the way down."

We might as well be direct on this point. If you are an utterly convinced hermeneut or Derridean, then you might as well put this book down right now and save yourself some time and trouble, for we cannot offer an air-tight argument that precludes all the possible flaws and traps of our approach. We can only offer what we hope are prudent and flexible answers to the above objections. We unabashedly admit that in some basic sense there is indeed a significant problem posed to our project by these objections, and no *a priori* arguments or methodological contortions are going to solve this problem for us with a wave of the wand. It seems indeed inevitable that any method will be part and parcel of the kinds of entities and properties invented by that method.

This is, among other things, true in the most consecrated forms of natural science, as recent scholarship has made abundantly clear. For instance, the ideas about the vacuum and ether, the construction and design of the air pump, and the social milieu where Boyle worked at the gestation of the Royal Society, were all inseparable ingredients of this fundamental advance in physics (Shapin & Shaeffer 1994). The vacuum is, as Latour put it, a quasi-object, partly social-instrumental, partly empirical-physical (Latour 1995). And if this is the case for the so-called hard sciences, it is all the more so for first-person disciplines which are still in gestation.

But this problem is also found in philosophy texts which concern, more or less, the experience of the author. Describing experience implies using a set of categories which will always make up an interpretive grid. Moreover, description is from the start an explication (an instance of *Auslegung*), at once reflective and comprehensive. Whether it is Husserl, Heidegger, or Ricoeur, each of these philosophers has clearly put at the center of his enterprise the explication of the meaning of experience, although they do so in distinct modes (Dastur 1992).

Acknowledging all this means not getting too shook up about the fact that *no* methodological approach to experience is neutral; they all inevitably interpret their phenomenal data. The hermeneutical dimension of the process is inescapable: every examination is an interpretation, and all interpretation reveals and conceals at the same time. But it does not follow that a disciplined approach to experience creates nothing but artifacts or a "deformed" version of the way experience "really" is. There are at least two arguments to support this stance.

First, the entire history of the natural sciences goes to show that although its objects *are* indeed quasi-objects, and inescapably hermeneutical to boot, they are nonetheless also inextricably constrained by their empirical appearance and reality. Vacuums and ether are not "mere" artifacts of social practices, nor are they simply "deformed" from some pre-given transcendental purity. *Mutatis mutandis,* the exploration of experience will suffer, along with all other methodological investigations, from cultural expectations and instrumental bias, but there is no evidence that the phenomenal data gathered are not equally constrained by the very reality of conscious contents. Thus the descriptions we can produce through the act of becoming aware as we describe it in Part I are not taken here as solid "facts," but as valid intersubjective items of knowledge, as quasi-objects of a cognitive kind. No more, but also, no less.

The second argument is that human experience is not a fixed, predelineated domain, but is instead changing, changeable, and fluid. If you undergo disciplined training in musical performance, the newly acquired skills of distinguishing sounds, of being sensitive to musical phrasing and ensemble playing, are undeniable changes in your capabilities of experience. But this means that experience is explored and modified by such disciplined procedures in non-arbitrary ways. Similarly, if we think of psychotherapeutic practices – even if one can be skeptical about their overall efficacy in dealing with human discontent at one level – the accumulated experience of psychotherapy indicates that the client's experience is transformed by the work they do in the therapeutic context. We might also consider the example of anthropological work on the practices, rites and customs of a given cultural group. Anthropologists do not remain untouched by their immersion in the foreign culture, just as the "natives" see their conception of the other modified by the presence of such strangers. However, this mutual intersubjective transformation is not without rules or results, as the example of the "observer participation" in ethnology shows us.

In other words, we are trying to avoid two unilateral extremes that we see as nonsensical or absurd: 1) claiming that experience is standard, raw, pure or ineffable; 2) claiming that all our experience is always already molded or even deformed by the language we use. All we have is experience at its own level of examination, depending on the kinds of effort and methods brought into play in that very examination. Experience moves and changes, and its exploration is already part of human life, even if the exploration has different objectives than the experience it explores.

It should be clear by now that we want to position ourselves in *a prudent but daring middle ground.* On the one hand, we wish to explore fully the tools available for first-person accounts. On the other hand, we do not claim that such an access is method-free or "natural" in any privileged sense. This mixed stance is yet another manifestation of the pragmatic spirit of this work.

Do I have to read Part II?

Perhaps not at all. As we have already said, Part II presents our motivations for exploring experience. We include it to reach out to all the different kinds of people we anticipate will read this book. It provides a kind of statement of what led each of us, to different degrees, to undertake the research project outlined in Part I. Reading Part II is therefore not essential to getting at what we want to say, but it may be of interest by providing a background to those domains that are *un*familiar to the reader.

Consequently, Part II is laid out according to the interests of the authors. Each essay is signed individually, with the exception of Chapter V, which is dedicated to practice, and which constitutes a synthesis of the different approaches to this question.

An invitation

We hope we have clarified some of the contents and difficulties of our book, as well as shown how important it is to open up this area of work. The ability to become aware of experience simply cannot remain unexamined and underdeveloped without seriously compromising our ability to meet a major challenge today facing several areas of research, practice, and indeed, human life. Please read on and judge for yourself how well we are meeting that challenge. Welcome to the inquiry. We hope you will be able to learn on the go, just as we did.

Acknowledgments

This work would not have been possible at all without the generous support of various people and institutions. We would first like to thank Amy Cohen-Varela, Evan Thompson, Dan Zahavi, and Bernardt Waldenfels for their comments on earlier drafts. Another special thanks to Amy and Evan who provided N. Depraz with precious critical comments while she was revising the whole manuscript before submitting the final version to the Publisher during the Fall 2001. Among institutions we would like to thank, first and foremost, the *Centre National de la Recherche Scientifique* (CNRS) where P. Vermersch is a research scientist and where F. Varela has been till his death intensively active. The CNRS was amazingly flexible in allowing both of them the time to pursue this unusual project. N. Depraz also benefitted from a position with the CNRS, *via* Fondation Thiers (1994–1997). We would also like to thank the ENS Fontenay-St. Cloud and the Archives-Husserl at the ENS Ulm, Paris.

The Section 1.2 ("Epoche") of Chapter 1 ("The basic cycle") (Part I) has been published first (though without the examples) in French under the title: "L'épochè phénoménologique comme *praxis*" (in: *Etudes phénoménologiques*, déc. 2000) and in English: "The gesture of awareness, an account of its structural dynamics" (in: M. Velmans ed., *Investigating phenomenal consciousness*, Amsterdam, Benjamins Press, 2001); it will be published shortly in German under the title: "Die phänomenologische Epochè als *Praxis*" (in: R. Kühn ed.,

Epochè und Reduktion, K. Alber Verlag, Freiburg). We want to thank the Journals and the Editors for having welcomed this core-section of the book and for having accepted it to be published again in its exemplified version in the present volume.

Francisco wrote directly in American English Chapter 4.1; John Protevi translated Part I, Christopher Macan Chapters 4.2 and 6.1/6.2, Matthew Sanderson Chapter 5 and Gregory Sadler Chapter 7; Amy Cohen-Varela kindly agreed (as a Psychoanalyst) to write the "example" concerning the Session of Psychoanalysis (in Chapter 2.1), to translate both Conclusion and Postface and (as a native American speaker) to check the final version. Antoine Lutz (Lena, Salpêtrière) formatted the final version and finalized the tapuscript for the Editor: we wish to express our gratitude to them.

PART I

The structural dynamics of becoming aware

CHAPTER 1

The basic cycle

1.1. Overall presentation

Entering into the inquiry

As we have already said, our work here springs from relatively independent disciplines. In one very real sense, it would be easier for you to enter into the structural dynamics of the act of becoming aware *after* you have been introduced to our motivations, since they would give you some concrete contexts for our results. Thus, although we only provide such details in Part II, logically they should perhaps be read first. However, since so much preliminary detail might be too tedious, we have decided to sketch out the bare outlines of these motivations and then plunge right into the heart of the act of becoming aware. We will thus relegate the detailed discussion of motivations for studying the act of becoming aware until later, where they can be treated more fully. This strategy is consistent with our main point: what we are calling "the act of becoming aware" is a human act that is so basic that it is quite independent of the contexts in which one becomes aware of one's own conscious activity. Consequently, the act of becoming aware has a variety of names; we use several of them interchangeably, depending on context and ease of presentation: *reflecting* act (*acte réfléchissant*) in the psychological context, *reduction* or reductive act in its peculiar phenomenological (and not scientific) meaning, *mindfulness* (in the buddhist meditation).

The term "reflecting act" is a technical term for us. We distinguish it, and the specific mental act it designates, from "reflection," "reflexive" and "reflective" act. To avoid stylistic stiffness we also use as synonymous with "reflecting act" the English phrase "becoming aware," (though the French expression "*la prise de la conscience*" has a more distinctly psychological and indeed Piagetian connotation). The expressions "motivated reduction" or "reductive act" are meant to underline the practical and embodied dimension, the *praxis* of this central phenomenological method. Finally, the Buddhist term "mindfulness" (in the sense of "attentive presence") is also sometimes used as synonymous with the above terms.

Although we leave for later the detailed presentation of the sources of our motivation, we will sketch them here for the sake of clarity before embarking on our discussion proper. There are essentially four points of view you need to keep in mind:

The Scientific Researcher: in Chapter IV we take up the issue from the point of view of the scientific researcher seeking ideas and tools for further research. The motivation for a researcher needs to be formulated by means of two distinct but interrelated scientific traditions.

On the one hand there is the current field of the *cognitive sciences.* The main issue here is the recent re-discovery of consciousness as a legitimate, even crucial, scientific problem. Relegated to the margins since the inception of the new sciences of mind, consciousness is now making a rapid comeback, in response to which many philosophers have weighed in with their views and many researchers have taken up the challenge in the laboratory. Within this context the first-person approach finally finds a home.

On the other hand we refer just as much to the older tradition of *psychology* in all its guises, especially those concerning the role of introspection and subjective experience, only a part of which is alive in the contemporary cognitive sciences. Since these two streams are both historically and sociologically distinct, we discuss them separately.

The Psychological Practitioner: in Chapter V we present the motivations relevant to those psychological disciplines concerned more with *practical applications* and interventions than with basic research. This area is important since, as we will see, a client's request for assistance provides a hands-on, pragmatic setting for issues that basic research has for the most part neglected. At the same time, these concerns highlight the central role of *praxis* in our work.

The Philosophical Thinker: in Chapter VI we take up *philosophical* motivations, that is, the philosophical stakes of our inquiry. We take our orientation here from the phenomenological tradition as begun by Husserl and continued by others. The central concern of this tradition is entirely consonant with what we want to explore, and phenomenology has been a constant source of philosophical insight for us. Here it provides an explicit conceptual framework for many of the ideas we develop, including the central notion of *reduction* as the method of phenomenology.

The Spiritual Seeker: in Chapter VII we address the realm of spiritual traditions, since here too we find a phenomenological *praxis* of human experience, albeit one uniquely oriented to human transformation and improvement. The Buddhist tradition of mind examination and training serves as an exemplary detailed case study for other traditions of human wisdom, Western and non-Western alike, which, although they might be just as concerned with phenomenological *praxis* as Buddhism, did not develop such precise practical techniques.

All these motivations pervade what we present here, but must now disappear as such, so that we may examine our main concern: the act of becoming aware.

The methodological stakes of phenomenological practice

The goal of this insert is to define more closely the *practical wager* that our description of the act of becoming aware represents. What is at stake here is the unified logic of our proposed journey. The general line of demarcation delineates what is effectively accomplished by a given subject and what is only thought, what is only the object of theory, speculation, or even discourse.

1. Methodology

In order to develop a method adequate to the act of becoming aware we must learn as we go along. We have to discover what our question entails as we explore its contours, that is, we have to have an open exploration, without positions staked out ahead of time and without establishing concepts definitively defined at the outset. In light of our disciplinary fields, we will speak of the "logic of emergence or non-linearity" (cognitive sciences), of "circular causality" (Piagetian psychology), or of "genetic or generative logic" (Husserlian phenomenology). In all these cases, an open questioning whose answers are not given ahead of time but instead surge forth from the research itself, is opposed to a system presented from the outset via a grid of definitions, such as Spinoza's *Ethics* or Kant's *Critique of Pure Reason*, or indeed, any static exposition of the research results of a theory.

2. Practical Horizon

This is the heart of the general method put into practice here. For us, *practice* means the level of action as opposed to theory. Practice is thus opposed to declaration, to contemplation, or to a discourse *on* practice; it is synonymous with "doing" [*le faire*]. According to the field and author in question, we will refer to *pragmatism* (in Anglophone philosophy), to *praxis* (in continental philosophy of a Marxist inspiration), or to *practice and practitioners* (applied psychology). Let us define how we see each term.

Pragmatism: the implementation of techniques, means and know-how. In pragmatism, one cares about how well something adapts to its situation rather than how well one formulates *a priori* principles. From this viewpoint, truth consists in the success, efficacy, and functionality of the realized action.

Praxis: the plane of action as self-sufficient conduct. In *praxis*, conduct finds its truth in itself and does not need a prepared blueprint. *Praxis* also entails changing the world and yourself by concrete action.

Practice: this term has at least two distinct meanings. In philosophy it is often associated with morals and ethics, what is done in the light of an ethical criterion or preference. In this sense, it is attached only to the decision behind an action, not to the results of that action. On the other hand, in applied industrial psychology, practice designates doing something, the accomplishment of a task. In this book we are concerned with this second sense of "practice."

Practitioners (professional) [«*les praticiens*»]: even though any professional has, in going about their duties, a practice (thereby including theoretical practice, a practice that uses the imagination, and so on), we will reserve, in accordance with its current meaning, the term "practitioner" for all those whose work is measured in terms of its "bottom line," its "practical success": teachers, psychotherapists, consultants, trainers, and rehabilitation therapists, of course, but also technicians, artisans, instrumentalists, athletes, clinical physicians, surgeons, midwives, and so on.

Practitioners (spiritual) [«*les pratiquants*»]: rather than the usual sense of "practitioner," which refers to someone with professional know-how, "practitioner" can also have a religious and/or spiritual connotation, designating whoever concretely invests religious ritual by embodying it in specific gestures or attitudes, whoever puts into practice the specific techniques of a given meditative path.

Despite these differences, one hears both instances referred to as types of *practice*: "practicing an instrument or a sport," and "a religious practice, practicing meditation."

3. The character of our descriptions

We want to stress the "working" [*en acte*] or "in process" [*en devenir*] character of our descriptions, that is, their "processual" character. Our descriptions are made on the move, they work themselves out as they go along, rather than having some sort of internal coherence based on the rigid and fixed univocity of the categories they employ. That doesn't mean our categories are not precise, but it does mean that they are born from the very movement of description as it works itself out, rather than being established in advance.

Here again, in light of our various background disciplines, we will use distinct yet convergent expressions when we need to.

Procedural description: This is a step-by-step description of an action, detailing the time it takes and the parts involved at each step. This notion originates both from industrial psychology and from the scientific study of education. By extension, in artificial intelligence and software engineering, it designates the presentation of information (instructions, operations) that allows you to accomplish some particular task with the software, rather than a declarative presentation, which defines each and every element of the program without reference to any one particular task.

The couple *declarative/procedural* in fact emphasizes an uncoupling of the two kinds of knowledge. Procedural knowledge – even if in principle founded on declarative knowledge – has no need of it in order to be successfully put to work, while declarative knowledge – even if it grounds the reasons which makes procedural knowledge successful – is not sufficient to accomplish something practical. For example, knowing the rules of grammar is not sufficient for putting them to work in producing sentences, because their application implies other knowledge than the sole knowledge of those rules. Thus, the rules governing the past participle imply that you know how to identify auxiliary verbs and how to put the different elements of a sentence together. Similarly, just knowing the principles of an internal combustion engine doesn't make you a mechanic, while you can know how to fix a car without knowing anything about the principles of the internal combustion engine. In other words, just knowing what something is doesn't let you know how to run it. Or in another formula, as Aristotle liked to say long ago, experience is better than theory when it comes to practice. Now if you don't keep this distinction in mind you can fall into the all-too-common mistake of confusing a declarative statement *on* a particular practice (the practice of the phenomenological reduction, for example!) with the procedural description *of* that particular practice. They are not the same sort of thing at all, and must be distinguished.

Operational/functional description:
— In Husserlian phenomenology, these two adjectives are equivalent and designate the plane of the *genesis* of an object in perception or of a concept in logic. Operationality and functionality are thus associated from the outset with the temporal dynamic of the advent of an object or concept. Producing a description situated on this plane implies embracing the very movement in which an object or concept is formed, capturing the moment when it is there immanently, experienced without yet having been seen. In this sense, phenomenologists speak of an operative or functional [*fungierend*] intentionality, which is opposed to a static and objectivating intentionality that has the intended object in view from the start. As opposed to such stasis, genetic intentionality intends the movement of the temporality of emergence of an object, the dynamic lived through by the subject. Synonyms for this would be an intentionality that is passive, non-objectivating, practical. Merleau-Ponty has a usage very close to the notion of "operative intentionality" in *Phenomenology of Perception*; Fink, for his part, has elaborated a precise distinction between "operational concepts" and "thematic concepts" in his *Nähe und Distanz*: the former are effective but operate in the shadows, as unthought, while the latter have been defined and explained.
— In Piagetian psychology, "operational" means that which is effectively inscribed or inscribable in the realization of an action, or more precisely, the property of structures of the intelligence which describe the organization of mental actions (operational structure, operational theory of intelligence, operativity). It is therefore opposed to the "figural" (mental image, differentiated imitation).
— In cognitive industrial psychology, "functional" can be employed in the sense of that which is effectively embodied in an action: functional knowledge is what is effectively employed in solving a problem. Thus among nuclear plant operators, we can distinguish between what they can knowingly declare and what they effectively use during the course of an accident: the difference between them permits one to see what is not yet functional in their knowledge. The term "functional representations" means the same thing; they are representations effectively used in doing something. These are vitally important for effective practice, which allows only a functional knowing, the kind that is immanent to a practice.

A working description: Three temporal horizons

In starting to describe the *procedure* of the act of becoming aware, we necessarily have to get up to speed, to prime the pump, by sketching out a seemingly strange and complex process: a beginning that has to be always already re-accomplished. We sketch out below an overview of this dynamic, but this remains formal and indeed schematic, in as much as one has not concretely run through the different steps in the deployment of the act. This is the heart of this book: a *procedural description* of the reflecting act.

Our proposal revolves around a three-layered temporality, which provides the actual mode of operation of our practice:

1. a *basic cycle* consisting of the *epoche* (Chapter 1.2) and intuitive evidence (Chapter 1.3);
2. the global structure of a *session*, which also includes expression (Chapter 2.1) and validation (Chapter 2.2);
3. the *temporal context* of the act of becoming aware, which comprises the preliminaries and after-effects of the session as well as the more long-term temporality of an apprenticeship in a specific practice (Chapter 3).

The apprenticeship dimension is to be reawakened at each step, by continually re-enacting the act of becoming aware, so that each one is more sedimented and incarnated than the one before. This pattern provides room for different scales of temporality, from the fraction of a second which it takes for a trigger mechanism – an essential facet of becoming aware – all the way up to the historical temporality of the transmission of the act between generations of teachers and students. At bottom, only by taking into account such temporalization does one appreciate the on-the-job learning of which we speak. Our description is thus at the same time a preliminary logic for elaborating a methodology and the product of jump-starting this method, of learning it as you go along, as we had to our first time through.

Why a session?

In formulating the schema of the act of becoming aware, we focus on the time-scale inherent in *a session that lasts a few hours*. Our notion of a session is not very precise, but refers to actual social practices which set the boundaries to the way in which most of us are able to develop the practice of becoming aware. Typically such explorations are done in small groups in a private or institutional setting. Given the usual time constraints, sessions last a few hours (a seminar, a discussion group, a meditation session, a psychotherapeutic visit), although occasionally they can extend over days (a weekend workshop) or months (more rarely). The reason why we center our analysis on the temporality of a session is simply because it corresponds best to the way in which most people are likely to encounter these practices. By referring to the session as the context of the act of becoming aware, we maximize its situated and embodied dimensions to the detriment of more theoretical or structural dimensions.

The basic cycle, formed by the two first steps of the act, the *epoche* and intuitive evidence, form the indispensable kernel of its accomplishment, the necessary conditions of a session. There are two main differences between the basic cycle and a session. First, a session is more temporally and socially situated than the basic cycle, which is relatively context-free (it can be carried out in a mobile, autonomous manner). Thus the basic cycle is necessary but not sufficient for a session. Secondly, and more importantly, a session includes the expression and validation of the findings of the basic cycle. Expression and validation respond to needs for objectivation which are certainly optional, but without which any accumulated know-how or theoretical articulation, and thus any transmission across generations of a refined practice would be impossible.

The temporal horizon surrounding a session contains essential elements we must consider. In the long run, we find the motivations for learning a practice, and the actual learning of the practice itself, both of which can stretch out over years. In the short run, we find the preliminaries of setting up a session and the after-effects of a session. All these elements are interrelated as the changing background to a session.

Exemplary variations

Just as we have run through the different steps of the act of becoming aware, we will now describe a number of experiences which intrinsically reveal the act of becoming aware without entirely saturating it, that is, without so exhaustively describing it that no further examples are illuminating. These descriptions are exemplary variations, which reveal the *eidos* (essence in Greek) of the reflecting act. They represent what we call after Husserl eidetic variations, which designate in a technical way the process through which the invariant element of an object can be isolated and identified out of a number of relative and contingent features of that object. Such eidetic variations make its essence appear in a facet which harbors in its own manner the complete *eidos*, but without restricting it to any one of these possible variations. In this way they show that the act must be able to be concretized in a variety of ways.

Two points are important to stress here:

1. All our examples come from very diverse traditions and practices, in order to underline the plurality and variability, indeed the heterogeneity, of possible approaches to the reflecting act.
2. That amounts to saying, correlatively, that such a diversity accentuates the absolutely singular character of each of these ways of putting the reflecting act into practice.

With these two preliminary remarks we want to legitimate the diversity of our examples vis-à-vis the identity of the general structure. We also thereby want to legitimate the way in which we express each of these examples in the specific discourse of each of the authors; this variety of "native" expressions or endogenous categories illustrates at the same time the plurality and yet the absolute singularity of the act of becoming aware. The general structure furnishes, to be sure, the regulated context of each example, but this general structure is nonetheless able to pave the way for a particular practice that is singular in both content and form. Here are the examples we have chosen:

— a debriefing interview (guided introspection)
— *shamatha* (seated meditation)
— stereoscopic vision
— the heartprayer (orthodox tradition)
— a psychoanalytic session
— a writing session
— a beginning philosophy course

It is all we feel we need to say at this point about the *articulation* between the act of becoming aware in its overall structure and its practice in these examples. There are two facets of this articulation, each of which mitigates the difficulty of a methodology which wishes from the outset to be a *putting into practice* and not an *a priori* form. Both of them attest in this sense to the *embodied and situated* character of such a methodology.

First, you will have noticed the inherent difficulty in the "functional logic of learning on the job." On a strictly logical plane, one is always confronted by an aporetic circularity which goes something like this: "you can only be sure you've described the act you say you have, rather than something else, if you've already defined it. But the only way to check your definition is to experience an act, and that's something no definition can ever do for you: you have to jump in there feet first and experience it yourself!" Hegel, with Descartes in mind, noted the same kind of aporia in describing the impasse that all sub-

jective philosophies face from the outset. To deal with this difficulty Hegel invented the dialectic, which we can call a *"speculative* logic of learning on the
go."* In our case, taking to heart the Husserlian slogan of the "eternal beginner,"
it's a matter of nothing less than an "empirical-transcendental logic of learning on the go," which, to distinguish it from Kant, does not furnish *at first* the
a priori conditions of singular experience in order to deploy them *afterwards*,
but which draws from empirical examples the resources for a co-occurent typ-
ification, that is, the process by which each independent and equal example
typifies the act, is an example *of* the act. The examples in this sense constitute
the putting into practice of the general structure itself.

Second, it is here that the method of eidetic variation forged by Husserl
makes sense as part of our project. Husserl's method implies two joint movements:

1. Each example is not a simple illustration or anecdote, for it retains from the
   general structure the status of a possible paradigm, of a potential model.
2. The general structure *draws from the examples* its character of concrete
   rootedness, for it is definitively commanded by them in its very formalization – it's nothing without them, it doesn't pre-exist them in Kantian
   transcendental formality or Platonic ideality.

Consequently, (1) each example is formally sustained, typifying on the average
of the structure of the act; while, (2) the act itself draws its singular vitality
from its concrete variations.

In fact, in order to understand the precise role that one example played for
us and that the current examples might play here for you as you follow our
description of the reductive act, let us briefly retrace how the articulation between the act of becoming aware and its examples came about for us. These
examples were at first the different steps of the reflecting act which progressively imposed themselves on us. Let us be clear that we had in mind "learning on the go" in a more or less diffuse manner – let's say in a pre-reflective,
lived, or pre-noetic mode – cases of concrete exemplary figures or situations
where this structural description took shape, which "spoke to us." But in the
beginning, spontaneously and tacitly, we "bracketed" these different concrete
contexts, these particular situations, in order to foreground the more global
description of the act of becoming aware.

It was only afterwards that we "became aware" of the importance of these
concrete anchorings for our descriptions. We had thus been looking for the
most paradigmatic descriptive materials for our own personal investments in
these different areas, either because they offered from the outset a rigorous

structuring of the act of becoming aware, (the debriefing interview, the session of *shamatha-vipashyana*, the initiation session of the heartprayer), or because they responded to the fact that the "practice of the reduction" is also a human act inscribed in the most open and everyday contexts (stereoscopic vision, a philosophy course, a writing session). We were thus led to formalize them, to structure them, in order to make the different steps of the reflecting act in each of their move more apparent.

There is thus an incessant *boomerang* effect between the act of becoming aware and its exemplary variations: the method takes shape little by little, following the tempo of the way the structure of the reflecting act is engendered from examples that are concrete supports for its formalization, and engenders from itself, at the same time, the already typified production of variations which are thereby raised to the rank of paradigms. Eidetic variation thus receives a clearly *dynamic* sense. In this arena, there is a necessary overhaul of the eidetic in its Husserlian version by its inscription in the genetic process of the engendering of the act and its very own variations.

1.2. Epoche

The three components of epoche

As we have said, our attempt to describe the act of becoming aware means we have had to learn on the job. That means we are not going to give you ready-made results; instead we are going to try to thematize an individual experience brought to life in each of the authors. After reflecting on our experience, we then submitted our perceptions to group discussion so we could have a feedback from other people. In this way, learning as we went along, we came upon the structural dynamic of the act of becoming aware.

What we found was the following: *epoche* and intuitive evidence form the *minimal* but self-sufficient *cycle* of the reflecting act. That means they call for one another: *epoche* is naturally completed by an intuition that crystallizes for the subject and which serves as strong internal evidence; this evidence is prepared for and qualified by a gradual process of completion [*remplissement*] that has its own quality of suspension.

One accomplishes the *epoche* in three principal phases (Figure 1):

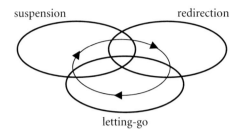

Figure 1. Three principle phases of *epoche*

— *A0: Suspending* your "realist" prejudice that what appears to you is truly the state of the world; this is the only way you can change the way you pay attention to your own lived experience; in other words, you must break with the "natural attitude."

— *A1: Redirecting your attention* from the "exterior" to the "interior."

— *A2: Letting-go or accepting* your experience.

Epoche: Greek meaning, roots in Antiquity and phenomenological Husserlian appropriation

Epokhè is a central term in Ancient Scepticism, introduced by the Pyrrhonian school of philosophy. Its meaning varies dramatically in function of the many different philosophical systems that have used it. For our purposes, it signifies the interruption of any quest for truth, which is the first step toward a happy and blissful inner mental state, called *ataraxia* by Sextus Empiricus in his *Pyrrhonian Hypotyposes*. In Cicero's stoistic approach the freedom of the wise man consists in suspending his judgement until he has an absolutely certain knowledge. Montaigne, in the sixteenth century, retakes the Stoic-Sceptic claim in his *Essays* (Raymond Sebond's Apology): "Their ritual word is *epekhô*, that is, I sustain, I do not move. That is their refrain. Its effect is a pure, total and perfect stay and suspension of our judgement".

Husserl does not refer specifically to the Greek lineage nor does he retrace the genealogy of the concept (Claesges 1972). Yet there is a general structural similarity between the phenomenological gesture of *epoche* and the Greek ethical attitude of suspension. From the sceptical meaning, Husserl retains the move of interrupting the flow of our current thinking or active attitude: it is a willful act which puts aside our beliefs and prejudices and refuses to endow the real world with an unexamined truth; however, contrary to the sceptical attitude of radical refusal of any truth, Husserl proposes an attitude of suspension of the truth until an absolute certainty (what he calls apodicticity) can be found. In this regard, he tends to be closer to the Stoic move, which leaves open the possibility of truth but promotes the freedom of the philosopher to suspend his judgement. Yet despite this proximity, Husserl remains attached to the search for knowledge and does not produce an ethics as such; nonetheless the stress on the attitude of suspension may be interpreted as a general *ethos* of life and knowledge.

Both following the greek-phenomenological meaning of *epoche* as suspension and breaking with it by enlarging it in a holistic way, we call *epoche* the organic whole of the three phases, because phases A1 and A2 imply that phase A0 is always reactivated at each step. Moreover, we will see that this gesture of suspension is also at work, albeit with different qualities, at each of the other steps of the reflecting act (i.e., intuitive evidence, expression and validation, which we will discuss in the following chapters).

The suspension and its follow-ups

The initial phase of suspension can begin in three basic ways:

1. an external existential event triggers your suspension. For example, you might be shocked into suspending your realist prejudice by a death or by an aesthetic surprise;
2. another person tells you to suspend your prejudice or models the gesture for you;
3. you tell yourself to suspend your prejudice. However, it will take a lot of training before you're able to stabilize the suspensive attitude on your own.

These three possibilities of jump-starting the suspension are not mutually exclusive, but can support each other: they are simply worldly, intersubjective or individual motivations to suspend your realist prejudice. All three, unequally present in anyone who's working on becoming aware, come together to make possible and then sustain phases A1 and A2, redirection and letting-go. You must therefore hold onto the suspensive disposition while you're shifting your attention and while you're accepting your experience.

A session of guided introspection

Social context

Guided introspection or the debriefing interview (Vermersch 1994) aims at describing in detail what you've done some time ago in the past. We use this technique in cognitive psychology research for retrieving detailed and precise introspective data.

These techniques were developed in practice, for example in classroom or training situations, to help students describe after the fact how they accomplished an exercise, so they could reconstitute the detailed unfolding of their mental actions ("What did you do when...? How did you start?"), their intake of information ("How did you recognize that...?"), or their criteria for the completion of the task ("How did you know that you knew?"). Guided introspection thus helps students become aware of their mental actions, of the types of representations or criteria they implicitly use; it helps teachers point out to students what's going right or wrong. This help in explicating things is also used with professionals, in debriefing sessions after a mission, an intervention, or an exercise in a simulator, to help them analyze and perfect their practice.

Context and goals of the session

The give and take of explication can last a few minutes during a class or several hours in a debriefing interview or a research interview. The most important technique we ask our interviewers to bear in mind – precisely what makes this type of interview useful in research and in the professions – is to ask non-leading questions (you can't whisper the answers under your breath when you're asking these kinds of questions!) so that interviewees can gain access to their own experience, that is, to an eminently pre-reflective material which is not yet conscious, but can be made conscious.

The structure of the debriefing interview

First of all, you as the interviewee must agree to be guided by the interviewer.

— The social context of the exchange, the time taken up by this, *interrupts* the "natural" accomplishment of the tasks to be done, so you can turn your attention to some already finished tasks. During this time you're not going to be doing *anything* productive. Whether you're at work or in school, whenever you're too swamped with work to do everything that needs to be done, you should right stop trying to be so efficient then and there, even if that sounds counter-intuitive.

— At the start of the exchange, the interviewer first asks you to "take the time to let the moment come back to you when you finished your task." Interviewers won't ask you for an *immediate and direct description*, because they want to help you attain the conditions for a living relation to the past situation. To let a specific moment of the past come back you *turn your attention* to your interior world, to the content of what is evoked, by simply remarking upon what the interviewer says while leaving it in the background. Thus in trying to recall a specific past moment you re-orient yourself to your interior world.

— The primary characteristic of the debriefing interview is thus to guide you to a type of recall that simply accepts what comes back: "take the time to let it come back to you." You're not going to be asked to recall anything actively (in the mode of explicit conscious memory), for that is a direct voluntary activity, but on the contrary you're going to be asked for what used to be called a long time ago "concrete memory."

— Your accepting stance is not necessarily going to immediately produce a completion, a strong and complete re-presentation (*présentification*) of the past. This intermediate time means you have to *stick* with intending your own lived past in the provisional mode of non-fulfillment, in the mode of something which is at first present as an emptiness. Now you are probably going to want to try to *prematurely* fill in this emptiness by verbalizing more easily accessible information (commentaries, judgments, generalities), or you're going to want to try to cover it over by a denial ("I don't remember, I don't know, I can't tell"), without entering into the experience of letting the past content come back to you, following what used to be called in the 19th century "involuntary memory." You have to remember that completion can happen in different rhythms and modes (either there's nothing and then everything happens all at once, or the past situation gives itself up step-by-step, and so on).

Expressive fulfillment: Difficulties or even failures
On its own accord what you say spontaneously is most often poor and generalizing, which won't let you or your interviewer figure out what went wrong or let you understand how you succeeded with the task you're trying to let come back to you. Experience shows that in schools or in professional training, most people are going to answer "I don't know" when they're asked "how did you do that?". The main difficulty for interviewers is to avoid having people reflect in such a way that they can only say what they already know and thus stay stuck with what they *believe* about the way they go about things.

If the interviewees spit their words out rapid-fire, or preface things with a little story, or if they won't say "I," then we know that correct positioning has not been attained. In that case we want to tell them to slow down and to make sure they're really in touch with the past situation.

An example of the very beginning of a guided introspection in the style of the debriefing interview.

Presentation	In this example, one of the authors is being guided to an intuitive fulfillment or completion of a specific past situation, determined at first solely by its temporal position (two months before). What we're going to present here – in the context in which it took place – is precisely the unfolding of that act of gaining access to a specific moment of the past. This description is thus not the transcript of what I said at the time of the reflecting (then, I said almost nothing: I just nodded my head or grunted to signal my approval), but rather the narration after the fact of my lived experience of reflecting. The notes in brackets aim at rendering precise the relation between this description and the cycle of the reflecting act.
Starting point	*Context:* in the middle of conducting a training course in debriefing I propose *to study the mental act of evocation,* that is, how one gains access to a specific moment of the past in the mode of "living it over again" [*revécu*]. I let myself be guided in this access by one of the trainees, with instructions to return to a specified moment in the past training session.
Suspension	*"We have decided to start, and I settle down a little better in my armchair with those little gestures your body makes on its own without you having to pay any attention to it. I feel that my waiting, my attention is turned to the other, I am used to all this and I know that the other is going to run the session, and that I don't have to be in charge anymore* [first step of suspension], *I abandon my other activities* (I'm usually the one in charge of the whole group), *and I ask one of the trainees to start up a debriefing with me in front of the whole group, in order to orient myself to this listening to my experience.*
	I hear the person accompanying me ask me to let a certain moment come back to me [this therefore orients me to pay attention to, and to accept, what-

Redirection

ever it is that comes back]. *I let go what I was in the middle of doing, I pull back my directed interest from the group, my visual orientation is modified, but I'm still listening, and it's as if my attention is turned towards the interior and that my body has turned (without moving) to the left, the direction of the past* [I've suspended my activity and redirected my attention, retreating from the world, thereby modifying my physical posture].

There immediately comes to me an idea, like an orientation to a few weeks ago, I note that I've changed direction, that I'm oriented toward a field of the past, but one without any content, some visual images of the context appear in the fringes but without any relation, in bits and pieces [in this very beginning of the *epoche* a

Receptivity

first completion arrives which is like what William James called a feeling of leaning, a sense of being directed to the past, but without content, that is, a *noesis* without its *noema*].

Completion

I feel the company of the other who invites me to let come back to me whatever impressions there are of the past moment which are in the process of coming back to me, I feel that this lets me remain centered on the activity of allowing a past moment of that particular period of time to arise [my companion indirectly helps me to remain in suspension and to open up to the acceptance of everything which comes back of that past moment].

Suspention (2)

The beginning of a rough outline of an image, like a mist, like something impalpable containing sketches of a place, pieces of faces, is beginning to take shape. I remain open to what is happening, oriented towards its acceptance; my attention is organized around this acceptance, the rest of my presence is detached from the present context: it's the beginning of being absorbed by something [continuation of suspension, more centered on maintaining the passivity of fulfillment, still very fragmented and partial].

Completion (2)

Bit by bit, a situation takes shape in the space of my representation, the impression of being grabbed, appearance of colors, presence at my side of C and M [sensory content of fulfillment is developing, which is very typical of this mode of recall]. *Suddenly and rudely a veil is torn apart, it's a café during a meal* [the fulfillment becomes precise in some determinations, but it is not yet felt as complete]. *My thought visualizes various possible places, I'm seated at different places in thought, (locations where I'm already seated at other moments with other people), but it's not right, confused feelings of inadequation, I try on the situations like you try on clothes to find which ones fit* [here there's the *mélange* of a reflecting activity that tries out various environments in order to infer which one is correct, and an intuitive evaluation which weighs the sense of what is adequate or not without rendering conscious the criteria]. *A particular place breaks free and comes to occupy the foreground, the other elements appear, the moment appears to me completely re-presented, I can now describe what is going on there...*" [The intuitive fulfillment of this past scene has worked, I can now start to put into words what went on and what was said in conditions that allow for a true reflecting on lived experience].

To speak of an *initial* phase of a suspension means we're going to have to deal with an issue that's been with us all along. This "initialization" or beginning of *epoche* has already taken place, yet at the same time, it's produced as if it were new each time. Let's ask ourselves: What do we need to do to put the reflecting act into practice? The answer: we need to suspend our realist prejudice, that is, break with the "natural attitude." But the very fact of asking this question shows that there's a problem. Considering its behavioral indicators or the products of its activity, the difference between the reflecting act [*l'acte réfléchissant*] and the act of reflection [*l'acte réfléchi*] may not be so apparent when you're learning how to practice the act of becoming aware as you go along. But as a result it's not possible to describe the reflecting act other than by having put it into practice. This has several consequences: you find yourself in a provisional circle of having to describe an act entirely by putting it into practice; the question of beginning is hidden in its radical character by the fact that the beginning has already taken place for whoever sets out to describe this very conduct.

Ways to bring about an initial suspension

individual mobilization	*shamatha*, heartprayer, psychoanalysis
prescribed cognitive attitude	*shamatha*, debriefing interview
bodily attitude	writing exercise, stereoscopic vision
modification of speech	
by slowing down	debriefing interview
by stopping	*shamatha*
by exhaustion of answers	psychoanalysis
real resistance to the completion of a task	stereoscopic vision

However, we can relieve part of this circularity by different techniques that *induce* or catalyze the beginning of the *epoche* (even if these exercises have not been thematized in the sketch we've just presented). The techniques will also let us size up any difficulties to be avoided or overcome so that we can put the act of becoming aware into practice, and will thus accentuate the unexplored character of the act of becoming aware. Giving lots of examples puts meat on the bones of the act.

Redirection and letting-go

The last two phases, redirection of attention and acceptance of what comes back, are complementary, and imply, as we've said, that you have accomplished and then actively maintained the initial phase of suspension. They correspond to two fundamental changes in what you do cognitively. First you change the *direction* of attention, which tunes out the spectacle of the world, so you can return to the interior world. In other words, you substitute an *apperceptive act* for perception. Now let us not fool ourselves: it is sometimes really quite difficult to turn away from your usual cognitive activity, which is most often locked in to the world around us. But do not worry: it can be done.

Second, you have to change from voluntarily turning your attention from the exterior to the interior, to simply accepting and listening. In other words, in moving from A1 to A2, you go from "looking for something" to "letting something come to you," to "letting something be revealed." What is difficult here is that you have to get through an *empty time*, a time of silence, and not grab onto whatever data is immediately available, for that's already been rendered conscious, and what you're after is what is still unconscious at the start.

Thus what we're talking about here is reversing two of your usual thought processes, the first of which is the condition of the second:

1. You have to *re-direct* your attention from the exterior to the interior (A1).
2. You have to change the *quality* of your attention, moving from an active search to an accepting letting-arrive (A2).

This means that while the first reversal actively moves between the dueling poles of the exterior and the interior, the second reversal moves from activity to a passive and receptive waiting, thereby doing away with any duality remaining from the first reversal.

For example, to talk in terms of phenomenological philosophy, the two reversals are just as much a matter of the Husserlian version of the reduction as reflective conversion as the Heideggerian version of "the turn" (*die Kehre*), an affective pre-understanding which lets-be (*Gelassenheit*) and lets the event come forth (Bernet 1994, Introduction; and Courtine 1984; Marion 1989; Henry 1991). Likewise, in the mindfulness tradition of Buddhism one makes a principled distinction between basic *shamatha* as a voluntary gesture of paying attention, and its natural development with training into an awareness (*vispashyana*) marked by the relaxing of the voluntary seeking into a receptive mode that is lived as more expansive and restful.

We know that these two reversals are going to seem unusual or even un-natural. We ourselves have felt all sorts of resistances and difficulties in doing them, and know that you have to take advantage of indirect strategies for doing them so you don't have to puzzle yourself over the paradoxical command to "be spontaneous."

A shamatha-vipashyana practice session

Brief background to the practice

We take this example from the basic practice of sitting meditation, widely referred to as *shamatha* (Tibetan: *zhine*) or *shamatha/vispashyana*. Al-though it's usually referred to in the West simply as "mindfulness medi-tation," this practice is a highly specific framework for cultivating certain mental qualities of stability, focus and openness, unlike some medita-tion practices in other traditions, which seem to aim at relaxation. As a practice it has been refined and explored by large numbers of peo-ple of multiple cultural backgrounds over 25 centuries. In this sense it represents a very elaborate experiment in human capacities, with an enormous body of empirical and theoretical developments behind it.

You should realize that the basic sitting meditation common to all Buddhist schools, albeit with important variants, is considered a basic training. You won't be able to do much in this area without working at it every day for at least a few years, with at least some periods (weeks or months) of more intensive dedication. You should also note that al-though it's a fundamental practice that everyone undertakes, *shamatha* is by no means the only recommended practice; a number of more "ad-vanced" practices are brought into play as your practice develops over time. We're not going to get into all those other practices here though.

The overall setting
A *shamatha* meditation session is highly structured. We focus here on the daily routine of cultivating a *shamatha* practice. The time is precisely set (never less than 30 minutes, usually up to 1 hour), and you clock in and out. You can practice *shamatha* either alone in your home, or with a small group in a meditation hall. It can be done either morning or evening. Since the routine is very explicit, there is no need for guidelines to the content of the sessions; everything is arranged ahead of time.

Getting help learning the practice

Starting point   You learn *shamatha* practice according to methods which vary from school to school within the Buddhist tradition. Here we follow the *Mahamudra*-inspired *shamatha* (Namgyal 1984; Trungpa 1995). You're usually introduced to the practice by an "expert" or a meditation instruc-tor who is there to clarify doubts about how to do things. As time goes by the same person (or others with the same standing) can also discuss with you larger issues, such as obstacles you might encounter, what all this means to your life, and so on.

A daily practice session

Suspension

1. *Shamatha* practice is based on an attitude of non-doing, expressed by a dignified sitting on the ground (the recommended posture, although you can also sit in a chair). You sit with a straight spine, your neck and arms are relaxed, and you rest your hands on your knees or over one another. Your eyes are open, and you breathe through both nostrils and mouth.

Redirection

2. Once you've settled into the basic posture, you explicitly decide to "merely" follow what is going on without engaging in it. Since you have to keep breathing, your breath becomes a guideline or a track for your attention. Although this doesn't mean all other sensations, thoughts, and emotions stop, you should consider them from afar, as an abstract observer would, like clouds in the background; the foreground is the breath as you follow it into the lungs and out the nostrils. This is in a nutshell just the sort of presence you're trying to cultivate: you're mindful of what's happening in the present. (As all kinds of experience appear within this attentive space, you explicitly avoid engaging in their contents, but rather pay attention to their arising, their emergence into full form, and then their subsiding into the background.)

Letting-go

3. As you get distracted you're suddenly aware that you have *not* been simply following your breath and so forth, but attending to thoughts, images, daydreams, bodily discomfort and the like. As soon as the sudden jolt of realizing that you have not been following instructions passes, you simply let go of the distraction and come back to the breathing. (If you're being bothered by too much activity or outside distractions, you enhance the attitude of being a neutral observer and you relax your body further by sliding back into the posture.)

Looping through cycles

4. As the session unfolds you relax as much as you can the position of being an abstract observer, and use a lighter touch regarding thoughts, merely watching them arise, present themselves, and subside. As you watch your mind, you see it moving through various "positive" or "negative" states; it either swims with content or is empty as it can be, you're either dull as dishwater or sharp as a tack or anywhere in between. You glimpse the constant impermanence of your thoughts, regardless of content and texture. You clearly see the composite nature of your mind and sense of self. You find yourself going in and out of an identification with a non-centered, non-ego space with various degrees of expansion.

Now if your attentiveness begins to become discursive, you start all over again with your basic technique of focusing on your breathing, reminding yourself that your main goal is to distance yourself from your thoughts.

	After the session
End	Your session ends at the scheduled time, and usually nothing specific follows. In particular, discussion, debate or expression of any kind is *not* part of the session. It's certainly off-limits for you to analyze what's going on in a session during its course. You're reminded to remain faithful to the technique itself.
After-thoughts	All discussion and clarification happens outside the session: you might seek out your instructor or one of your fellow meditators to talk things over, or you might just reflect on things on your own and try to figure out what went on during a specific session or during a certain length of time of your overall practice.

The difficulties of redirection

Most of the time during the day we're so occupied with other people, with daily chores, tasks at work, and so on, that we hardly ever spontaneously turn away from the world to reflect on what we're doing. The German philosopher Eugen Fink thus speaks of *Weltbefangenheit* ("imprisonment in the world") in his *Sixth Cartesian Meditation*. It's really quite rare that we turn away from the world and disinterestedly consider our thoughts or pick up on the emotional tonality of our actions (as opposed to *having* emotions or moods), since there aren't really all that many chances for us to do it on our accord, or in response to a school or training session.

When Husserl thought about how we turn away from the world and reflect, he spoke of changing our attitude (*Umkehrung der Einstellung*) to the world, by which he didn't just mean we merely act differently, but that we drop our natural interest in whatever we're dealing with in order to consider the act which lets us have access to it. Strictly speaking then, we're talking here about the very movement of the reduction as a conversion from the object to the act, or as a passage from *quod* (what) to *quomodo* (how). Now it's rather unfortunately true that Husserl described this "passage to the act" in analytic rather than dynamic terms, that is, as already accomplished rather than as a process. Hence we don't find many references in Husserl to the difficulty of converting your attention from object to act. So we have to admit that Husserl's description of conversion is not very procedural or even functional, as we've defined them above. The only way you'd know in reading Husserl how difficult the conversion is would be by noticing that his writings contain some contradictions on this point, and that he's rather ambivalent about conversion, beginning all the way back with what he writes about the circularity of the motivation for reduction. Thus we would say that this ambivalence in the writing corresponds to difficulties in theory, and that these difficulties show up in practice as stresses and strains or even obstacles.

From a psychological angle, Piaget insists that we are much more attuned in to our goals and to "positive information" (what's given in direct perception) than to the "instruments" (mental acts or "tools") which allow us to access them. Piaget has his own theory of becoming aware, and it allows us to evaluate precisely how much the fact of turning the attention away from the exterior world, from the intention of the goal, from the perception of the effects of action, from that which has a material, human, palpable presence, is likely to happen more spontaneously than paying attention to mental acts. These aspects are working there without us having to become aware of them for them to function effectively. The law of "rendering conscious" [*conscientisation*], which moves from the periphery to the center (Piaget 1937, 1974) clarifies the hierarchies involved in converting our natural attitude, that is, in turning away from what we are doing to how we are doing it. This hierarchy also shows how much less likely we are to interest ourselves in what is not directly important to our tasks. Elsewhere, he (Piaget 1977) has shown the primacy of "positive information" (that is, what we directly perceive) over the sort of "negative information" which only appears in the absence of positive information. So powerful is the primacy of "positive information" – that which is right there in front of us – that turning our attention toward the instruments which organize our actions in the world can only come later.

Pragmatic difficulties and help in overcoming them

As well as these psychological difficulties we also face *factual obstacles* when it comes to turning our attention away from the world to ourselves, as most practices will attest. Turning your attention to the interior sounds to many of us like turning toward *your own* little private world, which means running the risk of becoming aware of things we'd rather not know about ourselves. Out and out refusal to turn attention inwards thus rests on the refusal to make contact with your own private sphere.

When we are with other people in an interview or in a small group, reversing attention means you have to let go of the social control we usually exercise over others by our looks and speech: are we controlling their action directly by looking at them, or are we controlling our projected image – how we look – and thereby indirectly controlling them? All the same, you thus have to be confident enough to authorize yourself to pay more attention to the interior world than to the social world. However, paying attention to our interior world is not necessarily an act of becoming aware. In fact, reversing attention is common to many practices, such as attentive presence, debriefing interviews, and psychoanalysis, and experience with the last two practices has shown that some people simply refuse to go down that road.

We have to admit that it is hard to explain what is difficult about putting the reversal of attention into practice when we're trying to describe the change in the direction of attention. Only if you know the sort of techniques that help people *produce* this change of attention (e.g., the tradition of mindfulness (*shamatha*) in Buddhism) can you take the measure of the sort of detachment that can constitute the reversal of attention for some people. The most evident symptom of just how difficult this can be seems to be that these techniques *aim only at producing* the change of direction of the attention, as if, once the change is provoked, the rest (its use in reflective exploration) is self-evident. These practical techniques commonly take advantage of the fact that reversing your attention coincides in part, in the name of *organic support*, with paying attention to your body, to kinesthetic and proprioceptive sensations. By paying attention to the position of the breath, or indeed to the difference between holding it and not holding it, you are led to center yourself on your bodily interior, then on your psychic or even spiritual interior, and to leave to one side the outside world.

Thus there are many practical conditions for becoming familiar with reversing your attention, which can concern methodological pre-requisites, theoretical difficulties, pragmatic obstacles.

The methodological pre-requisite means, as we said, suspending your actions in the world. In effect, when you are first starting out, you cannot perform the reflecting act while you're doing something else. In other words, you have to do nothing in a quite literal sense: you just have to stay and pay attention. Why? Because doing something in the world is going to grab your attention very powerfully and distract you from turning your attention around toward your inner life. However, as you develop your practice past the beginner's stage, your suspension can co-exist quite naturally with fully situated action. In fact, such flowing co-existence is the very hallmark of having acquired a degree of mastery. To help you in the intermediate stages, most practices include explicit transitional steps. A simple example is the alternation between sitting and walking meditation in *shamatha* training.

Although we have stressed that reversing your attention, at least while you're a beginner, entails not doing any worldly action, it is in fact a *cognitive action*: it entails (or is caused by) changing your attitude toward the world.

When you look at it from the point of view of techniques that help you put it into practice, reversing attention means you have to release your control over things. In fact, since the natural attitude is one of being in control (or at least wanting to be in control), it can be accused (if it makes any sense to "accuse" an attitude!) of hypnotizing you; and so you have to release yourself from its grasp. Letting yourself go in this way is like speaking a new language: you have to let it all hang out to be any good at it!

Supports for reflexive conversion
Mental supports for turning around
  breathing as anchorage: shamatha
By evocation of the past   debriefing interview
Encounter with an internal obstacle
  obsessing over the question: philosophical research
  helplessness: heartprayer
Encounter with external obstacles
  trial and error: stereoscopic vision

Letting-go and the quality of attention

With the third phase of *epoche*, acceptance, the very *quality* of your attention changes tenor: you move from that sort of active intentionality which *looks for* the interior, to a "passive" *acceptance*, a *letting-arrive*. Yet this acceptance is passive only in name, for it is eminently an action.

Acceptance as the last stage of *epoche* means that the reflecting act aims at *letting* the reflection on lived experience *work*. In other words, you actively pay attention but at the same time you *wait*, since what you're reflecting on is by definition tacit, pre-reflective or pre-conscious. Thus you have to balance your-self between a sustained act of attention and not having immediate fulfillment. Hunters on the lookout at least know what they're vigilantly and patiently wait-ing for, even though while they're waiting for it their attention has no content, they don't *know* anything about their target-yet. To various degrees, what you can reflect on is not immediately available, but is only potential and is only re-vealed *via* a particular cognitive act. Thus your waiting has to be focused and open, possibly empty of content for a time, without any immediate discrimina-tion other than "there's nothing there," "it's foggy," "it's misty," "it's confused," "there's nothing happening."

This relatively empty time (the period in which something first takes shape, but also the time in which you tune into what can compose the object of reflection) can be very brief, or it can last several minutes if not more. In so far as you can't voluntarily "grasp" anything at this point, you can only adjust to the structure of your attention, since you can't adjust to the detail of a content which has not yet been revealed.

This waiting time is easy to pick out when you are trying to perceive stereoscopic figures. Even when you are a practical expert at this sort of thing, there will be a time when you are not able to distinguish anything yet, even though you know that you're no longer seeing things "naturally." During this time, you sense the form emerging until there's a brute change into clear perception. In a therapy context, while something is coming back to you, perhaps you have had the impression that "it's on the way"; sometimes you can even pick out the fact that it's coming from very far away, but you don't yet know what the content of the past scene is or even the words which are going to come back to you.

Now even when it is objectively very brief, this empty time seems to last forever, like "dead air" interrupting a broadcast. It feels like a long time because our usual conscious activity is so rapid. When you are helping someone reflect, as in a debriefing interview, slowing of the subject's expression and pauses in order to access reflections are often good signs that he is putting the reflecting act into practice.

Acceptance can be seen from different angles. From one perspective, acceptance has two difficulties: first you have to abandon the natural attitude, and then you have to learn how to accept, how to do something involuntary – which is really quite paradoxical if you stop to think about it! From another perspective, you have to distinguish acceptance from two other states of attention: (1) paying attention to something outside, in the world; (2) not paying attention, not from choice, but simply because you've stopped paying attention (often without noticing it).

Paying attention to what might show up (the most strange, i.e., unusual, state) is such a waiting time, which is at once empty and subjectively long, seems to be the primary hindrance to discovering and spontaneously putting the act of becoming aware into practice. We know it's hard not to immediately succumb to the sort of fear or boredom acceptance or attentive receptivity can bring out in you. Piguet, under the expression "semantic reversal," puts this dimension of acceptance into evidence:

> The term *semantic reversal* that we use largely exceeds the framework of scientific semantics. In a general manner, it envisions a reversal of the manner in which man relates to the world *by determining it*, in favor of a "passive" relation, where man accepts from the start the sense of the world in order to be

able, without denaturing it, to pass it on by the path of consciousness (Piguet 1975:4439).

Piguet also writes:

> The critical question of language consists in suspending, on the part of he who wants to comprehend (and eventually know) an internal totality, any kind of "talkative" activity in order to methodologically plunge into an "accepting silence" (Piguet 1975:4422).

In a much more general fashion, Heideggerian *Gelassenheit* equally carries with it this dimension of an acccepting listening. This time will be troubling if you naively believe you can instantaneously, permanently, and mechanically master your thought processes. In fact, you *perform* most things, that is, do them without knowing how you do them. You can also be troubled to find out that you are now able to become aware of all sorts of properties and aspects which you previously had overlooked.

Let's recall that in redirecting your attention you have to inhibit your outer actions in order to leave open a place for apperception, for turning inward. In the second change, acceptance, what you have to inhibit is an immediately fulfilling intuition that you might be tempted to bring about by projecting your categories, presumptions, and identifications onto what begins to appear. Once again, the quality of suspension, here inhibitory, would appear to be singular even while keeping pace with each step of the act of becoming aware.

With this idea of suspending judgment we're very close to the general sense of the Husserlian *epoche*, or to the principle of the absence of presuppositions Husserl formulated in the *Logical Investigations* (§7, 1901). However, we have to admit that since Husserl stayed on the level of principles, he doesn't do justice to all the different qualities of suspension with which we're wrestling.

On a more practical level, we've coming close to the attitude you find in the practice of psychotherapy. Therapists give their clients all their attention, but all the while they're careful not to interfere with the open and patient acceptance of what the client brings to light by making interior commentaries or counter-transferential movements. The therapist is only able to simultaneously register the verbal, the non-verbal (modification of posture, gestures, breathing rhythm, depth, placement, mimicries, micro-movements), the epi-verbal (what is said by the manner in which the other says it – linguistic structures as well as anything from the categories of description of the immanent world to the semantic choices), and the para-verbal (the variations of intonation) by an open listening and observation ("floating", as the pyschoanalysts would say), without looking to seize hold of anything.

Perhaps we can say the same about the painter: "It is interesting to remark here that the phenomenological reduction [...] has a double effect. It must make us forget at the same time as it makes appear. The reduction is at bottom the philosophical equivalent of a technique of painterly vision. One must forget what things seem to be when one looks at them superficially and make the thing itself appear as what it is in reality. Thus, practicing the phenomenological reduction is less seeing than learning to see." (Piguet 1963:154; Husserl 1991:13–19)

In the tradition of mindfulness meditation, letting-go is part of the more difficult or more "advanced" methods. The strongest emphasis on it is found in the Mahamudra-Dzogchen schools in Tibetan, Chinese Chan and Japanese Zen Buddhism. In all cases, the introduction of a pre-discursive component makes the repeated practicing of letting-go non-paradoxical. In Rinzai Zen, the repetitive work with koans is the classic example; in Tibetan schools the emotional association with a living teacher ("devotion") is considered essential for being "drawn" into the learning through a pre-discursive constitution (Namgyal 1987).

Quality of acceptance: Gestures to bring it forth
specific mode of suspension: Time of relative emptiness

nothing appears:	stereoscopic vision
slowing down of speech:	debriefing interview
modalities of the quality of attention	
contemplation of thoughts from a distance:	heartprayer
patient waiting for meaning:	philosophical research; psychoanalysis
intensification:	advanced *shamatha*

The reflecting act takes off from the non-availability of what is reflected upon; you might say it takes off from the non-verbal, from the pre-reflected, from the ante-predicative. But that means that reflecting takes off from nothing, in the sense that whatever lived experience you can reflect upon is not immediately available (if it weren't unavailable, it would already be under your control; thus when you reflect you can only control the conditions of reflection, not its accomplishment or the reflected content). The reflecting act thus takes off from a "silent" or "empty" relation to experience. You have to accept and listen, you have to be filled with something about to come forth, you have to contemplate rather than go looking for something in a pre-determined manner. Accepting something is more passive than knowing something, even if this relative passivity is pushed into the background by our usual ways of thinking, our categorial filters, whose permanent activity can be difficult to suspend. In this sense you cannot rely on a conception of a passive and mechanical reflection when you are trying to describe the reflecting act. When you reflect, you are working with a mirror that is anything but passive or neutral. But you do have to abstain from immediately crushing your lived reality with your language and thought schemes, so that you can establish a zone of relative and provisional silence, and try to take off again from the way you relate to the reality of lived experience. We have to tap into a fertile void which escapes, experientially, the boundaries of our given worlds and languages, and reaches an ontological level that is more radically open, that can only appear in *chiaroscuro*, in the contrast provided precisely by suspension and letting-go.

This inversion of the spontaneous movement of looking for information about the world can only be relative; it's a matter of braking, of inhibiting the most gross cognitive movements, those which totally cover over acceptance and make the reflecting act impossible. However, the next fundamental step is changing the way you make your lived experience present so you can *express* it (see Chapter 2.1). But in this stage, while it lasts, acceptance is the paradox whereby you deliberately turn your attention toward the interior, not to look for something there, but to accept what shows up there, or even more strongly put, to accept what you can let show itself.

Now when you read this description of reversing attention and all its difficulties, you might think that we have painted a pretty bleak picture. You might think that the reversal is *always* very difficult, if not downright mysterious. But in reality, reversal can happen so quickly that you don't even notice it if you're not deliberately paying attention, for it sometimes happens that the information you're reflecting upon is easily accessible. So it's not just the practice of the reflecting act that makes things difficult, but also what you're aiming at, and how you're related to it.

The basic structure of becoming aware: The double fold of reflection and affection

Let us now take a second look at our diagram outlining the basic cycle (Figure 2).

You can see, at the heart of this process of becoming aware – the reflecting act or the phenomenological reduction at work – both sides of the *epoche*, a double correlative movement: reflective conversion/redirection and acceptance/letting-go. We can also describe these components as moments of emergence, as *folds* in the process. The first fold, leading to reflection (and

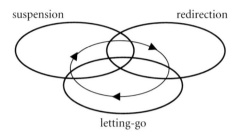

suspension   redirection

letting-go

Figure 2. Process of becoming aware.

eventually to expression) is a *return to yourself.* The second fold, leading to a letting-go (and eventually to tacit intuition) is *an opening to yourself.*

Let's now notice that the loop closes in on its interior, but without totally doing so, since this minimal opening of reflection is what opens up the second movement of acceptance of yourself and of the world. These two movements are like the double fold of diastole/systole, of contraction and dilation, folding together cognitive reflection and affective openness. In cognitive reflection, you take off from pre-reflected consciousness (pre-discursive, pre-noetic, ante-predicative, tacit, pre-verbal, pre-logical, or non-conceptual, as you like) (Brand 1955; Gallagher 1998; Bermudez 1998; Zahavi 1999) and apperceive this pre-reflected content, until it opens out a finalized structure. Affective openness, on the other hand, is rooted in pre-associative affection and involuntary habitual life (*habitus*) (Husserl 1966; Mazis 1993; and Montavont 1994), which means that if you haven't been systematically practicing a suspension, then you'll be led to focus on, by the very structure of affection, what the cognitive act feels like. That's not what you're after though, so when this habitual unfolding is suspended, and the fold of letting-go intervenes, you hit upon a revelation that is letting-go or acceptance, active abandon or available receptivity. This is the affective face of the process. Reflection and acceptance thus form a double fold of cognition and affection, dynamically recovering one another in linking one to the other, to the point that cognitive reflection and affective openness cease to be opposed to one another in the process of becoming aware, but form a non-duality.

We can therefore characterize the complete process of becoming aware, *epoche,* by four correlative movements:

1. The base: pre-given, passive, hyletic and kinesthetic intentional *emergence* in its immanent and incarnated corporeality, which impels intentionality toward its object and orients it to the perception of the world.

2. *Reflective fold*: conversion of reflection: becoming aware.
3. *Letting-go fold*: acceptance or letting-go on the basis of an originary affective hyletic dimension.
4. *Discursive explication* on the basis of the ante-predicative experiential situation.

The two folding-movements (2 and 3) face each other, are tied to each other in the non-oppositional unity of recto and verso, and form the very dynamic of the process of *epoche*. This process, as we've described it, is not all of a piece, but includes breaks and pressure points, thresholds and gradients. As we've stressed before, we can't enter into a detailed structural analysis of these folding movements here – something that will be necessary at some later date. Nonetheless, this sort of threshold and gradient is implied here, as you can see by comparing the use of the terms "thoughtless" [*irréfléchi*] or "unconscious" (in their Freudian senses) to the use of "pre-reflected" when we are talking about reflection, or "originary passivity" when we're talking about letting go of your habits. Consequently, this process contains limit or shadowy zones: on the one end of the scale, we run into the neuro-dynamical, the sub-personal, dimensions which, in principle, we can never become conscious of. On the other extreme, we find the philosophical ideal of a pure consciousness, of a pure or transcendental experience to which we might gain access in experience, but only in going beyond the activity of becoming aware. Only a profound and enduring exercise might *perhaps* allow us to surpass these limits. In any case, becoming aware remains a limited process, concerning either its grounds or its possible further expansions.

1.3. Intuitive evidence

Intuition as gesture and as process

Let us now move on to describe the second movement of the basic cycle, which we call "intuitive evidence." Intuition follows close on the heels of the *epoche* described in 1.2, and is necessary before one moves on to expressing and validating results in a session (Chapter 2). Intuition is thus a unique mental capacity that comes between the new awareness allowed by suspension and an inscription of results in traces others can read or see. The word derives from recent Latin *intuitionis* which meant image, looking into, from the root *intueri* (to look).

Our aim here is to provide a renewed understanding of intuition, based on its thematization in Husserl with the notion of eidetic intuition (see below) and refined and enriched thanks to the concrete and social context of the thought experiment process. In this respect, we will see how intuitive evidence contains a tension between two dimensions: on the one hand, an elementary intuitive component, more sensible and perceptive than conceptual or categorial, the fruit of an individual singular experience (it is the basic sense of intuitive acts as Husserl calls them); on the other hand, an intersubjective intuition established through eidetic variations, which paves the way for an extended, universalized form of intuition as a unique means of knowledge.

To begin with, since intuition is related to seeing and looking, it has nothing to do with symbolic knowledge, be it logical or discursive. But if it's not symbolic, then what kind of knowledge is intuition? In everyday language we talk about intuition as some sort of elusive and mysterious quality close to inspiration ("feminine intuition") or to the spark of genius (Mozart's musical powers were called "intuitive"). To move further on in our description of the act of becoming aware we need to go beyond this everyday understanding and bring out its precise structural components.

First of all, we have to clearly distinguish the product of intuition from its process, which is our concern here. Since we are looking for a *procedural description* of the act of becoming aware, we don't want to obsess over the question of whether there is or isn't a special genre of knowledge called "intuition" that orients us to the question of validation. Having said that, though, we do want to briefly consider some of the philosophical roots of the notion of "intuition" before we enter into our procedural description of how to bring it about.

The philosophical roots of intuition

In psychology, intuition has suffered as many complex misfortunes as introspection as an alleged access to the scientific study of mental states. We are not going to repeat that debate here. Moreover, intuition also has a long history in philosophy, and in order to have a useful notion for our purposes we have to disentangle it from the connotations it has accumulated along the way.

Via his process of systematic doubt, Descartes makes intuition bear the weight of that which is known *beyond doubt*. In this sense, intuition is already at work in the reflexivity of a thought that assures us of its certainty. When Kant comes along to take up the question of intuition, he localizes it and reduces its importance. Kantian intuition is primarily a form of a priori sensibility, as in the pure intuition of space and time. Intuition thus constitutes a faculty of perception which introduces a first level of order into chaotic sensation. But intuition for Kant is not enough to constitute knowledge of phenomena, which needs conceptual form. As Kant's celebrated formula goes, "concepts without intuitions are empty; intuition without concepts is blind." After Kant, the German Idealist tradition (Fichte, Schelling, et al.) turns its back on him and insists on intuitive knowledge as a foundation for knowing the absolute (Tilliette 1995). Now in all these traditions, intuition does not stand for something vague, private or ineffable. As a primordial form of our understanding, intuition retains the clarity and distinctness of Cartesian truth. At the same time, though, it is a form of truth that remains anchored in the subjective sphere.

Phenomenology changes this situation in two important ways. On the one hand, Husserl departs from Kant by making intuition a grounding principle of knowledge. On the other hand, since intuition is inseparable from its objective correlate (that is, the intended objects), Husserl departs from the subjectivist leanings of Descartes (Husserl 1970). The key issue for Husserl is what he calls direct "givenness", as expressed in the notion of *Fülle*, of plenitude, which is an integral part of intuition (Levinas 1973). Intuition refers to acts in which "objects show up in person" *(zur Selbstgegenheit kommen)* (Husserl 1982). In this sense, there are at least two major classes of intuitive acts: perception (*Gegenwärtigung*, or "presentation") and imagination/memory (*Vergegenwärtigung*, or "re-presentation" [*présentification*]). For Husserl, perception is the most primordial of these two acts, since it has its object "in flesh and blood" (*leibhaftig gegeben*).

We must distinguish the strict Husserlian sense of intuition from the kind of everyday evidence you can have without previous reflection, prior to the gesture of reduction, what is also referred to as perceptive faith (Bergson 1934; Merleau-Ponty 1968). Husserl names this weak form of evidence *Selbstverständlichkeit* (literally "self-understandability"), and relates it to the always "presumptive" way in which we relate to the world (Husserl 1960). As opposed to this, evidence in the strong sense (*Evidenz*) has a claim to apodictic certainty, (something is apodictically certain when its converse is self-contradictory), and can thus partake of the absolute and indubitable certainty of the subject (Husserl 1960: §8). While weak and presumptive evidence comes from a diffuse and anonymous subjectivity inscribed in an always already given world, (it is "self-evident", "taken-for-granted" in the sense of "of course, everybody knows that, it goes without saying!"), apodictic evidence, in virtue of its methodological strictness, can only appear to the individual subject. Thus in strict Husserlian terms, only apodictic evidence is the criterion of truth in the fundamental correlation of subject and object given by the intentionality proper to all acts of consciousness. "Evidence is in an extremely broad sense an 'experiencing' (*Erlebnis*) of something ... a mental seeing of something." (Husserl 1960: §5) The juxtaposition between experience and seeing is quite telling here. Its living, embodied quality gives intuitive evidence its appearance of being "in person" (*leibhaftig*). But the complementary side is also a quality of seeing, of conscious appraisal, from which springs the closeness of intuition and in-sight (*Einsicht*): the force of seeing, evidence as being-seen.

By now we have touched upon the constellation of evocative terms Husserl uses in locating intuition in his phenomenological project. But in doing so we have only just sketched the outlines of intuitive evidence as it occurs in the act of becoming aware. Thus let's move on to describe its embodied procedures.

A session of stereoscopic vision

	Background
	As researchers, we set up the session so you can experience for the first time the stereoscopic fusion of two-dimensional images. We will use various images, such as Julesz's random stereograms, scientific images, or the popular "Magic Pictures" (Julezs 1971). Our experience as researchers shows that these images remain impenetrable for most people at first glance, so you will need to stick with it through several re-starts in order to make the jump and to clearly see the figures in a convincing three-dimensionality.
Settings	*The overall setting*
	We structure the session so you can learn to see for the first time. You are provided with the images to work from, and you have the help of a teacher who has not only seen them but has acquired a stable mastery over them, and can provide some pointers on what you have to do. It will take a few hours to learn what to do the first time around, but after repeated practice, you will be able to bring about the three-dimensionality you are after in only a few minutes.
Suspension	*Help in learning what to do*
	You don't necessarily need to have a teacher standing over you, as long as you are reassured that many people have succeeded in the past, for this will give you the confidence you need to keep plugging away even though you fail in the beginning. There is evidence of non-accessibility (the image is flat), then imitation, and even competition between those who know how to "see". Helping different people to see can be quite var-

ied depending on circumstances. Almost always though you will be given these hints:

Conversion

1. Start by looking at the pair of pictures directly in front of you, ideally vertically arranged, and at such a distance that they cover most of the foveal region (i.e. at the center of the visual field). You will suspend your usual attitude when you are struck by the fact that you can't access the three-dimensional image. We call this "resistance by reality," by which we mean that your usual perception is not up to the task.

2. Cross your eyes by looking intently at the tip of your nose, while keeping your attention fixed on the (spatially superimposed) images of the two source figures. You'll probably then look for help "about how I'm doing this," and then do some trial-and-error work with variables like distance, location, and the use of reflections.

Letting-go

3. Let your vision find its point of focus over the images, and relax the grip of the eye-crossing effort. Your suspension is imposed and maintained by the failure of the 3D image to show itself. You'll then find yourself reflecting on the perceptive act by being "worn out," by exhausting all the easy solutions, and by constant repetition. You will keep at it due to all this glaringly obvious and maddeningly uncompromising failure. Here you will find a great example of "empty time": even the experts can't instantly access the 3D image, which will take several seconds to appear.

4. Let the 3D effect click into place all by itself. At the beginning it will be unstable and fleeting. But then you will notice a progressive fulfillment (relative to perceived content); you will see the surface begin to change and notice the unstable character of first successes, but also the simple character of what is intended (it is always just an image!).

Cycling through

5. You will find a lot of emotion welling up the first time you see a stable, sharp and crisp image, because now you've suddenly hit upon a hidden dimension; you will feel the usual certainty in which physical space is shaken up; you may even want to put your finger into the imaginary space in front of us.

End

After the session
The experience now becomes fluidly intersubjective: you can talk about what you have just done and can refine your procedure in subsequent tries. You and the researchers will want to validate your seeing with new and different test figures whose hidden figures are kept secret from you at first. You will feel a nice sense of satisfaction at having learned the task.

After-effect

Even after a few days, all you have to do is to return to this initial session and you will be able to reproduce the stereoscopic vision, and to carry it over to other types of images.

The temporal dynamic of the intuitive act

As a way to open up the inquiry and to lay open some basic themes we need to examine, let's begin by distinguishing two aspects that seem, at first glance, to be proper to the intuitive act: it is a form of becoming aware that is both *non-mediated and passive*.

Surprise and novelty: at the moment it occurs, the intuitive act is *non-mediated* by any conceptuality. Intuitive content doesn't fall into any of our usual conceptual "pigeon-holes." Having said that, though, we have to admit at once that intuiting remains inevitably mediated by your cultural horizon, your means of expression, and by the context of the intuitive act. Lived phenomenally as direct experience, without intermediaries, the intuiting act has no direct precursor that is able to prepare you for the emergence of a lived content as novel, as breaking the continuity of your experience, your vision of the world. Intuiting is thus both *discontinuous* and *novel*.

The discontinuity of intuiting is nonetheless incompatible with the voluntary and constant pursuit of innumerable attempts at it, which we will call later "variations," including entirely discursive, conceptual, and voluntary variations. With the 20–20 hindsight of the observer, we can easily show a causal relation of condition and product, but at the very moment when it is happening, in the immanent coherence proper to the unrolling of the action, intuition is *lived* as an emergence, as if there were nothing directly linking the content of the variations and what appears to you. Thus we have to ask ourselves: just exactly *how does* "the novel" emerge, or at least what we experience as novel? What is at stake here is the *creativity* of thought, which we have to sharply distinguish from the "mediate" activity which presents itself as a reflexive activity and whose every step follows the preceding one according to the laws governing the coherence of contents in our experience. As opposed to such coherence, what we are interested here in is the way the intuitive givenness combined with an *epoche*-move *ruptures* this train of experience. In that respect, Marion made a first attempt at thematizing the surprise as an event which takes subjectivity when all grasping fails (Marion 1989: 300–301).

Waiting and acceptance: relative to fulfillment, the intuitive act is *passive*. When we consider its temporality, we can describe the intuitive act as involuntary, since you cannot directly bring about either its accomplishment or its results. Rather, you can only create the conditions for it: this is the meaning of the decision you take in practicing the *epoche*. You cannot anticipate the results as such, but you can anticipate their form, their quality. In effect, all you can do is to try to see to it that nothing stands in the way of the eventual realization of involuntary fulfillment. There is thus the possibility – and perhaps the necessity – of a double movement: 1) passive acceptance (but not absence, it's very much a matter of a hidden presence); 2) holding-in-the-grasp (*le maintenir-en-prise*, after Husserl's "*im-Griff-halten*" in his *Phenomenology of Time-consciousness*) in a sufficiently light-handed fashion that the opening is not altered. This is learned and cultivated.

The fragile lightning-bolt of the process of intuitive fulfillment: From emptiness to givenness-in-flesh-and-blood

We can clearly see from this initial examination that the most salient trait of the intuitive act is its implicit temporality, which is quite complex and should be immediately broken down into three aspects:

1. on the most elementary scale, on the order of seconds or even minutes, it is a matter of *fulfillment* (or completion) or even of holding onto the void;
2. on the scale of the organization of an activity (a work session of several hours, a week or more of successive work sessions), it is both a matter of *renewing* the suspension in emptiness, of a non-completed yet nonetheless renovated fulfillment, and a matter of multiple tries at variations of all sorts which precede and follow each moment of empty, partial or complete fulfillment;
3. on a still larger temporal scale, it's a matter of continuing the research project (see Chapter 3).

The interplay between lived and seen extends as far as the interplay between what you immediately perceive and what you only think about, what you intend as mere signification without an embodied presence. Now the process of intuition is precisely the *filling-in* (*Erfüllung*, completion) *of such an intended meaning by direct perception* that Husserl thematized so brilliantly in his fifth *Logical Investigation* as a general structure of all acts of consciousness (Husserl 1970); when filling-in and intended meaning both perfectly coincide you have intuitive evidence. Conversely, when the intended meaning and lived experience don't match up perfectly you have a lesser degree of filling-in, and so a lesser degree of intuitive evidence – but still different in kind from the anonymous "of course" of "self-understandability" and "taken-for-grantedness".

Intuitive fulfillment of experience thus admits of degrees and also implies a certain passivity of the givenness itself. That is, the giving of evidence in flesh and blood is far from being able to proceed of its own accord. To take an example from external visual perception, recall how hard it sometimes is to identify the silhouette of a person you think you recognize but aren't absolute sure, and all the perceptual conflicts which ensue, before you can, after a number of delays, realize that you have been tricked, that it is not the person you at first thought you had seen. Besides, Husserl dedicated endless analyses to these perceptual conflicts, from *Thing and Space* (Husserl 1997), where he indicates that an absolute saturation (*Sättigung*) is impossible, to *Experience and Judgment* (Husserl 1939/1973, first section, §20 sq.), where he insists at length on doubt, probability, and possibility in the case of various modifications of perception.

Thus we can say that the synthesis by which you gain an intuition (*Veranschaulichung*) proceeds from a passive intention which *tends* to be realized in the knowledge of the object. In this sense you experience an emptiness in fulfillment, which is felt as a tension, a drive to the fullness of incarnated giving. In other words, the structure of fulfillment has an intrinsic lack: when we analyze the intention which aims at an object we see the *tendency* to intuitive plenitude, rather than the intuited object as an acquired and definitive result. Such a passive tendency Husserl calls driven-intentionality (*Triebintentionalität*) because it cannot be voluntary and corresponds to the very process more than to the access to the object as a result. Thus we have to see intuition as a graded and never totally achieved act, as a *dynamic* tending toward a plenitude which is never totally given, never saturated, but which is instead rare and fleeting. Such a graded and fragile tenor of intuitive fulfillment ends up *rooting* our very intentional relationship to objects. To see this connection we must 1) isolate the constitutive passivity of the synthesis at work there, very often without the full conscious awareness of the subject; and 2) show how the dynamic of what is intuitively intended comes from the drives underlying consciousness (Husserl 1966: 65–112; Husserl 1939/1973: §20 sq.; Nam-In Lee 1993; and Nagaï 1995: 453–459). In other terms, intuitive evidence is less a result or a product than an act and a *process of coming forth*.

A session of the heart prayer

Historical and cultural background

The "heart prayer" (also known as the "Jesus prayer") is one of the most venerable and most elementary practices of the Orthodox Church; it draws its strength from the *hesychast* tradition of the Christian East. "Hesychasm" comes from the Greek *isichia*, which means "calm," "silence," "contemplation." The essential teachings of this practice are found gathered together in a collection of Patristic texts (Clément 1995). Its incessantly repeated formula, in its most simple form, is: "Lord Jesus

Christ, have mercy on us, poor sinners!", or in its complete form: "Lord Jesus Christ, Son of God, pray for us, poor sinners, now and at the hour of our death." When said orally and then interiorly, the prayer puts those who entirely consecrate themselves to it at every moment, day and night, in the intimate presence of God, to the point of a quasi-sensible union. When you incessantly pray in this manner you develop a quality of being intensely present to yourself, which takes the form of an attention to your own body, or better, to the body of your body: that is, to your heart.

Originating on Mount Sinai and in the Egyptian desert in the first centuries of Christianity, the *hesychast* tradition corresponds to the mystical school of union with God via deification, and is opposed to any purely ascetic currents. The proper formulation of the prayer does not appear until the 6th Century, with John Climacus. Starting from the 11th Century with Simeon the New Theologian, the spiritual quest comes to be inflected with a taste for an experimentation that includes the psycho-physiological, directed to the heart in its organic dimension. Starting in the 15th Century the *hesychast* tradition is transmitted to Russia, where it is then published in a Slavic *Philocalie* (1794). But it is above all in the 19th Century, with the anonymous publication of *Récits d'un pélerin russe* (1870) (Laloy 1978), that the prayer of the heart knows a true, even popular, renaissance.

Overall framework
The main thing about the prayer of the heart is that it is supposed to become *perpetual*. Only an incessant repetition really fulfills the practice as it is supposed to be done. At the beginning, you are recommended to repeat the Jesus prayer a certain number of times each day, morning, evening, or both, perhaps with the help of a rosary in order to more easily remember how often you are supposed to say it. You usually say the prayer silently and alone, but you can also gather with others in a chapel for group prayer in which case you say it out loud.

How the Jesus prayer tradition is passed on
If we put to one side the psycho-physiological inflections tied to the reforms of Simeon the New Theologian and the "spiritual" reaction of Gregory Palamas in the 14th Century, as well as the popular diffusion of the *hesychast* tradition in 19th Century Russia, the practice of the prayer of the heart is constant and unified over the centuries. Beyond its Orthodox context, you can find incessant prayer practiced by Western Christian monks, notably the Benedictines, and by the Sufi strain of Islam.

When you begin the practice of the prayer of the heart you are going to need an initiator, such as a "staretz" (a Russian spiritual advisor), or a monk or a priest who gets you going. Often, especially at the beginning, regular participation in sessions of communal prayer will let you solidify

Setting

and sediment the elementary gestures and acts of the practices, so that you can recall them later more easily when alone.

Unfolding of the prayer in different steps

Suspension

The basic bodily position is to be seated, silent, and solitary. This is the most stable position, but you can also kneel, or even remain standing. You slightly incline your head forward, and close your eyes: more than the position of the body, it's the position of the head and eyes that is essential.

You then slow down the rhythm of your breathing, and direct your mind to the interior by centering yourself on your heart. You start saying the Jesus prayer by breathing in on the first part ("Lord Jesus Christ") and by breathing out on the second ("Have mercy on us").

Redirection

You re-direct your attention from the thought to the name by locking in on the task of making the thread of the prayer coincide with that of the breath. If a thought pops up to the surface which makes you lose the thread, you fix your attention on the word on which you slipped up, take note of it, and then take the thread up again.

Letting-go

You let all the thoughts which pass by pop up to the surface without trying to fix them or get rid of them: you let them come and go of their own accord, and contemplate them from a distance.

It is here that the heart breaks free of the mind. You experience an overflowing when the strength of the repetition of the prayer is such as to produce, at a given moment (suddenly, and yet prepared for by the long and weighty repetition), an intensity of self-presence, which sometimes has as its outcome an intense heat at the level of the heart. You feel a surplus of presence, a superabundance which *Diadocus from Photiceas* named *pleroforia* (plenitude). Such an overflowing often results in a flood of tears, which is traditionally called "the gift of tears."

In this context, neither expression, nor *a fortiori* validation, is required.

End

In so far as you intensify your repetition of the name of Jesus from session to session, the prayer becomes more and more a part of yourself: it is interiorized to the point of flowing like a piece of music in you, accompanying all other external or internal activity. You will thus be surprised to find yourself praying while you are in the middle of doing something else.

An immediate and direct giving of evidence hits you like a lightning-bolt of sudden clarity. On the cognitive plane, the lightning bolt is the "Ah-hah!" or "Eureka!" when you make an unexpected discovery of a clear and distinct truth; on the affective plane, it is the sudden feeling of a profound justice, of quasi-aesthetic success, often accompanied by an emotion of joy or even jubilation. In therapeutic practice, for example, we know we have hit upon a valuable

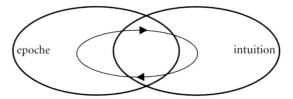

Figure 3.

interpretation of a symbol when the client is hit by the sudden advent of this feeling of plenitude; on the other hand, when nothing of the sort happens we know we are nowhere near where we need to go.

However, let us not get too carried away with all this talk of lightning-bolts. On the one hand, this instantaneous breakthrough of a threshold of intensity that fills us up, that satisfies or saturates us, can be very unstable. On the other hand, let's not forget that we are hit by this lightning bolt only because we have been out in a thunderstorm flying a kite, like Ben Franklin. It is like the old show-biz joke of the overnight success that was 20 years in the making. Thus we have to recognize that the concrete conditions of intuition are integral parts of its lightning-like temporality. In other words, the lightning-bolt temporality of intuition is in a full and constant circulation with *epoche* (Figure 3); what we have treated as different stages, are, although radically distinct, still intimately tied to each other.

We are always struck by how much most sufficiently detailed examples involve this double temporal dimension, both preparatory and passive, where, on the one hand, plenitude is already announced in outline, and, where, on the other hand, the complete confirmation of satisfaction is instantly realized in a lightning bolt. However, we have also noticed how, according to the case, one or the other of these dimensions is privileged, without one ever completely disappearing in favor of the other. Finally, in certain cases, a reiteration turns out to be necessary, a reprise due to the instability of the first intuitive giving.

We find these three dimensions (empty waiting, lightning fulfillment, reiteration) in each example: in stereoscopic vision, the fleeting moment of waiting, then the breaking free of the form; in writing, a pre-fulfillment that is open to many different possible fulfillments, then the right word comes to you like a gift; in *shamatha-vipashyana* or in the heart prayer, the time of the emptiness of fulfillment is determining, but it refers rather to the preliminary rhythm of the *epoche*; the lightning-bolt of intuitive giving is revealed either as a force of emptiness, of impermanence, or as a surplus of presence, as a superabundance.

Reiterated looking for evidence also belongs to all the above practices, but it is perhaps most developed in scientific or philosophical research.

Modalities of intuitive completion

insistence on the emptiness of completion and its progressive character
stereoscopic vision; writing

giving of intuitive evidence in a lightning-bolt:
shamatha-vipashyana; heart prayer

incessantly taking up again or repeating intuitive evidence because it's not there yet:
psychoanalysis

Concerning reiteration, let us note that both reiterated pre-fulfillment and fulfillment encourage internal, sensory, emotional gestures that allow you to evaluate the quality of fulfillment, its insufficiency or its completion. These cognitive gestures are just the sort of "variations of discovery" you can perform either to gain evidence or to regain it in order to reassure yourself that you had it in the first place. Thus the "before and after" of fulfillment, (pre-fulfillment and reiteration), form internal horizons of the lightning-bolt of intuitive evidence, like the "protention and retention" Husserl describes as internal to the "present impression" of internal time-consciousness, assuring its living presence.

Intuition and affectivity

As long as you don't have an example to refer to, you will be tempted to merely "think" the temporality of the intuitive act as a sudden flash. But when you return to the description of really experienced examples you will see that the intuitive act is slow – relative to a reflexive act – and that its fulfillment often occurs in steps. For comparison's sake, we have found that fulfillment usually takes about a minute – or at least more than a few seconds – but in exceptional cases it can take up to ten minutes or more, a stretch which is often experienced as being out of time. During this non-time you either lose any perception of duration or you enter the strange time of an exclusively non-intentional centering, in the sense of what is non-volitional as such. This resembles the description of the temporal quality of the act of evoking a past lived experience: its relative slowness, or perhaps its "viscosity" compared to the neatness, the discrete character, the rapidity of speech working over well known data; in contrast, the act of evoking the past is articulated, composite, often accompanied by microsteps, its qualitative order of sensory apperceptive fulfillment so different in each person.

We realize that in our analysis of examples we have confounded the strong emotional reaction to that which makes sense to you in a flash toward the end of fulfillment, and the quickness of fulfillment itself. Without a doubt the two events are related, but they don't work the same way temporally: the first is like lightning, the second like flowing water that always manages to find its course.

With this first facet of our description we have come to a central part of our project: the methodologically rigorous description of the *failure* of fulfillment. Now you can certainly achieve an instantaneous, first-time fulfillment, without preliminary attempts, right from the first try – even if, to be sure, you have indulged in a pre-reflective incubation that prepares the way. But there is nothing we or anyone else can say about this type of direct givenness, other than to register our astonishment that it is possible and to affirm that you can't discount its possibility. As opposed to the mere acknowledgment of this sort of dumbfounding instant fulfillment, we are much more challenged when we try to describe non-fulfillment or incomplete and unsatisfactory fulfillment.

In this regard, stereoscopic vision is particularly interesting because it's so clear-cut whether you've succeeded or not. As long as you haven't turned the corner, you simply don't see what there is to be seen; it stays hidden from you. With each new stab at it, you can vary the distance or intensity of focus; you can take a entirely different tack by glancing at the images, for example. You can even wait without doing anything, hoping that fatigue might produce new results. But this example shows well that, as long as access is not gained, the familiar perceptive reality is always there. When you see "nothing," in fact, you are continuing to see the motifs of the sheet: you look for a fulfillment on the basis of a naturally pursued activity; what is given in fulfillment happens on the downslope of an *epoche*, and what was not accessible becomes so.

Primordial intuition and imaginary eidetic variations

These observations concerning the temporality of intuitive fulfillment allow us to shift the focus from the perceptual dimension of intuition or fulfillment to intuition as eidetic, that is, as revealing an essence, a dimension which is grounded in imagination.

Eidos, eidetics and imaginary variations in Husserl

As early as the Logical Investigations (1901), in his critique of empiricism (and more broadly of psychologism), Husserl attempts to define a method founded on the intuitive evidence of what is directly given to us in our immediate experience but that nonetheless accounts for the universal essences and categories necessary for objectivation and truth. This will lead him to work out the idea, in the Sixth Investigation, of *categorial intuition*, which asserts (against Kant) that sensory intuition is a foundational experience inherent in all processes of categorization: I can actually *see* the category, have a sense of it. In *Ideas I* (1913), he broadens the scope of his investigation to include not only formal categorized language, but also perception and memory. Using the notion of the *eidetic intuition* (from the Greek *eidos*, which means essence), Husserl investigates the extent to which we can access objective (universal and necessary) features from within the contents of our subjective perceptive and remembering activity. The *eidos* of an object of perception or of my very act of perceiving it, is what is given to me in so far as I can isolate its invariant features from those that are particular and contingent. I look at each feature, and either keep it as essential or leave it as inessential: Husserl calls such a process of observing and discriminating an *eidetic variation*. The term variation comes from the mathematical context of the variation of a function, which means a process of substitution of one function for another (Husserl 1982: 7, 27, 132–141; 1962: 92: "The general description of the method of ideation is manifestly itself a description of the generality of essence; in a free variation, we can well and truly let each exemplary object on which it is practiced become an undetermined object in general, let it in a certain manner become a variable in the mathematical sense."). Now, he also names it *imaginary variation* because the object of perception or the act of perceiving as they are given to me are not given to me as mere raw facts: they entail potential dimensions which I will not necessarily see at first glance. So I have to vary, that is to modify or to change the features of the given object or experience (either using other perceptual ones, or including imaginary ones); this variation gives me access to the intrinsic possibilities of the object and, in the last instance, reveals its invariant structure.

Husserl's method of eidetic imaginary variation is one modality of what is generically called phenomenological reduction, which provides a detailed descriptive account of the passage from the object to the act through which I am perceiving it. The eidetic reduction, however, identifies structural invariants of our experience thereby accounting for the passage from the object to its essence.

One thing is clear: intuitive evidence is not a private subjective or sheer inner mental state. Although, as we have seen, the nature of evidence is multiple (Gil 1993) – or at least ambiguous – we can schematically render it by distinguishing between the intuitive and the conceptual, a distinction already present in ordinary language. Intuitive evidence results from an active interplay between perception and memories/imagination, as we have already mentioned in our brief discussion of Husserl.

Nature of evidence (Depraz 1995: Appendix)

intuitive	
primary	secondary
presentation	presentification
perception	memories, imagination
oneself	intersubjectivity

On the one hand, intuitive evidence *qua* memory/imagination is constructive, providing a unified understanding, an eidetic intuition of the totality of the objects that intuition embraces (Casey 1977:70–83). On the other hand, intuitive evidence *qua* perception is constitutive, as the primal impression isolates a singular aspect of the object being considered.

Thus the process of obtaining an eidetic intuition is always double: on the one hand, eidetic intuition can be detached from proximal or aspectual impression in the lived experience of phenomenal data: what is given can be varied without altering the final intuition of the essence of the phenomenon. At the same time, no intuition which *is totally isolated* from "the facts of life," from the experience of a situated subject, can appear as such, for that would render it disembodied, void of givenness, and shift it over to the side of purely conceptual evidence. In other words, eidetic intuition is *totally indifferent* to the facts of experience, for it is a matter of a completely different act, distinct from the act which intuits an individual sensible object. However, such indifference is not the same as isolation, for eidetic intuition is founded on individual intuition, not in a substantial grounding, but it cannot appear to consciousness without a subject having experienced the givenness of an intuited sensible object.

Our discussion so far has emphasized the key role that *eidetic variations* play in the process of intuition. To unfold the full procedural structure of intuition let us trace more precisely the way you put such variations into play. So far, however, we have concluded that the search for truth is grounded in the continued expansion of evidence. In this sense there is no need to contrast intuitive and discursive; we should, rather, contrast sufficiently developed evidence and incomplete examination. For Husserl, truth is "an infinite horizon of approximations tending toward the idea .... science and philosophy involve an order of cognition, proceeding from intrinsically earlier to intrinsically later cognition; ultimately then a beginning and a line of advance that are not chosen arbitrarily, but have their basis in the 'things themselves.'" (Husserl 1960:§5)

The three-part structure of insight

What is it, then, that we *do* when we access the kind of evidence that forms eidetic intuition? What Husserl calls "imaginary variations" is our clue to developing a structural account. For clarification, let us turn to mathematics, to which Husserl is also indebted for his elaboration of the imaginary variation, as we saw it, and consider the well-known procedure of a thought experiment (*Gedankenexperiment*). We borrow this insight from Rotman (1993). It is clear that we owe much to his analysis, but making it relevant to the question of the phenomenology of intuition is our responsibility. There are three *parallel actions* or processes in a thought experiment. First, there is a *subject* who performs the thought experiment itself, the narrator of the tale or the witness, as it were. Second, this subject builds an imaginary scenario in which some rules are arbitrarily posited, as in a game. This calls for a *virtual agent*, or collection of agents, who are projected proxies able to effect all the actions in the scenario set up by the subject. Third, the subject's story is explicitly directed to an audience, a human *community* of *embodied* subjects in their personal, linguistic and cultural setting.

Consider a classical thought experiment: Descartes' evil genius. Here we see the philosopher as a lonely, reflective subject who subjects his experience to an imaginary variation. He posits the scenario of an evil genius, whose virtual mission is to change the subject's first hand experience, for example, to make it appear real, although it is a dream. Thus the agent, through virtual or imaginary variations, produces effects in the subject's experience. Finally, note that it is Descartes who is writing. He submits his "reduction by doubt" to his audience, the European community of philosophers and religious thinkers of 17th century France: he uses Latin rather than French, he has a recognizable tone of expression, he uses typical rhetorical tropes, and so on. None of these three elements can be absent if you want to arrive at the kind of "Eureka" experience that Descartes' readers have had on the way to his core conclusion concerning the *cogito*. We have all had that evidence in the flesh at the moment when what was until then the ordinary knowledge that "I'm the one who thinks" (exactly the sort of anonymous "of course" Husserl called "self-understandability") becomes a piece of persuasive evidence, an extra significance that gives Descartes' text its weight.

Our main guideline here is that eidetic intuition is completely convincing, but let's not forget that *its convincing status is acquired through an active process*. To help us see what is going on here, let us spell out the analogy between the process of attaining eidetic intuition and a thought experiment: both have a three-fold structure constituted by a subject, an imaginary agent, and a listening community.

Acquiring intuitive evidence
actor 1   virtual agent, changing perceptions
action 1   imaginary variations
actor 2   subject
action 2   command agent, producing an account
actor 3   community, background for satisfaction
action 3   agreeing or not with an account

These three dimensions of the process of attaining eidetic intuition are all woven together and should not be taken as detachable sequences. Taken together they avoid the traps known to haunt many previous accounts concerning intuition. In fact, if intuition is a completely convincing evidence it is because of the directed actions of the virtual agent, and not because it is a form of originary truth that eidetic reduction would reveal from some hidden order. On the other hand, the mere fact of producing an account with an eye to a community – transcribing it painstakingly to make it convincing – embodies evidence and submits it to the judgment of the community as to whether or not it is convincing.

We would claim that when you attain eidetic intuition *via* a thought experiment – that is, *via* imaginary variations inherent to the intuitive act and to its incarnation in a community – you end up coming back to the really genuine phenomenological sense of intuitive evidence. To back up this claim, let's recall Husserl's distinction between *Selbstverständlichkeit* (weak and anonymous evidence of the type "of course, everybody knows that, that's self-evident, taken for granted") and *Evidenz* (strong and apodictic but solipsistic evidence). It should now be apparent to you how neither of these two notions of intuitive evidence does full justice to the intersubjective structure of evidence we see in a thought experiment, whether by default (solipsism) or by excess (anonymity). At bottom, there is another intersubjective approach which should be brought to light here, one which includes both co-reduction and inter-subjectivity. In Husserl, such an intersubjective constitution of evidence is primarily deployed in the context of what is called the "way of psychology," which places back-to-back the inherent solipsism of the Cartesian way and the anonymity proper to the way of the lifeworld (Blankenburg 1991: 144–179, and below Chapter 6.2).

In short, our notion of intuitive evidence is strongly intersubjectively structured: it finds all its richness in the intensifying convergence between the three-fold of the thought experiment and a renewed reading of phenomenological intersubjectivity.

A beginner's course in philosophy

	Context of the exercise
Setting	In this example, we want to help beginning or intermediate students develop their capacity to ask questions and to reflect. The teacher helps you out by choosing the subject matter, by orienting your reflection with questions, and by stimulating discussion between you and your class-mates through well-chosen interventions.
	The overall framework
Suspension	Each session lasts between one and two hours in the usual classroom, usually once a week or every two weeks. The sessions are not isolated moments, but are part of the on-going in-depth study of a theme or an author, stretching out for at least a semester or an academic year. We assume you are there for the duration of the course; this assures a certain constancy in the give-and-take and the going-into-depth.
	The stages of the course
Redirection	The teacher gets things going by problematizing a question or a text. You listen and take notes. The teacher's proposal provokes a response in you, but it stays un-expressed at first: questions well up inside you but stay unanswered. You are in a state of uncertainty, instability, and openness. Rather than look for a way to *answer* the questions you always ask yourself when you're listening with a critical mind, you turn your attention to the *way you ask* yourself the questions, their logic.
Intuitive completion	You stop searching and an inner work of maturation or sedimenta-tion begins, letting you find the right way of asking the question. Sud-denly, a trigger is pulled, and you have got it, you have got the question that has been hiding from you! Carried away by a sense of urgency, you interrupt the teacher, reversing the usual order of things in the class-room, begin an exchange. Now is the chance for the other students to intervene, either to ask another question on the same path or to return to the first discussion. In the best of cases, you all begin to discuss among yourselves, and the teacher steps back behind the debate (s)he helped start.
Expression	
After-effects	Once things start to heat up in class, you often find yourself contin-uing the discussion in the corridors or in a bar or café, with or without the teacher being there.

The mode of evidence as inserted in a background

Our approach makes intuition out as a kind of evidence which is distinct from that of natural science but at the same time not too far from it. In fact, scientific arguments are always an account (a scientific paper) by a subject who is considered a reliable witness by the community. This view is at the center of a recent understanding of how scientific truth and facts *become* what they are. In early European science, the figure of the English gentleman and his supposed moral standards for truthful reporting were at the base of what was to be counted as fact (Shapin 1995; Latour 1995). Robert Boyle, for instance, counted as a reliable witness, and it was in this fashion that he reported on the air pumps to prove his ideas on the nature of ether. But in reading his accounts you can't help but see the form of a *Gedankenexperiment*: "Imagine that you have a bottle where the air has been pumped out to such a degree, then you will easily see that ..." (Shapin & Shaeffer 1994). In this case, the instrumentation and laboratory manipulations play the role of the agent.

The similarities with intuition as a convincing argument through imaginary variations is clear. This is a "technology of witnessing," which, according to Shapin and Shaeffer, is "the production in the reader's mind of such an image of an experimental scene as obviates the necessity for direct witness and replication."

What makes us cross the boundary between community and subject is *dis-embodiment*: the historically situated narrator becomes a detached individual who examines the evidence as it appears to him "in flesh and blood." The passage from subject to virtual agent is one of *meaning*: what happens in the scenario obtained by variations is not supposed to be constrained by perceptual givenness. It is a move to induce or evoke a perspective which the subject will then convey to those to whom it is destined, to arouse in them a similar witnessing leading to a new evidence. This evidence is *at the same time* based on the primal givenness of the subject's experience, and yet incarnated in a historical community within which its value transpires.

What makes a bit of evidence convincing then? It seems that only the *simultaneous satisfaction of the three components* of the intuitive examination can be convincing. Now let us be clear that this is not a question of algorithmic certainty. Just as in scientific evidence there is a *degree* of force in the evidence which depends both on the nature of the subject scenario for variations and on the manner in which the evidence is structured for presentation. The nonmechanical nature of this harmony or accord between the three structural elements gives a new sense to the question of fulfillment that so preoccupies us. In the final analysis, we can't ignore the fundamentally *aesthetic* nature of the harmony among community, subject, and agent that gives fulfillment its punch. Now to be precise, explicitly expressing your intuitions (in the sense of the expressive communication (rendering worldly and available to a community [*mondanéisation et communautisation*]) of this intuition, as Fink puts it, (2000:§11. Cf. also Chapter 2.1)) is not a constitutive moment of the basic cycle, but an optional one, one which requires that you are motivated somehow to want to validate your intuitions intersubjectively (cf. Chapter 2.2). The simple fact that all intuition occurs in a situated context, with a community in the background, doesn't *oblige* you to make the experience public.

Here we can't help but find Einstein's phrase, "Conviction is an excellent prime mover, but a terrible regulator," extremely thought-provoking (Holton 1973/1988:8). Husserl says the same thing in the twenties, when he fully elaborates genetic phenomenology by valorizing genetic and heuristic intuition in the name of the phenomenological construction of meaning; all this amounts to recognizing the necessity of formalizing genetic phenomenology in a logic of exposition distinct from the logic of discovery itself:

> In a certain sense, moreover, every knower proceeds constructively and regressively; he does so in the reasonings of his inventive thought. All invention presupposes an anticipation; one can neither look for anything nor look to produce anything without having available from the start a directing idea of what one means to look for, or of what must be produced. The inventor will organize in imagination different possible ways which, by means of already established truths playing the role of steps, may be able to lead to the anticipated result. What one has thereby gained is only a preliminary hypothesis and a provisional probability (Husserl 1956–1959:191; Depraz 1996a:209).

Thus, contrary to a version of intuition perhaps closer to Husserl's early perceptive ideal, our view of eidetic intuitive evidence doesn't confer on it an apodictic value, but it does make evidence an essential component on the route to a new understanding. It preserves Husserl's demand for intuitive evidence as an "infinite horizon of approximations tending toward the idea," that is, a process of growth wherein different forms of evidence participate in establishing new knowledge in a corpus proper to a community.

Criteria of appreciation and of completion

If we now return to look, on the whole, at what we've said about the intuitive act in its sensory and eidetic dimensions, we find that the distinctions between incomplete, in-progress, failed or indeed full fulfillments show us not only that there are criteria immanent to the product of the act of fulfillment, a judgment on the result of the act, but also, in the same stroke, that there are criteria immanent to the one who appreciates, the one who has the taste for fulfillment, and who thus produces an act of judgment which accompanies the act of fulfillment. On these grounds we propose three ensembles of criteria, all envisioned at first from the point of view of the "first person":

1. First, from *the cognitive point of view:* on the one hand, confusion, incompletion, absence, whiteout, emptiness, nothingness, unreadiness, that which still moves within, and on the other hand, clarity, distinctness, evidence, completion, stability, coherence, being finished, "at peace."

2. Next, from *the emotional point of view:* the feeling of adequation, of justice, or aesthetic success, of joy, of a profound satisfaction, of global congruence when the criterion is fully satisfied, or of surprise and frustration or disappointment if it is not.

3. Finally, from *the properly intersubjective point of view,* participating at the same time in the cognitive (the constitution of objectivity) and the affective (conviction by means of empathy): the experience of an inner conflict or the force of assent, of being carried along by a convincing argument which makes you approve of it as soon as you agree to recognize its truth.

Chapter 2

The structure of a session

The next two phases of the act of becoming aware, expression and validation, are optional with regard to the basic cycle (*epoche* and intuition). But they are both equally necessary parts of a work session; thus we only present them here successively because of the demands of linear expression. In fact, in a research context, expression and validation are both methodologically necessary, so they appear side-by-side in the work session. They mutually imply each other: expression implies a (minimally) objective form, even if it is not verbal; on the other hand, complete validation implies a linguistic act.

2.1. Expression

Expression is an optional and multiform component

In the previous Chapter we saw how intuitive evidence contains a tension between two intrinsic dimensions. On the one hand, we found an elementary intuitive fulfillment, more sensible and perceptive than conceptual or categorial, the fruit of an individual and *singular* experience. This is the most basic sense of "intuition" – the sense in which Husserl calls perception, recollection, imagination and even empathy intuitive acts – as opposed to signitive acts, which imply only a non-intuitive, "symbolic" fulfillment. On the other hand, we found "intuition" to stand for an *intersubjectively* certain evidence which is established *via* eidetic variations.

Now we insist that intuition, on the whole, can be accomplished without expression. The initial intuitive completion can simply lead to something that remains unsaid. We can easily imagine that you can live out this experience of reflection as complete in itself, that you cannot put it into words, or even that you have no intention of expressing it (see Chapter 2.2). In any case, in order to focus on the particular qualities of the expressive act, we need to distinguish between the *expression of the product* of the reflecting act and *the expression of the reflecting act itself.*

Expressions and linguistic descriptions

Expression and verbalization are not, of course, equivalent. We therefore can get confused when we juxtapose the use of the term "thematization" in psychology to designate "putting into words" with the use of the same term in phenomenology. In Phenomenology, "to thematize" has a very large and yet at the same time technical sense: it means to take any objet whatsoever as a theme, as an object of investigation, to explicitly grasp it under the aspect of an act of apprehension, and is opposed to "operative" (*fungieren*), which means "functioning without having been remarked upon or put in view". (Fink has clearly formulated the distinction between thematic and operational concepts in *Nähe und Distanz*). In other words, in phenomenology, thematization in no way implies an expressive nor *a fortiori* linguistic action. We will thus use "verbalization" (*verbalisation*) to name the linguistic aspect of expression. Thus expression is larger since it covers all the means of signification and not just the use of language. In certain therapeutic techniques, you might be asked to express yourself in free sketching, sculpting, free dance, improvised song, and so on, in other words, in whatever medium is able to translate the content of the experience. But of course, neither here nor in the case of meditative traditions would this type of thing necessarily be part of a research project.

On the contrary, verbalization means exactly that, putting something into words: we require a *linguistic description* of the content intended by the reflecting act. In effect, if you can't produce a linguistic description, the rest of our methodology stays in the dark. In this case, all the work of segmenting the description, and all the criteria we give you for separating things, will thus not be made explicit and you won't work on them to bring about an intersubjective confrontation. *A fortiori*, you won't work on the subsequent steps of reformulation and synthetic resumption. It would be as if you jumped directly from reflecting on something to the polished public presentation of distinct essences. This would bury all the *intermediate* work needed to get to that point; all that work would remain private and would seem to be completely implicit knowledge, folded away in yourself.

Thus producing a full description is a *condition* for validating future analyses, but also for learning on the job so that you can get past the intrinsic interpretation belonging to all descriptions in natural language. A full description allows us to confront you during a session with whatever it takes to show, after the fact, those interpretive aspects that are still invisible when they are produced. A full description also allows us to make very useful term-by-term comparisons between your descriptions of different experiences (variation of content), your description of different moments of the same experience, and between your description and those of other people.

When should a description be produced?

So far we have presupposed that you can gain access after the fact to an individual, delimited and singular experience. This *a posteriori* access wouldn't sit well with those cognitive psychologists who insist on simultaneous verbalizations, which they claim gets rid of the inherent deformation and incompleteness of memory. It seems like they are after a practice which least resembles introspection and which, because of that, can the most easily be recognized as "scientific" (Ericsson & Simon 1993).

But their insistence on simultaneous verbalization supposes that reflecting on lived experience doesn't soak up most of your mental capacity. We have found that when you are truly working on new solutions, you're not really all that available for an additional task of verbalization. In fact, usually you are silent. Furthermore, simultaneous verbalization means that the verbal "encoding" has to be rather accessible, but that can unnecessarily limit the nature of the task and the degree of finesse of the description. Finally, there should not be a big temporal gap between the moment of the lived experience and its being put into words.

We find that those psychologists who gather verbalizations haven't paid much attention to the very *practice* of reflecting access that we are describing. Thus they don't appreciate that you can have a recall that is a "letting come back," a "reliving", a concrete memory (Gusdorf 1951) of a past moment which lets surge forth a detailed episodic memory anchored in the sensory mode of lived experience. Being able to obtain detailed descriptions after a significant lapse of time seems entirely to rest on this type of memory, on the renewing of a reliving sufficiently incarnated that it recreates the past. Of course, such a contention raises difficult epistemological issues: anyone who is familiar with research on memory in cognitive science, or recent debates about memory in the context of psychoanalysis, will immediately want to question it: is one gaining access to something and subsequently actually living it in a fresh way or is it a recreation, confabulation or even an induced false memory? Our general phenomenological contention is that such a re-living, though including a recreation-component, is, as such, a genuine act of recalling. We can be genuine enough in our recall to attempt not to include any invented element, and if such fictious elements find themselves intrinsically included in the recall, it means that they genuinely participate in the genuine texture of such a recall.

The specific quality of suspension proper to descriptive verbalization

Thus, if the re-emergence of lived experience requires different levels of time, expression itself – as an act more than a simple product – does not proceed of its own accord – far from it – but requires a certain specific suspension. When you engage in philosophical research for example, since natural language is the milieu in which thought is formed, you have to let the right word come to you; this takes some time, you have to slow down a bit, or in any case not be in so much of a hurry. Moreover, the work of writing as such, poetic or narrative, seems intrinsically inhabited by this suspension, this inhibition, voluntary or not, of the spontaneous act of writing, in order to let meaning arise in all its intensity: the latter is *constituted via* the act of writing understood as an act of "secondary spontaneity." Thus from the point of view of expression, we have to deal with the extreme inverse case in examples coming from spiritual traditions: expression, which is here verbal (but in the case of painting or music, this expression remains non-verbal), appears constitutive of the very process of experience.

A session of writing activity

	The general context The goal of writing is to transform a subjective or emotional experience using a verbal or textual medium whose stylistic and rhetorical qualities communicate the power of the sensation.
	The setting A regular period of time, most often 2 or 3 hours spent sitting at a desk or table, pen in hand or keyboard under the fingers. Sometimes this rhythm is interrupted by time spent walking in the apartment or outside. This rhythm may continue for weeks, months, and even a year ... until the work is finished.
Stages of the activity	1. Once seated, attention is focused on the meaning to be expressed rather than on the form that expression will take. 2. When attention turns to seeking the pregnant meaning, there emerges a second suspension, not of the expressive form, but of the act of expression itself. At this point I refrain from writing anything at all. 3. Patiently, I await the formulation of meaning that will "congeal" in this moment of holding back from writing. Here, it is as if time slows down; I am passive, expecting an event whose content is not yet clear. 4. An expressive donation of meaning emerges from this waiting: the co-emergence of form and meaning.

5. Written remarks, renewed attempts, erasures indicate that the process 1–4 (*epoche*-intuition) is activated as often as necessary until I consider that the work is finished. Drafts and erasures play an analogous role as moments of suspension.

After-effects

Although I am unaware of it, an interior process continues between these periods of work (from one day to the next). It is like a kind of secondary attention that functions when I am doing other things. The writing project thus matures and clarifies itself even when I am not paying conscious attention to it.

Piguet is certainly one of those authors who has best theorized the suspension prior to expression (Piguet 1975:8158). He always insisted on the practice of a language which is respectful of reality in the sense that one takes one's time in order to let the thing be revealed on its own, in its own perceptive or affective "language" (so to speak) "before" being "translated" into one of our everyday talk. He takes care not to determine reality *a priori* by the immanent categories of language, but tries to let language reveal itself by itself. Suspension will thus have as its outcome a silent time, an inhibition or a holding back of the first words which come forth: Piguet speaks in this regard of a non-talkative time.

We thus find it remarkable that, in the *Cartesian Meditations*, Husserl formulated such a requirement, without thoroughly understanding it *via* a precise analysis in all its practical implications. Husserl underlines the essential necessity of "letting the still mute experience [*die stumme Erfahrung*] come to the expression of its proper meaning" (Husserl 1960: §16); he clearly understands by that an ante-predicative expression, which was for him the intentional language of perception itself. Isn't this Husserl's injunction to grasp what the thing itself says in "its own language"? Merleau-Ponty, for one, was not mistaken in stressing Husserl's desire for the native language of the thing itself while conducting his very judicious commentary in the Preface to the *Phenomenology of Perception* (Merleau-Ponty 1962). In another more recent attempt, the contemporary phenomenologist Michel Henry tries to discover the language of the thing itself not *via* the paradigm of perception but according to the immanent logic of affection. His point can be formulated in the following manner, on the basis of his work on Maine de Biran, *Philosophie et phénoménologie du corps*: what is the intimate language of our feelings and emotions? How can we intuitively find adequate words? In making this non-predicative level of meaning a primordial dimension of satisfactory expression and verbalization, we feel that these philosophers are searching for the suspension that is singular and proper to expression. Fink himself, in §10 of the *Sixth Cartesian Meditation*, insists on the necessary loss of words (*Sprachlosigkeit*) of the phenomenological spectator, as well as on the requirements of a "transcendental language" which takes charge of, in an analogical transposition, the terms of natural language. However, despite the intrinsic interest of their work, none of these philosophers focus on the phenomenological *practice* of suspension and expression. None of them focuses on the bottom line, as we see it: they never bother to ask themselves how they're able to write as phenomenologists!

The quality of the intuitive evidence proper to verbalization

If we want to do justice to our inquiry, we have to be precise about "expressive fulfillment or completion." We find the extent to which the idea of an expressive fulfillment remains a blind spot in phenomenological analysis to be very interesting. Despite the few allusions we evoke above, Husserl barely treated it, obsessed as he was by the dichotomy between intuitive and categorially signitive acts. Derrida (1973) very early critisized such a dichotomy. We therefore have to account for a phenomenological writing, the requirements of which would be to be adequate to the *epoche* (Depraz 1999b). In that respect, we need to speak about expressive fulfillment in order to do justice to the very specific quality of the emergence of a meaning that is indeed pre-categorial but nevertheless intuited. It is remarkable, in this regard, that in the *Critique of Judgment* (§59 and §74) Kant knocked a hole in the opposition between intuition and concept that he himself had established in the first Critique, by showing the necessity of an "aesthetic intuition" or a "symbolic intuition," in the name of an event of meaning irreducible to the categories (Richir 1984). Thus we find once again, though of course with a different quality, the *basic cycle* of *epoche* and intuitive evidence. This time however, we find another form of fulfillment, no longer sensible-eidetic as with intuition, but expressive, conforming to the immanent logic of putting into words.

In pursuit of such expressive fulfillment, we find that in conducting a debriefing interview we often have to ask you to slow down your speaking; in self-mediation (or interiorized mediation), you have to go back over what you said; when you are writing – which is here paradigmatic – expression leads you to run back through the whole of the initial cycle of *epoche-intuition*: when you hold yourself back, or are prevented, from writing (cf. Mallarmé's famous anguish!), you are dealing with the waiting necessary for a more dense formulation.

We find the impression of poverty, even of destitution, in this first movement of expression to be fascinating. It is as if, despite all our preparations or expertise, there's so little to say about a lived experience. Putting into words happens in successive layers which complete themselves, which bring forth complements, details, layers of meaning that each new reduction gives birth to. In autonomous work, the after-effects of the work session can last for weeks by renewing and enriching themselves.

A session of psychoanalysis

The background

The practice of psychoanalysis was originally developed by Freud through his work with his first patients. In some cases explicitly, in others by implicit demands, they indicated the design of an experience that Freud spent his remaining lifetime elaborating, and whose basic form is intact today. The following brief description of selected aspects of an analytic session is written *from the perspective of an analyst's experience*. Certainly writing it from the perspective of the analysand would highlight different levels of the experience. That being said, it is worth noting that it is proper to the analytic project to problematize the very question of its protagonists' experiences by establishing a specific kind of intersubjective space which resists reduction to either perspective (even if this does not exclude "accounts").

The setting

Beforehand

Whatever different traditions or schools analysts come from they all agree on the necessity of a fixed frame for the psychoanalytic process. At the outset of an analysis a contract structuring the alliance between analyst and analysand is established. This contract stipulates the groundrules and frame for the work to be done. Sessions are scheduled for a certain time, a certain frequency (variable), and have a specific length (variable or pre-determined). The analysand comes to the rendezvous, and pays a fee to the analyst. (S)he may be seated in a chair, or lying on a couch, with the analyst seated next to or behind her/him. Maintaining a constancy and regularity in this frame is an obligation for both parties; any departures from it, on the part of either analyst or analysand, are subject to examination in the context of the process.

Suspension

Within this stable frame the analyst is to exercise a certain kind of listening, that Freud called *evenly suspended* attention. In this particular mode of listening the analyst must refrain from developing her/his own trains of thought or theoretical preoccupations, and follow the trail of the unfolding discourse of the patient, making no judgements nor foregrounding any particular content. As for the analysand, (s)he is subjected to a symmetrical rule, that of saying all that comes to mind without censorship (free-association) (Freud 1912, Vol. 12:111–120).

The beginning of a session finds the analyst in a position of expectation. An anticipatory, albeit relative, emptying of mental content is conditioned by the frame, and most certainly triggered by the ritualization of the greeting process (imagine the audience the instant before the curtain rises). As the session continues, reflections or emotions emerge and are passed over or "put aside" as the listening process goes on. Some will perhaps be retaken later in the session in a retroactive movement, for example a punctuating intervention or interpretation. At times the analyst's thoughts may be polarized by something (s)he has selected from the analysand's associations. This polarization, which often is actualized by the emergence of a theoretical construct, corresponds to a break in the listening process; this very gap signals the analyst to re-suspend her/his attention.

Redirection

The experience of analytic listening thus leads us to understand Freud's injunction to evenly-suspended attention as a technical horizon that foregrounds the interplay between suspension and its breakdown in the listening process. The rule of free association also functions similarly as a kind of horizon or limit for the analysand faced with the difficulty of suspending censorship and thereby suspending the production of (conscious) meaning.

Letting go

In concert with this continuous interplay, the analysand's associative flow triggers the redirection of the analyst's listening within a twofold (double) context: the first, which might be called the microcontext, is that of the flow of signifiers during the session itself, considered as a closed unit or individual event (like a poetic unit); the second, or macrocontext is that of the analysis, the preceding sessions and the dynamics of the transference. These contexts, which are clearly specific to a particular session and a particular analysis, are grounded in the material produced by the analysand. They are obviously interwoven, inseparable; nonetheless they are both present to the listening analyst, serving as a filter for his/her own mental contents during the session, and conditioning the style, content and timing of his/her interventions. This is perhaps why it is often the experience that interpretations (enunciated or not) tend to "appear" to the analyst as opposed to being consciously "thought up", since it is the analysand's signifying material itself that conditions, insists toward its own interpretation.

Modalities of linguistic expression from the perspective of a research program

Let us suppose you agree with us that a full description of the act of becoming aware is necessary for research in a variety of scientific areas. How are we going to go about it then? There are several types of description we need to consider:

1. Simultaneous or deferred description
2. Written or oral description
3. Autonomous or mediated description

The concrete practice of description brings together all these different aspects: temporal phases, means of expression, and modes of mediation (internal or external). We have found that producing a full description useful for research implies we use all these parameters. We have found a mutual enrichment when we ask for both an immediate description and then a reconsideration later; for both an oral and a written description; for both autonomous and mediated descriptions as well as a solitary reprise.

Right now we can't go into all the details of validation, since for that we will have to clarify the status of intersubjective mediation as such, as well as the second-person pole, as we will do it in the Chapter 2.2, which treats of the precise fashion of mediating intersubjectivity in the name of the objective validation renewed in scientific work itself; nor can we get into the precise nature of descriptive categorization and the eidetic method pertaining to validation. These will come later. Right now, we will just present two concrete and pragmatic arguments which support these three research necessities for our subjects:

1. an external or internal mediation
2. the repetition of exercises
3. the complementary use of written or oral expression

In case 1, we find that our research subjects, even when supposedly left by themselves, have recourse to mediation by interiorizing the criteria and procedures we trainers or counselors use, since in the research context we are living examples or models to be imitated. Now this sort of self-mediation (that is, an already-interiorized mediation) requires a specific know-how about one's own cognitive activity. 2. Now it can take a long time for the sort of research subjects we are likely to have come to us to acquire this sort of self-mediating expertise. Usually we lack this time because of the relatively short time period during which we are supposed to carry out a research project. 3. However, we have found we can refine some of this difficulty by having our subjects write down their descriptions or by transcribing their words from recordings, since these practices materialize expression and make coming back to reconsider it all the easier. Given all these problems with self-mediation, we have found that it is quite important to develop expert external mediators who know how to guide description without leading it, know how to facilitate suspension without being intrusive, know how to question without feeding the responses or providing any information that interferes with description.

Our experience with psychologists and psychotherapists, and our work in focusing the technique of the debriefing interview, lead us to argue for the utility of an external mediator who can listen and guide you in your descriptions. In the same way, we would argue that becoming a philosopher or a scientist almost always implies having a mentor who helps you develop your research skills by sharing his or her experience.

However, despite the necessity of mediation in research as we outline above, the arguments we present below are mostly derived from the experience of practitioners rather than researchers, since the former are without doubt those who, in the West at least, have done the most to develop techniques and to stimulate the internal self-mediating relation of subjects with themselves. Nevertheless, despite their origin with practitioners, these arguments should also be taken up by all researchers who wish to reconnect their scientific approach and their subjective experience. These arguments can thus serve as useful points for a *practice of research*:

You express more than you meant to say: this case justifies our claim that we need a witness who notes non-verbal, para-verbal, and epi-verbal indicators. Now of course a video recording would have been able to capture all these bits of information. But a camera cannot, having spotted a mimetic or metaphoric gesture accompanying verbal expression, direct your attention to a gesture which expresses more, or something else, than what you say, nor can it make you come back to that point and start over again. That sort of intervention requires someone with all the tricks of the trade of a psychotherapist to exploit these extra-verbal signals, which are sometimes contradictory enough to signal strongly that your verbalization is conflicting with something which is not being expressed. You cannot exploit these signals yourself since they are unconscious (try as you might, you can only displace the limit of the conscious without being able to abolish it).

Now we are not calling for an ideal observer who could tell everything about you just from looking at you (that is, an observer who is capable of an absolutely overpowering interpretation). Rather, we are calling for a companion attentive to what is expressed across the grain of what is said, and who uses these signals to get you going again so that you can explain what you meant but didn't say.

You say less by yourself than you could with mediation: this second remark might seem to contradict the first, but it really doesn't, since they don't address the same point. In the first case, you furnish – unconsciously – more information than you think you do, and the interviewer helps you to start all over again with what you showed but *didn't* say. In the second case, we focus on what you *want* to say, but can't. In this case, we can help you to go further than you could on your own.

We can enable this progress for several reasons. We have already seen the first one: as long as there is a need for delay, for inhibiting the most immediate responses, the presence of a mediator facilitates suspension and at the same time plays a formative role. Most of what you gain access to is pre-reflected: thus your verbalization is accomplished following the rhythm of what is revealed, that is, rather slowly. Exterior guidance can help you to take the time needed to accept this form of expression. External mediators can also help you to curtail those moments when reflected knowledge gets in the way of the reflecting act, as when you sketch a rectangular table because you *know* that it is rectangular, even though you *see* a trapezoid. When you are working at writing, it often happens that you write too quickly; this leads to erasures and drafts, which are concrete manifestations that evidence is not yet there, signs of the discrete presence of an other in you who tells you that you are not yet there, marks of a clarification, of a necessary relaunching that, *de facto*, you work on alone, even if famous others – the creators who have preceded us – are present in the background of our writing process.

Staying within the limits of a putting into words that confines itself to what effectively appears is a delicate thing, and demands that you remain in a meta-position with regard to what you say. You can do it alone, but not without a long apprenticeship. It is easier with a companion, even when you are gifted or already an expert (Vermersch 1994, Chapter VI).

We can also help you say more than you could on your own by asking questions which focus your attention on those aspects of your lived experience for which you do not yet have the right *categories*. Thus we have found that interviewers with the right kind of knowledge and experience possess keys to describing that are more developed, complete or differentiated than those possessed by the interviewee.

We thus have plenty of positive arguments for introducing a mediator into a research context, but we can't forget that the mediation itself will be limited by the *competence of the mediator*. On the one hand, acquiring all the competencies of an expert interviewer is a long process, demanding a lot of training to master the various techniques involved and to make them operative in the exchange. On the other hand, despite the distance mediators can attain, they remain limited by their culture, pre-conceptions, implicit frames of knowledge, and unconscious projections. It would be vain to think we can find mediators who can absolutely free themselves from these limitations. Assessing the limits of individual mediators leads us back to the necessity of *intersubjective* regulation.

Modalities of the role of expressive fulfillment

Expression that is different from and non-constitutive of experience
heart prayer, shamatha-vipashyana
Constitutive expression that is spontaneous and open to multiple forms of symbolization
stereoscopic vision
Expression in which verbalization is constitutive
oral mode: debriefing interview
mixed, oral and written mode: philosophical work
Expression in which verbalization is constitutive and exclusively written
writing activity

A sketch of the problems with descriptive categorization

If we want to establish a scientific program based on a descriptive eidetic, we certainly need individual subjects to undergo the work needed for the temporal suspensive base of expressive and intersubjective fulfillment. But we are also going to need to create a community wherein the rules of expression and description are formulated. And when we consider verbalizations realized in a *research community,* we see descriptive categories unfold, often in an unanticipated baroque profusion, laying bare the multiplicity of descriptive points of view, the diversity of objects and planes of description.

Other people have observed this phenomenon as well. Fink, for example, stressed the intrinsic difficulty of establishing a scientifically communicable phenomenological language. In his *Sixth Cartesian Meditation* §10 he pleads for what he calls a "transcendental language." However, he remains caught in a theoretical tension: on the one hand, he proposes the development of a transcendental language as an analogue of natural language, while on the other hand, he nevertheless continues to use the words of a mundane language which he invests with a transcendental meaning, but without making precise the con-

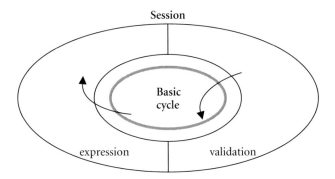

Figure 4.

crete procedures for doing so. We welcome his efforts, but they remain, in our opinion, insufficient. The defenders of the primacy of language can only state that a "transcendental" language is quite an odd language, and see in Fink's claim an unsurpassable or indeed useless aporia.

As opposed to his previous insistence on a transcendental language, in the *Sixth Cartesian Meditation* §11 Fink insists on the necessity for the spectator to come back to the world. In other words, Fink insists here on the necessity that phenomenologists communicate with each other within a research community. Even if he often notes that a language made worldly [*mondanéisé*] is not a language that is simply worldly [*mondaine*] – since it has stood the test of a transcendental *epoche* – he doesn't say nearly enough about the concrete problem of how to realize an eidetic description which might be intersubjectively communicable, thereby becoming the source of a renewed objectification. Concerning this issue, we find that the only way to get beyond the theoretical aporia of phenomenological descriptive language is the long and laborious communal elaboration of descriptive categories in which each researcher can recognize his own experience.

2.2. Validation

What expression and validation have in common

We have already seen two things expression and validation have in common. First of all, neither expression nor, *a fortiori*, verbalization, is necessary for the basic cycle of the reflecting act, which need only consist of *epoche* and intuitive fulfillment (Figure 4). As we have said, the basic cycle can culminate in something that remains non-said, or even in something that could not be said even if you had wanted to. In the same way, having what you express validated by others is also optional. Secondly, we have also already seen that linguistic description requires an intersubjective mediation, which has certain modalities and constraints. This is obviously another common point between expression and validation.

Beyond these commonalities, since we are now focusing on validation, we are going to systematically discuss the role of mediation, which we have already met up with several times along the way. First of all, we have noticed that intersubjective mediation belongs to any meaningful research practice of description: we can only elaborate a descriptive categorization if a community has already put into place the intersubjective conditions for validating the categories in question. Furthermore, we can only effectively deploy these validating conditions by supposing a project of verbalizing the concretely engaged reflecting act. Thus we have already anticipated, in the context of descriptive verbalization, an essential trait of our proposal – intersubjective mediation. Here we will explicate it in the context of validation, under the rubric of *the second-person*. Elsewhere, we have also met with intersubjective mediation in the initial step of *epoche*, as well as in the categorial constitution of intuition in the form of eidetic variations conducted in the manner of a thought experiment. Now, just as *epoche* receives its specific quality at each step of the deployment of the act of becoming aware, so does mediation accompany the course of the global structure, with a specific coloration at each step.

Validation is an optional and multifarious component

Validation is thus only necessary when inscribed in a project which gives it its specificity. In particular, it need not be restricted to the single perspective of natural science. As we shall see, validation is a multifarious aspect of the dynamic of the act of becoming aware. Everyone knows that the empirical sciences (in this context, the cognitive sciences) have their own well-worn means of dealing with the issue of validation. However, we shall see the way in which a disciplined exploration of experience opens a number of *other* horizons for validation.

Meditative traditions, for example, also give instructions for evaluating and validating achieved results, by demanding the careful verification of the presence and properties of the results arrived at along the way of their own paths of experience. Phenomenology, for its part, does not pose the problems of validation in the same perspective as empirical sciences do – though this different strategy is certainly not developed in order to relax the rigor of its method. Rather, phenomenology deals with validation by putting forth the strong, and extremely strict, criterion of apodicticity and the internal intuitive criterion of lived experience.

In what follows, we hope to be able to do justice to these various approaches to validation by focusing on the problems we have encountered in developing a form of validation that is inspired by (1) empirical science and (2) phenomenological philosophy.

We must also admit right up front that we don't yet have the means of differentiating between the problems of validation specific to different domains of research. For instance, each of the following would pose its own issues: (1) types of objects (temporal research objects like the unfolding of an act, or even non-temporalized ones like the description of a state); (2) the scales of temporality such objects imply (the macro-temporality of the after-effects of a session, the time of a session, the micro-temporality of an act of fulfillment); (3) the articulation between individual knowledge and its collective inscription (modes of descriptive formulation, criteria of falsification, work context of a collective phenomenological project). You can be sure that anyone trying to work with this methodology, as with all others which have been developed over the course of the century, will encounter original problems and hence will need to develop specific methodological tools for the class of research objects being studied.

In fact, in the year 2001 we find ourselves in the paradoxical situation of treating problems of validation without having the means of presenting detailed research projects using the proposed methodology, apart from certain incomplete cases to which we will do justice at the very end of this discussion. Moreover, the analysis of the structural procedure of the reflecting act that we have just set forth was established on the basis of a methodology which we are trying to specify. We can provisionally plead the case for the limits and coherence of the results we have *learnt on the fly:* it is the very fact of deploying this research which allows us to better understand the requirements that it imposes; this is all the more the case because what we study is at the center of the methodological practice we propose.

Now there are two main axes we need to analyze here, each of which is orthogonal to the other:

1.   First, the multiple gradations of the collective or intersubjective dimension: the gradations between what we call the first-, second- and third-person *positions*.

2. Second, the various *stages* of the actual unfolding of the process of becoming aware as they concern validation.

Structures of mediation: First-, second- and third-person positions

1. Outline of the three positions

Validation intrinsically concerns the intersubjective establishment of criteria of veracity in an investigation. The standard *de facto* method of validation in science is the so-called scientific method. Now, as contemporary history and philosophy of science have made abundantly clear, this is far from a simple gathering of empirical data by a detached Cartesian observer, which is then checked against falsifiable hypotheses. We might as well face it: the reality of science is far from this regulatory ideal. Establishing an empirical fact as "scientific" brings with it the entire edifice of the scientific enterprise as a network of social actors, including their aesthetic, political, and geographical idiosyncracies (Latour 1991; Stengers 1992). The visible product of the scientific process is of course the article published by a more or less reputable journal or research institution; these make up the core of the social network of scientific life. Thus, although the received view is that scientific truth is objective in the sense that every reference to subjective judgment is removed by the scientific method, we insist that *a social mediation is always at work*. The validation leading to scientific objectification is, to be sure, a very unique and specific way of placing social actors in a structure that can appear free of any reference to individual experience; on this very freedom from reference to individual experience rests, in part, the ability to forge facts as independent world entities. However, we insist that this position or objective stance is a specific form of a socially distributed mediation. We refer to this objective stance as a *third-person position*.

In stark contrast to third-person accounts we find *first-person accounts* (Varela & Shear 1999). In its received interpretation, such a stance is singular and individual, inaccessible except to the one who experiences. This option needs to be examined more closely than is usually done, and the experiential or subjective must be sharply distinguished from the private or inaccessible. As we discussed above, there is no *a priori* reason why what we experience – what is closest to individual subjectivity – cannot *also* be examined, expressed, and opened up to intersubjective validation. This is in any case what all those traditions for whom lived experience is important – introspective psychology, phenomenology, various professional practices in education, therapy, but also the traditions of human transformation (mindfulness meditation, and in a certain way, the heart prayer of the Orthodox Church) – have always claimed, even though they might seem at first glance to be far from any need of validation.

Our attitude is thus a far cry from the idea that the first-person point of view is a solipsistic privacy forming the polar opposite of objective validation. Others share this attitude of bridging the seeming gap between first- and third-person: for instance, mathematical validation clearly straddles subjective and collective validation by means of disciplined descriptions. How phenomenologists and practicioners validate their own data remains, of course, less clear; to clarify this is partly one of the goals of this book. Just as Husserl himself was looking for a new science, the "object" of which would be subjectivity itself (Husserl 1960: §8), we are trying to institute the concrete means, in the methodology we develop here, for a scientific study of the experience of a singular individual.

In this respect, the first- and third-person positions we have just outlined make clear the need for the introduction of a less obvious position we call the *second-person* (Thompson 2001). The second-person position is neither the disembodied scientific community to which the validation of an empirical fact is addressed, nor is it the direct experience underlying the first-person position. Rather, a second-person position is an *exchange between situated individuals* focusing on a specific experiential content developed from a first-person position. The second-person position is thus typically instantiated in a tutor or guide, someone who has more training in or exposure to a certain domain, and who tries to help the expression and validation of someone else.

From the list of our examples, let us take the debriefing interview as a paradigm. In that situation, a skilled interviewer is able to bring forth a number of pre-reflexive contents of a particular type of knowledge or know-how by means of carefully chosen, and thus non-leading, questions.

The second-person position is central to all the traditions invoked in this book, with the possible exception of the sciences. In science, the second-person position is certainly to be found, but only in the training of the scientist. Younger researchers often seek the help of a more experienced scientist who will tutor them, thus helping them develop their scientific skills by broadening their imaginations, honing their intuitions, refining their evaluative abilities, and so on. Although scientific culture has a variety of informal ways of paying homage to elders who form the lineage of a scientist's training, all the second-person mediations so important in the training of an individual scientist are studiously ignored in the article published in a scientific journal.

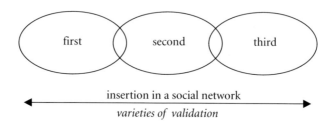

Figure 5.

Figure 6.

In short, then, the three positions are not differentiated by the content they address, but by *the manner in which they are inserted in a social network*. The particular roles social actors take in each case determines their belonging to one or the other position; gradations between roles are also possible, as represented by the overlaps in the diagram below. (We discuss gradations between positions below.) We therefore reject a strict opposition between public and private, or objective and subjective, in favor of a continuum of positions in a social network. We can illustrate the situation as in Figure 5. Compare this continuum of positions with this diagram of a subjective–objective opposition (Figure 6).

2. Multiple gradations in the three positions

Precisely because validation depends on the exact way in which an intersubjective network is constituted, there are possible gradations between positions. In other words, the three positions are not hard and fast categories, but convenient ways to talk about a complex social network. Thus each of them has multiple gradations, defined as a function of the *emphasis* one puts on accomplishing a particular mode of validation. Let us re-examine the three positions in light of the above nuance.

The third-person position, instantiated in the standard observer of scientific discourse, is the most extreme way of creating the apparent dualism between internal experience and external objectivity; it is the basis for scientific reductionism in all its forms. This "pure" form of observation, is, however, directly challenged by the cognitive sciences, since their object specifically involves the social actors themselves. Thus the cognitive sciences form a singularity in science; no other science has this self-involving structure that co-implicates observer and observed. Now, to the extent that the scientific content of the cognitive sciences focuses on biochemical and neural operations, this circularity is not an important issue. However, as every neurobiologist knows, animal behavior and expression are also an integral part of the relevant data, even when such behavior is studied *via* classical recording and measurement. An extreme case in point is verbal behavior – not necessarily when taken as an expression of mental life, but as acceptable data.

Now to impute a mental correlate to such verbal or behavioral correlates is another matter, and as we all know behaviorism based its entire research program on just this distinction. In contemporary practice, most cognitive neuroscientists do not make this into a principled distinction; they assume, more or less explicitly, that such behavior comes from a cognitive subject or agent, but don't push the matter very far. Although such practices are squarely within the norm of third-person accounts, they already involve the other's position in a way that studying cells and crystals does not. That's why we single it out here as a gradation within the third-person position that edges toward a second-person position.

From a second-person position, what appears above in strict behaviorist third-person accounts as mere overt behavior is taken explicitly as traces or manifestations of the mental life of the other, and furthermore as the *only* access to this mental life. Dennett has recently called this very position *hetero*phenomenology (Dennett 1991, Chapter 4). For Dennett, heterophenomenology is the position of an anthropologist studying a remote culture. For anthropologists, merely collecting tapes, pictures, and notes is only the beginning. From these "raw" materials, (they are of course the product of selections, conscious or not, as to what is important to notice and what can be ignored), anthropologists must then infer models of mental – that is, cultural life, using what Dennett famously calls the "intentional stance." As he puts it in *Consciousness Explained*:

> We must treat the noise-emitter as an agent, indeed a rational agent, who harbors beliefs and desires and other mental states that exhibit *intentionality* or 'aboutness', and whose actions can be explained (or predicted) on the basis of the content of these states.

As Dennettian heterophenomenologists, we do *not* take our sources at face value by baldly subscribing to *their* interpretations of their behavior! In other words, in remaining in the anthropological stance, we do not become a member of the tribe. We include this stance within the range of second-person positions because, even though when we are heterophenomenologists we strictly use external traces, we are nonetheless present as a situated individual; we must explicitly and consciously, indeed, methodologically, adopt the intentional stance and undertake the interpretations it involves. These procedures are of course not necessary when validation does not take up the intentional stance and stays with the study of neural and behavioral traces, as in animal studies and many types of human studies.

We know this might infuriate some people, but now we are going to investigate just what happens when we give in to the temptation to become part of the tribe! In this gradation within the second-person position, we observer/interpreters give up some of our detachment and identify with the understanding and internal coherence of our source. In fact this is how we see our role: as an empathic resonance with the experiences of the source, based on our familiarity with this type of experience and on our ability to resonate with others having this type of experience. This empathic position retains something of heterophenomenology, however, since a modicum of critical distance and critical evaluation is still necessary. You can't just melt into the other person! Rather, we want to meet on common ground, as members of the group of people who have all undergone the same type of experiences. We have encountered many examples of this type of mediation in our overview of practices and traditions.

Thus we have moved from the position of anthropologist to that of coach or midwife, whose trades are based on a sensitivity to the subtle indices of the interlocutor's phrasing, body language, and overall expressiveness. As this sort of sensitive empathic mediator, we are looking for more or less explicit indices which can serve as inroads into a common experiential ground. Such encounters would not be possible were we not steeped in the domain of experience in question; nothing can take the place of that first-hand knowledge, nothing can take the place of having been there yourself! Empathic resonance is thus a radically different style of validation from anything we have seen before.

Let us move even further toward the first-person position. Here we see that the second-person stance can also be seen from the point of view of the source, the person undergoing the experience to be examined. Here we focus on you as a subject who, having decided to seek a validation for an expression, moves into an examination session in which you submit to the mediation of another. As we have seen, this opening up to intersubjectivity is not obligatory at every moment or in every session. The converse though *is* necessary: at some

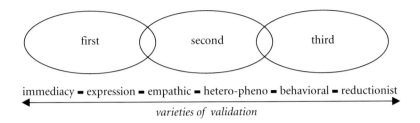

immediacy ▪ expression ▪ empathic ▪ hetero-pheno ▪ behavioral ▪ reductionist

varieties of validation

Figure 7.

point, in order for it to be fruitful and socially-engaged, all first-person work must eventually, sooner or later, assume the position of a direct experience that refuses continued isolation and seeks intersubjective validation. Without intermittently opening up to the other, the process of becoming aware risks a vicious privacy or even solipsism. We do not deny that such a radically enclosed position is possible for human beings to adopt; as we all know, many people do in fact create completely self-contained worlds, which, from the vantage point of a social network, appear as delusional and thus in some cases as excuses for intervention. We do not want to pass judgment here on whether or not such social treatment is justified. We simply note here that the passage into a position open to second-person mediation is necessary at some step for the process of becoming aware to fall within our search for a methodology.

Leaving to one side the issue of delusional isolation, we should note that the first-person position contains a form of internal validation, which draws its force from the nature of intuitive fulfillment. As we have noted previously, at the core of becoming aware there is a certain force of evidence in intuitive fulfillment. This experience, while it is certainly not incorrigible, does at least hit you with an *aesthetic* force. The immediacy of fully accomplished intuitive insight, then, is the most "pure" subjective form in the spectrum of validation, but we must be clear that it has this place only to the extent that it *belongs* to that continuum: it is not in any way isolated from the other types of validation available to the other gradations of first-, second- and third-person positions. We can now represent the gradations of validation (Figure 7).

Stages in the process of validation

We now turn to the second axis, to examine the various *stages* of the act of becoming aware. Validation is present at every stage of putting the methodology of the reflecting act into practice. At each stage, we can see a form of validation from the perspective of any of the styles of validation we have just described.

They can coexist without contradiction, as some cover aspects tending more to the first-person pole, and others cover aspects tending to the third-person pole.

Thus we can reconsider our exemplary variations in so far as they range from the exclusively first-person pole to the third-person pole.

Modes of validation
Intrinsically internal validation
artistic quest: painter, composer, poet, novelist: "writing activity"
first person
second person in background [I–(II)]
Internal validation including a mediation which proceeds by being interiorized
spiritual work: *shamatha-vipashyana*, heart prayer, philosophical work:
first, then second persons [I–II]
Constitutively mediated validation by the second person
debriefing interview: *second, then first person,*
completed by the third person [II–I + (III)]
Primarily third-person validation, but able to be rechecked in its objectivity
by an appeal to the second person
scientific session, stereoscopic vision
third person
complemented by the second person [III–II]

Now, the interface between first- and second-person positions appears more sharply when we distinguish at least four stages in the process of validation:

1. The existence and determination of the *reference experience* [*vécu de référence*] (E1), that is, what is grasped as a target by the reflecting act.
2. The *qualities of the act* by which this lived experience (E1) is reflected upon; this act of reflection is thus another lived experience (E2).
3. The *qualities of the verbal description* of E1 (truth, completion, fine-grained quality).
4. The *analysis of results* that have issued from the descriptive verbalization.

Each of these steps implies one or more of the preceding steps, but the fact of having lived through one of these steps does not render necessary one or more of the subsequent ones (Figure 8).

1. The reference experience (E1)
The reference experience cannot be the object of a validation as such, but it does constitute the reference point of all the other steps. What grounds our research into the act of becoming aware is experience, that is, an individual (lived

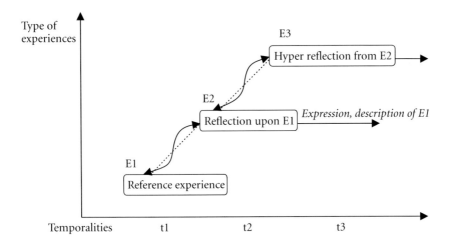

Figure 8.

through by a person) and singular (possessing a thematic, spatially and temporally unique site) reference experience. At the moment you are reflecting on
this lived experience and trying to describe it, we can legitimately ask you: are
you verbalizing a lived experience that has really taken place? Are you indeed in
the process of describing the lived experience you should be and not another?
Is what you are describing the same experience you lived through? Is it at least
compatible with the *a priori* properties of the lived experience in question? Is
your verbalization of facets of the experience we can't observe at least compatible with the traces you leave behind and with those observations we were able
to collect at the moment of the lived experience?

We will have to face all these questions at other steps of validation, but
we will be able to answer them better if all the means for gaining access to
later validations have been collected at the moment of the lived experience.
Concerning this step, if we record the traces you leave we can constitute data
independent of your volition, allowing us to validate:

1. the existence of the reference experience,
2. whether what you say is true, that is, able to be validated in the second- or
   third-person (what is objectifiable),
3. whether what you say is compatible with what we know about the properties of the situation.

Between the extremes of the internal side (the lived experience) and the external side (the traces), there are thus varied relations following which the lived ex-

perience is more or less the creator of its own traces, or depending on whether recording devices were put in place or not.

2. The reflection on the reference experience (E2)

Here we focus on the reflecting act related to E1. Whatever is the case in the almost immediate retentional present (but there will always be a temporal gap proper to reflexive access), or in forms of re-presentations in the evocative mode of remembrance, reflection on this lived experience merges with the basic cycle of *epoche* and intuitive fulfillment.

In this step, the question of validation seems to split off into two problems: the validation of the *content* of what is reflected upon, and the validation of the *act* which reflects upon this content. In so far as the content is only accessible to validation if it is expressed, we will tackle this question in the next step.

The reflecting act itself can be made the object of an evaluation after the fact, and this appreciation can affect the value of the collected verbalizations. However, this evaluation of the access on which verbalizations are based calls for a new degree of reflection, or implies the putting into play of a new reflecting act *regarding* the putting into play of the reflecting act relating itself to E1. There is thus a third time, a new lived experience, E3, which differs from E2 only by the fact that, in precisely grasping E2, it thus supposes the existence of E2; this new act thus constitutes a second degree act or a *super-reflection* [*hyper-réflexion*]. This super-reflection constitutes a new reduction, the condition of possibility of this evaluation.

In the end, putting this super-reflective evaluation (E2 = simple re-presentation; E3 = re-presentation of the re-presentation) into practice supposes that we determine some criteria for its proper use. We propose three indices in this regard. This evaluation will thus take place after the fact, when we are questioning the act of reflection on E1. Most experts will be sensitive to these points *during* the very reflecting act itself and will thereby regulate themselves.

a. Index of the individualizing singularity of the reference experience. Access to a lived experience is singular; if it is not singular, it is not a matter of a lived experience but of a class of lived experiences – and a class of lived experiences is not a lived experience! It is not on the same logical level nor does it even have the same ontological status. You can appreciate this singularity in temporal terms: "it's that moment there", you can say; you can identify it as being effectively unique in your life. This temporal character doesn't necessarily imply you can situate it on the calendar, by day, week, month or year. What is fundamental is that you are conscious of the uniqueness of the moment you are accessing. Now if you cannot so testify, you must be sure to focus on the nature of the modification, imprecision, or distortion of the index of singularity. Even if you can't grasp the temporal singularity of the reference experience, you might still be able to pick out the singular circumstances of the experience. Thus this index allows us to evaluate the type and the degree of the singularity of the reference experience. This is not only a matter of gradation, for it can be expressed, even when it is not fully complete, following diverse qualitative structures (superposition of situations, flashes, etc.).

b. Index of the presence of, or of the re-presentation of the reference experience. Whether in present access (the experience of being present to something) or in retrospective access (the re-presentation of a past moment – experienced as a re-living) – the evaluation of this index is based on the appreciation of the strength and effectiveness of the relation of presence or re-presentation. The latter case raises the question of the subjective identification of this lived experience as belonging to your past, and the question of the extent to which you really re-live it or merely think about it. In the debriefing technique this is called the position of embodied speech. Experience with debriefing has shown that a strong re-presentation allows one to gain access to very detailed levels of description and facilitates the activation of recall, as described by the theories of concrete memory (Gusdorf 1951; Vermersch 1994).

c. Index of fulfillment and clarity of intuition: Liveliness, precision, sensory completeness of access. This index aims at determining the *sensory modalities* implicated in the evocation of the reference experience, their degree of liveliness or evidence. Moreover, it concerns your different positions relative to this re-living. (Is it really your own point of view, or is it based on somebody else's, or on the dissociated point of view of an observer?) The experience of practitioners in this domain seems to suggest that the type of sensory modalities, or their number, determines the impression of the experience lived through again. For example, the only time vision comes into play is when it is accompanied by the apperceptive position of an observer; here you see yourself in the past situation from the exterior in a more or less strongly "dissociated" manner. Sometimes all we have to do is help you make contact again with other sensory impressions of the past experience (external or internal hearing, smell, or taste, bodily sensations, emotional tone) for the impression of a re-living to be intensified.

3. Validation of the content of descriptive statements

Let us suppose that, on the basis of a reflection on the reference experience, you have been able to produce a verbal description. We then run right into all the questions that haunt first-person research. How then do we clarify, in all their gradations, the passages or bridges between the first- and second-person positions? This is the crucial point which has served as the focal point for all sorts of critiques, doubts, and re-thinking of the question. We can structure this step of the validation more specifically on the basis of these two major objections:

a. First-person statements are infallible or incorrigible (Rorty 1970: 399–424; Searle 1992).

b. Descriptive statements are embroiled from the start in pre-theorizings that are implicit in language; in other words, they are always already interpretations and not descriptions (Ricoeur 1969).

a. First-person statements are incorrigible. If you are the only one able to gain access to your own experience, then whatever you say cannot be doubted or even checked, for it seems logical to think that if someone else tries to do so, then *they*, the checkers, would have an insight into what *you* have experienced; such access, however, seems to contradict the singular character of subjective experience.

We have already seen that in its extreme formulation this argument seems to question any project of validation of subjective accounts, or at least to imprison it in an interiority (in our view, falsely) opposed to objectivity. This objection however completely neglects the fact that first-person accounts are intrinsically open to intersubjective validation, which is not an all-or-nothing affair, but a multiply graded structure of social agents ranging from immediate experience all the way to established scientific procedures.

We can turn this objection around by a productive counter-criticism: the incorrigibility argument errs by sweeping aside two sources of the *perfectibility* of first-person statements. On the one hand, let us suppose you don't have an expert practical knowledge for describing your own experience. Regarding your experience, you are no more an expert than you are regarding the world: there's so much to learn and discover in both arenas (Piaget 1950: 282). You may be the only one to have direct, first-person access to your own subjective experience, but you can learn how to increase the stability of the attention which allows the holding-in-the-grasp (*Im-Griff-Halten*) of such an experience (Husserl 1939/1997: §23b). This apprenticeship can in part be replaced by an expert mediation, as is the case in the practice of mindfulness or debriefing. With this last allusion, we have already touched on our second point, the unsurpassable role of the second-person position and its insertion in a dense network of intersubjectivity. Even though you are the only one able to reflect on your own lived experience, others before you have had the same *kind* of experiences (at least in structure); on this basis we can help you reflect, we can guide your attention to certain descriptive traits we know are present in this genre of experience.

To be sure, the ultimate criterion in this purely internal facet of validating descriptive statements seems to be the direct intuitive evidence we have already discussed. But it also seems just as important to us to focus on the *mediation* possible for help in describing what this criterion of evidence is related to. For example, if my access is not singular, if there is no true re-presentation, then instead of describing my experience, I am going to be talking *around about* my experience. I won't even be aware that the diffuse feeling of intimacy associated with this experience is not a matter of discursive knowledge.

If every first-person statement is a subjective truth, we must not be mistaken about *that of which* it is the subjective truth. Since this statement can concern what you believe about your experience (that's the truth of your belief), according to the naive theories relating to the type of experience you have just had (that's the truth of your comprehension or knowledge), the statement can in the end concern what you reflect on in accepting the experience that constitutes the reflecting act. In this sense the skeptical heterophenomenologist ignores such possible reflection and mobility in describing his sources.

In short, the incorrigibility argument can receive numerous developments which in fact render the description more complete, more detailed and more pertinent. But we can still leave behind the first- and second-person points of view and, on the basis of more traditional third-person methods, envision all the modes of recovery and confrontation which can make the descriptions more plausible. In this discussion, which belongs to the incorrigibility argument, we have touched upon the perfecting of individual testimony, the means of mediation which improve expression. In an enlarged methodological perspective, we would have to add on all the styles of validation made possible by the second-person point of view as well as the multiplicity of first-person points of view, and, on top of that, the contributions of the third-person point of view. We don't have the space for such an extended discussion, however, so we move to the second standard objection to the first-person position.

b. First-person statements are embroiled from the start in pre-theorizing.
From a research point of view, the fundamental critique leveled at all descriptive approaches is that descriptions use natural or ordinary language and because of this implicitly contain pre-scientific theories carried along in language.
About this critique, in principle so devastating, we can make several remarks.

If the argument is taken in all its radicality, it bites its own tail, rendering implicitly suspect, if not downright incomprehensible, its own statements,
which are themselves manifestly embroiled in non-explicit pre-theorizings.
The only position which lets us escape from this argument would be a position outside culture – if such a thing were possible. At this point we might
ask ourselves, how are we going to even begin to so thoroughly comprehend
the culture in which we are embedded that we are able to transcend it and
enter a presuppositionless sphere of pure observation? Let us then leave aside
the radical dimension of this argument, which like all extreme skepticism self-
destructs. It is not at all that we are anti-intellectual, but at some point you just
have to let the skeptical serpent bite its own tail: we have work to do!

We would claim that the soft underbelly of this argument is that it invents
as its object of critique the naive belief in a transparence of language which
would make what one says into a description of the thing itself, or make the
thing itself appear without any contamination by the medium employed in its
description. But this is manifestly not the case, and we never claimed it was so.
This manner of posing the problem tends to restrict itself to the taking into
account of the statement by itself, as if what was described didn't have its own
structure and could only be grasped by language, without having left behind
behavioral traces or having structural properties which allow us to *corroborate*
the description by sources independent of language.

Take the example of a mental action (solving a problem, adding sums,
memorizing a musical passage, working out an anagram, and so on): we can
compare what you say about how you're going about the action to your response to our questions, to our observations on present behavior, to delays in
the action. We are not going to accept that what you say is true just because you
say it. Like all data, what you say can be corroborated by other complementary
aspects. We thus enter here into a logic of exploiting verbalizations in principle
very close to what goes on in judiciary hearings: a testimony only counts in so
far as it is compatible with the facts of the case (logical constraints, time and
space considerations, causal factors, and so on).

We find that it is precisely those disciplines whose research objects don't
have their own structure (the study of representations in sociology, for example), and which gain access to their object only by constituting it *via* verbaliza-

tions, which have been most often subjected to this critique of the research use of verbalizations. In these cases, the technique of analyzing the content of verbalizations is at the same time the only mode of constituting the results and the intended reality. This is not the case, however, with the mental acts we describe.

With the same aim of not letting verbalizations stand without corroboration, we can also try to *falsify* them. For example, if a pianist describes the playing of a score as being, among other things, constituted by a detailed visual image, then it is possible to ask complementary questions which involve an impossibility if it is not truly visualized. In this way we can systematically search out questions which can be the source of falsification (Schotte 1997). Piaget has already opened the way to this sort of approach by developing counter-propositions which seek to test the stability of the system of transformation proper to the establishment of an invariant.

Finally, it is still possible, whether we are conducting a debriefing interview or re-reading of our own written descriptions, to moderate or even "catch in the act" a language which has become abusively interpretative. In effect, the language we all use is drawn out along the axis of description–interpretation, and common sense lets us catch ourselves or others slipping toward interpretation; we can then pull ourselves back closer to description. It is not a matter of fantasizing an ideally descriptive language, which is in any case fundamentally inaccessible. Rather, here again, it is a matter of conceiving and putting to work a practice of improving a description. For example, if *describing* one event as having been produced before another carries with it a pre-conception of time proper to our society, it is palpably different to qualify an event as having been premeditated, a qualification which clearly *interprets* intentions. But one knows in following judicial reasoning that an interpretation of intention can be justified by meeting certain criteria: thus qualifying an act as pre-meditated implies establishing the material, contextual, preparatory elements which allow it to be so determined.

We can also always re-take a description by critiquing it after the fact on its precise descriptive value, and show in what way it deviates from the descriptive pole. Recording traces and observations of the object of study allows us to bring them to bear on a verbalization. In this manner, we can hope to zero in on what we can at present grasp of the descriptive traits which make sense to us. The fact of fixing a description in writing allows us to learn on the job by exploiting the comparison afforded by the gap in time and by intersubjective comparisons. Every experienced researcher has encountered the surprise and strangeness of descriptions jotted down several months ago, even though other descriptions have been produced, even when exchanges have uncovered interpretations there where we saw only a strict description. We are always learning on the job when we are engaging in a process that starts from a minimum which we can improve upon.

4. Validation and intersubjectivity

At this point, in order to concretize the process of validation in all its complexity and richness, we want to take stock of what really happens on the spot in intersubjective validation. First of all, let us be upfront about the fact that in being effectively put into action, intersubjective validation runs into some real problems which the quasi-idyllic harmony of the three-pole configuration (first-, second-, and third-persons) set up by the originality of the second-person perspective can tend to make us forget. These problems occur when you take the diversity of individual experience seriously. You can't just ignore such diversity when you are trying to come up with a methodology which focuses precisely on individual and subjective singularity! We must thus do justice to the whole range of *inter-individual variability*. However, far from being the aporia it would be were it to remain in a purely theoretical context, this practical difficulty is instead a source of richness: it helps to enlarge, to universalize, the sought-for objectivity, to re-qualify it. Rather than erecting an autonomous vision of the world (a *Weltanschauung*) as any number of phenomenologists have done, thereby absolutizing an intuition into a truth alongside other thesis-truths, and rather than, inversely, hiding out in the neutral and anonymous objectivity of reductionist science, the middle path of intersubjective validation sets itself the task of drawing out the fecundity of *conflicts in validation* themselves.

Thus contradictory or antinomical descriptions can very well constitute not so much a theoretical aporia about the universal truth of experience as an invitation to produce a more nuanced description, that is, one that is more finely tuned, more differentiated, one that takes into account supplementary dimensions. In other terms, intersubjective conflict in validating descriptions can deepen both description and the quality of validation.

We have had such an experience of turning conflict into an opportunity for enrichment during our 1996–1998 *Seminar in Phenomenological Practice*. There we explored the intersubjective description of sound – of its retention, of its being-held-in-grasp – and also the intersubjective description of the emotional quality of a precise moment of time. After several meetings, we realized that careful comparison of inter-individual variations led to the discovery of several (two or even three) invariants of experience – instead of the one we might have expected! Thus, after an experiment based on Husserl's time lecture

§7, we found that the description of the retention of a sound and its immediate duration was presented by some in either its passive persistence, or in its active being-held-in-grasp; sometimes we even experienced the escape of the sonoral impression – the quasi-impossibility of holding on to it. During the course of a meeting dedicated to the experience of the emotional quality of a brief moment, we met up with several apparently contradictory and conflicting experiences regarding the existence of a single emotion at time T1, or even regarding the co-existence of several emotions at the same moment, the limit-case being the presence of an emotion of super-abundance of joy which is instantly analyzed as an abyss of suffering. Is it possible to speak of the *quasi*-coincidence of emotions? What is one to do with such contradictions in experience? Let us be clear that this is only a sample of a work in progress which will treat of practical phenomenology on the basis of the phenomenology deployed here. As such, this sketch allows one to more precisely embody the global structure of the three positions presented here, whose exemplary variations have already furnished a first concretion.

To begin with, let us mention two possible deformations of this work of intersubjective regulation: (1) when subjects are cowed by an expert; (2) when subjects cling to an *a priori* principle. Rather than dwelling on these problems we find it is without a doubt better to deploy all the richness of contradictions so that we can relieve contradiction by making a practical differentiation. In all cases, overcoming these categorial obstacles implies that we individually re-do experiences, and consequently that we refine each description so that the experiential arguments can be intersubjectively compared. Intersubjectivity at work, in the heat of exchange, is thus preceded and prolonged by an more interiorized intersubjectivity, which one can call "intra-subjectivity". Here we find ourselves going so far as to take into account the descriptive horizons opened by others, something which contributes to enlarging our own experience, to enriching it by opening up unsuspected dimensions and thereby questioning our own limits. In this way, intersubjective validation already begins to operate in a dimension of alterity internal to oneself, what was recently called a "self-alterity" (Depraz 1995b).

Now, in order to even conceive of the workings of intersubjective validation, there has to be a community of expert researchers or a sufficiently advanced mastery of mediation which can allow less expert subjects to be guided in their access to, and thematization of experience. While science has for some time had its own frame for validation, nothing of the kind exists for most of the other styles of validation. A major exception, however, is the mindfulness/awareness tradition, where the issue of validation has been the object of meticulous attention for centuries.

On the phenomenological front, it is interesting to remark that the question of a community of researchers has been very rarely evoked and even less explored, the exception being Spiegelberg (1975). A little bit of intersubjectivity would have let Sartre (1940) avoid generalizing certain of his manifestly abusive analyses. Husserl, in a letter from the 30s (Kelkel 1957), speaks of a gnostic community, and Fink (2000: §11) claims a transcendental communication among phenomenologists. On the other hand, a true expansion of styles of validation, encompassing a wider range of phenomenal data from third- to second- and first-person sources, will entail a necessary and important restructuring of the social edifice of contemporary science. This is a long-term challenge which we cannot explore further here. In short, the intertwining of these three forms of validation (first-, second- and third-person) brings to light a validation which we would like to call a *validation by practice*.

CHAPTER 3

Surrounding events

The specific temporal logic of training, motivation and postsession work

3.1. Upstream and downstream

By introducing the notion of different temporal scales, we were able to see how the repetition of the basic cycle of reflecting activity (Chapter 1) fits within a session's work. Then, we analyzed the session itself (Chapter 2) as part of a research project or a personal exploration. A session is an element in a socially embodied practice, that is, it is sedimented and reactivated within the institutions, meanings, and struggles that bring it about and make it become an integral part of a laboratory, a training course for researchers, or the topic of defensible academic theses.

Now this simple schema of basic cycle and session – even when put in social context – has to be supplemented with practices which are both *upstream and downstream* of the basic cycle and session. Indeed, one of the most important things we have to say in this book is that becoming aware is a *practice*: it takes work. We have found that if you want a well-ordered, fruitful practice of becoming aware, then you have to be *trained*. Now in an abstract "logic," training happens "before," or "upstream" of a session. But we have insisted again and again that *our* logic here has to be that of apprenticeship, of learning on the job. Thus, since the act of becoming aware is a practice, it can only be learned through experience – through its own effective practice. And so your training will have to take place during a session. You are only going to be an apprentice if you get your hands dirty: book learning is no replacement for doing it yourself.

But you don't just learn on the job; you also learn after work, when you can sit down and think about what you have learned, or talk it over with one of your mentors. Thus one of the high points of this apprenticeship comes "after" the practice, after the session, "downstream" from it. This is when you can reflect on the *practice of the practice*, talking it over with experienced mediators by repeating to them the descriptions you produced.

But it is not the end of the story. Every time you analyze your practice in the hopes of getting better – whether this happens after a session or in the second part of a session after you have put in some work – you are working "upstream," you are preparing for the next go-round.

We seem to have gotten ourselves tied up in knots. But that's only if you stick to a linear notion of time. Apprenticeship has its own temporal logic, in which you are always ahead of yourself. With apprenticeship we are obviously dealing with the learning on the job we have been talking about since we started. The peculiar thing about apprenticeship is that you can't prepare for it, you can only do it! To learn this practice is to do it, even if it means starting all over again in order to do it better, to make it yours, to discover what it's all about; like all lived action, apprenticeship in the practice of becoming aware is largely pre-reflective. You have to become aware of the way you are always implicitly becoming aware of yourself!

Thus, we are always ahead of ourselves in becoming aware. To make becoming aware your own you must begin by becoming aware of becoming aware, you must describe it by reawakening the reflective activity oriented to the practice of reflective activity. We will encounter a similar temporality when we approach other important questions: think about the motivation to engage in this methodology, or about the manner of exploiting the post-session period in order to pursue the resonance effects which can largely overflow the time of the session and be themselves deliberately cultivated as a methodological time in itself. In other words, the temporality of this aspect of becoming aware is large-scale. In long-term training, we focus on transforming ourselves so that we can stabilize reduction as a know-how or skill, that is, making reduction a spontaneous or internalized gesture, less dependent on either external mediation or existential shifts.

When we emphasize the practice of apprenticeship we have to depart from the *strictly linear time*, which, resting on the dichotomy of anterior/posterior (*hysteron/posteron*), was perhaps the most famous part of Aristotle's treatise on time in the *Physics*. That doesn't mean that we are going to turn around and embrace the totally cyclical temporality, the identical and unitary sealing off of an always already mediated immediacy, that we find in Hegelian dialectical temporality. The unique temporal logic of apprenticeship, which draws its strength from both its incessant verification and its very *praxis*, means that the gesture of becoming aware *never ceases to self-anticipate itself* when it is really truly of work. Thus each new session opens you up to a new apprenticeship that nevertheless remains embedded in what you have gained in the previous sessions. The temporality of learning on the job is thus double: sedimentation/rootedness and novelty/surprise.

In this chapter, then, we are going to deal with all those points we couldn't deal with when we were focusing on the articulation between the basic cycle and the work session. After having articulated the different times and facets of apprenticeship in its practical unfolding, we will return to the questions of motivation and after-effects in a more positive fashion, taking into consideration the singular quality of the temporality mobilized by them.

3.2. Apprenticeship and training

We have to count training among the more fine-grained aspects of the basic cycle and the work session. In fact, unless we consider reduction as a skill or capacity that we can stabilize, the entire ability of reduction to become a *fact of life* is put into question. In other words, without training and stabilization, not only would reduction be *somewhat* un-natural (since we admit that it is, to some extent, in the sense that it is contrary to the natural attitude), it would be *wholly* un-natural, i.e. beyond the reach of human abilities altogether. We stake our claim here: if reduction means anything, it means that, with proper training, it can become part and parcel of a human life.

Let us compare reduction with acquiring a musical skill: the problem with reduction is that you are not just learning a sensory-motor skill (although reduction is that as well), but cultivating the conscious ability to shift from the natural attitude to suspension and redirection. As we all know, cultivating a musical skill – playing, conducting, composing – takes years, even decades. However, becoming more sensitive in listening to music is not so time-consuming, and this is perhaps what we want to strive for in our first steps in the apprenticeship of reduction: become proficient at letting the music speak to you in all its force.

We can already see the limits of this comparison, though, simply because it is so very self-evident: if you want to learn how to sing, to play an instrument, or even just to read music – or certainly to compose it – no one would dream of denying that you need rigorous training, and lots of it. Thus the first difficulty to surmount in training for reduction is precisely *realizing the necessity of an apprenticeship in the practice of reflecting activity!*

In other words, here we face the need to build up an expertise that is only acquired step-by-step, but to which we have no birthright – no more than having a body makes you a dancer, even though in a non-technical sense the sole fact of having a body lets you spontaneously dance for joy. Singers don't need to create their own sound apparatus, but they do indeed need to create, on the basis of this apparatus, the expert instrument which allows them to sing. Pianists don't need to construct hands in order to play, but they spend years creating the hands of a pianist: strong, dextrous, calibrated in space with an extraordinary precision which let them become *virtuosi*.

Mutatis mutandis, we are certainly equipped with all the cognitive functions which allow us to develop this reflecting activity, since it is a matter of nothing more than what is at the basis of becoming aware; this doesn't involve inventing, but only identifying the relevant cognitive gestures and exercising them assiduously.

What you might find scandalous in all this is that, for a gesture as intimate and personal as reduction, you have to work at it, that there are degrees of expertise which condition the possibility of access to certain aspects of subjective experience that, without them, would remain inaccessible. Thus the multiple manifestations of non-expertise allow one to apperceive the practical implications of the lack of competence. The American psychologist E. Titchener underlined the negative consequences of believing you could dispense with training in these areas when he discussed introspection, whose practice would seem to be self-evident (Titchener 1912:485–508). On the other hand, his insistence on the necessity of training and on the mistakes of students who hadn't been through the first steps of practice and thus hadn't been confronted with their own incompetence, can do a disservice to the reflecting approach by making it look like a bizarre, furtive activity. During Titchener's time, his Cornell colleagues and students were looked on as a "sect" organized around him, as if the whole idea of a mandatory training was unacceptable and could easily be ridiculed as an "esoteric" activity (Boring 1953:159–189). In fact, even though we are entirely justified in claiming a disciplined training for anyone who wishes to engage in the study of becoming aware, we want to say that such an ability is also given to each of us from the very start. So there are not insiders as opposed to outsiders in the practice of the reflecting act. We want to emphasize the fact that such a capacity is open to everybody. All the same, though given to everybody, it is not a given in the sense that you would just have to go and buy it. It needs an real exertion in order to be reachable, but again, each of us can really do it.

3.3. Facets of apprenticeship

We insist on training for *all the facets* of the act of becoming aware, even though we have until now been concentrating on the structure of the reflective act. As we have said, the general temporal framework of apprenticeship, motivation, and after-effects resides in a new temporal logic, which we have highlighted by the structural convergence of notions drawn from: (1) cognitive psychology, for example, the development of Piagetian circular causality, which brings about the idea that learning is non-linear, that presupposes repetitions and variations; (2) cognitive science research, notably the theory of emergence, the peculiar dynamics of which lies in the irreducible arousal of global mental properties out of local neuronal connections; (3) phenomenology, for example, Husserlian genetic and generative phenomenology, which is crystallized in an open temporality of contingent self-anticipation, neither dialectical nor dichotomous.

Thus we will have to get to work on the practice of the act, on the stability of attention, which allows you to "hold on to" the object of attention without it disappearing. It will only stay there by being held in place, as opposed to the spectacle of the world that you perceive, which is always going to be there again after you have closed your eyes or been distracted. But more than that, we need training because we are not experts regarding the objects which make up our experience and toward which we can turn ourselves (Piaget 1950, vol. 3), any more than we are botanists because we can turn our attention to the plants in our gardens! The content of subjective experience is not any more directly given to us than the content of the experience of the world, although we are in direct contact with pre-reflective consciousness.

But, still more profoundly than with these difficulties, your apprenticeship is going to be hard because of the personal character of the process: learning to practice reflecting activity is learning to practice the relation to yourself, learning to listen to yourself, learning the letting-go which supposes the acceptance of non-immediate fulfillment that often follows the gesture of suspension. Even if it is a matter of a technical motivation, of a research aim, outside of any salvational, religious, or simply personal development project, the practice of attending to your subjective experience is going to implicate your entire person, since it is going to be a matter of working on your own self-relation, on the details of your own experience.

Moreover, you don't just undergo an apprenticeship on the basic cycle conditioning access to experience, but also on the latter steps, such as oral or written description. Certain practices are going to require an apprenticeship in spontaneity, as with advanced techniques of *shamatha* (resting the mind) or when doing the *heart prayer* while in the middle of everyday life. You are going to have to learn how to describe, and then you are going to have to work at it, refine it. Describing your own experience is no more a natural act than drawing. In fact, that's a pretty good analogy, if you abstract from the difficulties of learning how to draw the line, the actual embodied skill of your hands, for just like in learning how to draw, you have to translate what you have observed of yourself into what you note. All these apprenticeships take months and years, except for stereoscopic vision, which can be picked up quite quickly, and the debriefing interview, since there the expertise is on the side of the interviewer.

3.4. Progressive generativity of expertise

When you practice the reflecting act you are accompanying yourself, engaged in a meta-cognitive activity. When you practice the reflecting act alone, you have to do two things: (1) turn your attention to *what* appears, to the content reflected upon; (2) pay attention to *how* you conduct the act of reflection itself. You want to develop the ability to perform this second movement without disturbing the first, and for this you need a light touch, something which is going to take many years of regular practice in order for it to be exercised alone with success.

You should not get discouraged, but you have to face the fact that for a long time the second movement, which regulates your practice, is going to be something of a spoilsport because of the strength and "heaviness" with which it lumbers about chasing down various differences it wants to hold onto. We have seen this very clearly in meditation. As we noted before, the transition between a relatively heavy-handed observer in basic *shamatha* gradually gives way to one with a light touch in *vipashyana*; such a transition is the condition of possibility of the "advanced" stages of exploration in, for example, the *Mahamudra-Dzogchen* tradition. Being able to not react to these reactions and to return to them with a very light attention is a long-term objective for the meditator.

To avoid some of the burden of long-term commitment, we have noted that you can turn over some of the task of regulating the practice of becoming aware to another person who can put you back on track when you stray, who can guide you without giving you the answers. This sort of approach is appropriate when we are conducting a short-term training aiming at a precise and terminal goal. But since this is not one of our main interests in this book, we are going to drop it here.

It is obvious that training has many levels, from beginner to expert. Gauging where you stand with regard to these levels is not easy, because the only valid criterion is how well you *perform*. However, a trainer with several years of experience can spot regularities in overcoming various difficulties: discovering all the different spaces reduction helps you access; the sorts of efforts which damage the stability of holding-in-the-grasp; the confidence in putting different suspensions into practice, and so on. We still have to follow up and thoroughly study the microgenesis of competence in reductive practice.

But, in any case, we should not count on a mechanical growth of capabilities; it is impossible, for instance, to make a one-to-one correspondence between time spent and level attained. As with all other learning, everything depends on other factors besides the mere amount of time spent. In other words, we are dealing here with a non-quantifiable temporality which involves a structure and some qualities of always having to start over again. Some of the factors involved are natural aptitude, quality of the learning situation, and the motivation for a genuine engagement. It is not easy to formulate all these factors precisely, but they are all relevant.

3.5. Relation to mediation

We can analyze apprenticeship in the practice of becoming aware from the point of view of the exercises involved, the learning curve of the individual, and the pedagogy behind it. In the same way, we can analyze the types of mediations which make this apprenticeship concretely feasible. We focus on two: the role of the *context*, and that of the *mediator*.

The context of mediation. When we analyze the context of mediation, we are really talking about the session, but from a different point of view. When we first talked about a session, we emphasized its structure in itself. Now we want to emphasize how that structure facilitates apprenticeship.

Let us recall that we are trying to develop, indeed to provoke, a mental gesture that is difficult to define and difficult to maintain, whose result is not immediately striking and whose object is not only changeable, but only graspable by an effort of attention which makes it exist for me (but at the same time an effort that isn't too great or too much of a strain). It would be very easy to get lost, to no longer know if you have or have not had such an experience. Can you just jump right on in and start going on your own? All our experience suggests not. Here we see all the importance of a framework for practice sessions, which calls forth, proposes, or suggests the first tries at determined targets, which manages the time, gives directions, sets the start and finish times.

We have found that it is very important to help you give yourself some external indicators so that you can more easily pick up on the indicators of more interiorized activity. But as Spiegelberg (1975, Chapter 3) also emphasizes, even if lots of pointers were given on the arrangements in his phenomenological summer Colleges (and the trial-and-error rearrangements they caused), it is important to rapidly cut the ties to authors you may have read and to other participants in the workshops in order to confine yourself to the reality of your own lived experience, the only one you can describe. Mediation by the directors will be there to solicit from you your own personal resources, since you are the only one, with your truths and your limits, who does the apprenticeship.

Let us turn our attention once more toward our examples so we can dwell further into the pedagogy of leading an apprenticeship in the act of becoming aware. Here we can distinguish two types of cases. The first is when you are isolated and without direct mediation. In these cases, largely found in philosophical apprenticeship, the only thing which allows progress is having a precise objective: to write and to return critically to your own production. In all the other cases we find rather similar training arrangements: these pedagogies put you in a situation in which the goal is accessible and comprehensible to everyone from the start. The important point is that this goal should be at the same time interesting in itself (if it isn't, it won't be motivating) and yet secondary, in the sense that it is only there to create the conditions which permit the deployment, recognition and identification of the basic cycle. It is not possible to have someone else perform the reduction for you; all the other person can do is propose a task whose pursuit creates the conditions of reduction.

Contexts for apprenticeship

1. *Buddhist Meditation session*: assiduously pay attention to the *shamatha* technique; create the conditions for attention to turn around on itself; make the efforts to surmount the difficulties in maintaining the goal of having attention engage without fail (after a few tries); bring about a posture of acceptance of everything by paying attention to stabilization and continuity without any voluntary disturbing contradictions.

2. *Heart prayer*: constantly and patiently repeat the prayer, for it is the incessant re-iteration which triggers the conversion of the attention from the name to the heart itself.

3. *Debriefing interview*: let the moment come back to you when you were in the middle of realizing an activity which you wish to describe; this orients you towards an apperceptive attention completely occupied by the act of evocation; by accompanying this act of evocation you let the reliving of the past situation happen in the mode of accepting it.

4. *Practical phenomenology seminar*: like Spiegelberg, we organized a seminar for three years in Paris (1996–1998). The manifest task was to perform the experiment, for instance, of listening to a crystalline sound. Here we used Husserl's experiment on the difference between retention and resonance (Husserl 1964: §12); the necessity of describing what this experience consisted of – its unfolding, its different facets – led each of us to retrospectively pay attention to what happened for each of us and thus to try to reflect on our experience. This direction of attention led each of us to different reductions.

Trust and mediation. When you are an apprentice in the act of becoming aware, you are going to have with you a person helping you, serving as a model, or you will be in a group or community which will help you make sense of what you are trying to do. By definition, all effective training in becoming aware starts from what is produced in the basic cycle. However, here we need to pay attention to the nature of the relationship that such mediation involves, a very tricky aspect of the claim that training is possible at all. As we have seen with validation, all the forms of external and internal intersubjectivity play a determining role in the very possibility of attaining the reductive act. Intersubjective mediation, except in very rare cases, seems to furnish the constitutive structure of the apprenticeship for such an act.

We can distinguish three basic modes or *stages* in mediation. First, no mediation is possible without a little *trust*, a little willingness to think another person is competent enough to set up a learning situation. In the case of reduction there are quite a few proven formats:

1. being introduced to the reading of a text by a teacher, thereby producing the shift to reductive reflection;
2. being engaged in an active exercise of encountering *epoche*, such as in the context of the workshop or debriefing interview;
3. seeing an analyst for a weekly session of psychotherapy;
4. completing a formal workshop on meditation practice.

These are all situations in which we seek mediation in order to reproduce reliably the reductive gesture. It is quite obvious that unless we are willing to sustain this form of mediation for a relatively long time (a semester or school year, a whole series of debriefings, a good bit of analysis, a complete meditation retreat) we cannot even begin to cultivate our skill. This is the grounding for all that can come later.

Interestingly, from the point of view of the learner, the only safeguard needed here is *critical* trust. "Trust" because we enroll ourselves in the situation for a considerable amount of time. "Critical" because we demand to see evidence that we are learning something, that we are being transformed in our experience, even though the mediator is telling us that it is "too soon," or that "you haven't worked hard enough." True as these caveats may be, it is essential that we preserve our freedom to move on and discontinue our engagement if the trust (or transference) doesn't take root.

Close apprenticeship. In all the domains we have used as examples, the initial stage of critical trust lets you enter an active learning that leads to an *initial* degree of competence. This initial degree is one clearly beyond the beginner's stage, but is not yet a full mastery. The exception would be learning to see stereoscopically, where merely trusting that someone else can do it and is competent in it is enough to get you going.

In all the other situations you need to take a further step to move into mastery. This is an apprenticeship as well since the link with the mediator – the second-person role – becomes for a time both more specified and more intense. In close apprenticeship, you become part of a sustained effort, you don't question the adequacy of the training or the competence of the mediators (except in sudden attacks of doubt). Thus young scientists will start talking about "their" mentors and labs, analysands about "their" analysts, meditators about "their" teacher and lineage, and philosophers about "their" school of thought.

In terms of stages of training, close apprenticeship is where the more substantial vocational, psychological, or physical obstacles to learning really show up. Only a closer relationship than "trust" (which can be relatively diffuse and hence involve less commitment) permits enough openness for the painful realization of shortcomings, reluctance, and resistance that must be confronted head-on. Hence the universally ambivalent love-hate character (or at least resentment) of the teacher-student relationship.

Notice that although trusting in someone's temporary guidance is a relatively common occurrence in many people's lives, close apprenticeships are more rare. Only a few manage to find and maintain this closer relationship for long enough and intensely enough to attain a degree of mastery sufficient to let you return to self-reliance. This is also where all those dangers occur that are the converse of deep trust: blind allegiance, manipulation, dogmatism, the whole True Believer syndrome. You can never bypass these dangerous waters;

you must navigate them. Refusing to enter them because they are dangerous means you will never make a breakthrough, you will never get where you want to go. The only thing to do is to engage a trusting realism – or to indulge in an even greater oxymoron, a trusting cynicism – that is, to cultivate an awareness always on the look out for traps and blind spots. Here the best teachers show their worth, by refusing the mantle of infallibility, by defusing the cult of personality, by constantly provoking critical doubt and demanding that learners verify for themselves and not rely on the teacher's say-so.

Now we do not want to say that close apprenticeship is completely necessary for everyone to become a master at becoming aware. There certainly are a number of gifted people who seem to manage to find their own ways of sustaining their training by simple self-motivation. These people are quite rare though. One has only to think about how many truly creative philosophers or scientists have ever popped up *ex nihilo*, without have been immersed in a previous tradition. Similarly in contemplative traditions: the self-made individuals known to history are sufficiently rare that they are usually counted as famous reformers or sources of a new tradition.

Our reflections on apprenticeship are still only a sketch of what will become the training of young researchers in such a methodology. The examples drawn from training in debriefing or in mindfulness provide leads that should be developed in University curricula. What appears certain from our perspective is that you have to undertake experiential training, and if you don't, you will only ever have book-learning about awareness. And the fact of being a trainer, director, or teacher doesn't exempt you from your own experiential process. The fact of being a researcher and only wanting to receive the testimony of others doesn't exempt you any the less from the need for a true engagement in becoming aware of your subjective experience.

The absence of University training courses means that each of us who have put this approach into practice had learn to practice it in another field first before trying it in research or disciplinary training. We thus have had to take a detour before putting it to work in research: this is clearly one of the facets of the question of what motivates us to undergo this training and to return to put it to work in the service of a socially contextualized project.

3.6. The temporal generativity of motivation and after-effects

With this question we find once again all the scales and facets of our temporality put to work: what can engage you in an apprenticeship whose results you cannot by definition anticipate? What can be so evocative that you return, over and again, to an activity which will deeply change you but which you will never fully master? And what after-effects lead you to want to apply this approach in a field as narrow as that of scientific research (rather than the search for personal development or spiritual quest)?

This second period, which puts the accent on the so-called upstream and downstream of apprenticeship – but in reality it is integrally constitutive of apprenticeship, indissociable from it – lets us pose the problem of the temporal logic deployed here more clearly, and to specify its status.

Motivation. Let us begin with the first of these questions: why does someone stick with this practice when you can't know what it is going to be like to get better until you do so? To explain motivation in an apprenticeship whose re-sults cannot be anticipated, it seems enough to invoke a "circular causality" which is modified favorably or not by variables of individual difference and educational influences: in the end, all the classical factors. Now, your perfor-mance in the reflecting act is based on your cognitive possibilities. In a "logic of emergence," your capacity to learn the reflecting act is thus only one of the innumerable particular spaces where you must find yourself led. It therefore doesn't seem necessary to engage in the philosophical difficulties – the apor-ias – which lead you to wonder how you can anticipate something, how you can look for it, even when you can't know it ahead of time. This aporia, like many others, is solved by life itself: it is only contradictory to an observer who knows what is going to happen to you even though you don't know it yet.

From this point of view, the vicious circle of motivation for the reduc-tion, excellently described by Fink in the *Sixth Cartesian Meditation* (2000: §5; Waldenfels 1998) dissolves itself when one "plunges" into the practice of the reduction. The aporia of transcendental motivation for the reduction rests on conceiving temporality in terms of a punctual beginning in the Cartesian style. But we have said all along that to become aware you have got to get rid of this naive notion of time and dive into the temporality of the incessant genesis of the reflecting act in itself.

Precisely, you *don't* need a reflexive knowledge of where you are going in order to go there, for, otherwise, how would the first ones have done it? Such an immanent social transmission lets you hook up with this type of process, and, with a little luck, enter an organized training process. The variety of our examples shows that numerous practices engage and solicit reflecting activity without having conceptualized it.

But what is lacking today is training that can be articulated with philo-sophical and scientific research. Moreover, we note that people trained in, for example, debriefing interview techniques, leave as soon as they cultivate this process of receiving data, without being encouraged or called upon to cultivate a more personal becoming aware. Indeed, the general response to the question of motivation appears to be ethical. Beyond all the good reasons can be given in the first part about the methodological and epistemological necessity of taking subjective experience into account in science, the need for personal motivation to stick with a long apprenticeship makes it hard to imagine a research practice that is called scientific – and thus *a fortiori* philosophical – that ignores that most profound dimension of personal motivation (what Plato unforgettably called philosophical *eros*). In the end, the motivation for re-iterating the ges-ture of becoming aware, for always coming back to renew its conditions when expertise in this area does not entail being sure of the results – all this assuredly is tied in with ethical necessity. Now the invitation to be closer to your own experience in a careful self-transparence and self-responsibility also brings a *pleasure*, indeed a certain joyfulness, to the explorers of this domain. If there is a motivation to become aware, it would seem to be more properly ethical, in a large sense, than cognitive! (Varela 1999a). In that respect, Husserl (1956/1959, Introduction) stresses the importance of vocation (*Berufung*) as the primary structure of philosophical and scientific responsibility (Depraz 1998a/2001a).

The "after-effects". Just as with motivation, the after-effects of a session put the temporal logic of self-anticipation into play. It is thus the complement to motivation, the downstream to its upstream.

The after-effects of a work session are only the preliminaries of the next, in the sense that they are going to pursue, amplify, even intensify the work begun during the session – in particular description and the levels of the re-duction – but also in the sense that they are going to prepare you for future sessions of phenomenological practice. In other words, it is always in the after-effects (Husserl used the term "*Nachträglichkeit*" to designate genetic tempo-rality, whether it was retention, remembrance, or more generally genetic) that the meaning of what have been lived through immanently shakes free, and that a more dense, more intense reliving of the same experience is undergone.

You might be tempted to question the notion of an "afterwards" or of "after-effects" relative to our reference point, the session. If you take another reference point, for example, the object of research, or indeed the unfolding of a research project, that would *displace* what you can consider as having a place before, "during" or after. We take the session as our relative reference point because of its temporally delimited character and its structured organization and use of time. You won't spontaneously find these features in the other steps which temporally surround it.

In our Paris seminar in practical Phenomenology, we noticed above all that we could let the basic cycle be developed in the days and weeks following a session, by subordinating it to the motivation which consisted in leaving open and living all the questions about the description of the reference experience. Similarly, in *shamatha* training, the time between sessions is referred to as *post-meditation*, and you are enjoined to let what you have learned during the actual sessions reverberate in your daily life through many gestures of mindfulness: the way you step on a bus or talk to a colleague, for example. Only in such post-meditation can you figure out what the practice means for your life, and decide whether or not you want to go on.

After-effects are also felt in expression. Often, the first time you express your experience, it can seem summary, poor. Sometimes something appears that doesn't really seem all that noteworthy. What shows up after several tries, however, is that the several levels of description (the detail of temporalization, for instance, of the differentiation between sensible properties and properties of the act, or the distinction between the act of perception and the more intimate act contained in the attention in holding-in-grasp, or the emotional climate which underlies the different associated acts) are only shaken free progressively. For these different levels to appear (at least it was that way for us), they need to be repeated, and we have to wait patiently for intuitive/expressive fulfillment. It is also the case that this progressive movement can be maintained well past the time in a session dedicated to a first expression.

Because of this, the elaboration of a description can be stretched out over several weeks, and can thereby continue to be enriched. We can thus conceive *a second type of work session*, based on reliving the same reference experience (this will have, after all, a common structure for the whole work group) and focused on elaborating the description.

There is still another fundamental aspect of the after-effects, which we have already broached in examining training procedures: the reflexive/reflecting return to the practice put into action. Here we meet up again with contemporary professional training, as well as the advanced training of professionals by means of the analysis of practice. In other words, we are referring here to a period within the after-effects when professionals, with the help of an expert mediator, verbalize their experience in order to improve it, analyze it, and think up ways to overcome problems and limitations found in real situations.

This is thus a crucial aspect of apprenticeship in the methodology of reflecting activity, since we can't teach it as such, but can only create the conditions for you to have the experience. On the other hand, we can rely on the description of someone else's effective experience in the after-effects, precisely to help you recognize your own action, help you identify the internal criteria for realizing your goals, become aware of the effects of projection or of hangups which have blinded you to your own experience. Expert mediators in this area, with their own way of practicing, don't need to be omniscient; it's enough to have a technique which can help other people describe their own actions.

Synopsis of different temporal modalities in the act of becoming aware

1. *The temporality of* epoche, whose quality, specific to each time it is accomplished, nevertheless rests generically in a *waiting* attitude which is slow, patient, continuous and graded. This is an open anticipation of a general given context whose singular content remains undetermined.

   Creating such a temporality of open waiting within yourself is indeed a difficult apprenticeship.

2. *The temporality of intuitive fulfillment,* whose singular quality is the *unexpected,* the improvised. This surprise-time is, to be sure, self-anticipated in its global context, but the singularity of the intuitive tenor remains new, unexpected, unheard of.

   Learning to accept intuitive givenness as it is, in its own contingency, is assuredly far from automatic, as we have insisted all along. The exemplary variations which most purely show the double temporality of suspensive waiting followed by intuitive "lightning" are: (1) stereoscopic vision and (2) heart prayer.

3. With the more global structure of a session, we move on to *the temporality of reprise, of re-iteration,* of a return motivated by the care for expression, then communication and finally validation. This gesture of iteration and repetition, the key to apprenticeship, is certainly already there in the time of suspension, but in a preparatory mode and must be reactivated each time. Iteration is employed on another plane in the expressive, verbalizing, and validating context, each time with an eye to a new quality of objectification. It properly characterizes the time of a session in its open linkage with what happens before and after.

   The most pertinent exemplary variations here are: (1) writing (for the period of expression); (2) the debriefing interview; (3) psychoanalysis session, (4) the tradition of mindfulness.

4. Finally, *a temporality of generative, generational and historic, transmission,* which, by sedimentation and interpersonal re-activation, roots intersubjectivity in a community and a historicity. It intensifies and deepens the whole of the dynamic structure of the re-iteration proper to the context of a session.

In this way, contemplative traditions such as the heart-prayer or mindfulness, or even philosophical and scientific research (for the conjoined period of expression and validation), have cultivated such a requirement of interpersonal inscription and generative transmission.

PART II

The motivations for the study of experiencing

CHAPTER 4

The point of view of the researcher

As announced in the Introduction, the Chapters of Part II gather individual statements of the motivation that has nourished the work presented in this book. For this very reason, they are signed by one author individually, (with the exception of Chapter 5, written by all three, and of Chapter 7, written by two of us). These Chapters are given here as extended context and background, in order to make the understanding of the foregoing more clear and accessible. They are not essential for our main presentation (Part I), but the reader may want to read through one or more disciplinary threads that are pertinent for him/her.

4.1. The cognitives sciences
(F. J. Varela)

The recent consciousness boom

In the modern cognitive sciences the issue of human experience has surfaced recently under a peculiar turn which manifests itself as a sudden interest in the question of human *consciousness*. Let us be clear from the beginning: such an interest describes the situation in a field largely dominated by anglo-american philosophical background which is, whether one likes it or not, an unavoidable ingredient of modern research in cognitive science, a recent scientific invention incorporating, as is known, the neurosciences, linguistics, artificial intelligence, anthropology and some aspects of experimental psychology (Dupuy 1993; and Varela 1996a). Within this literature, in fact, we are currently witnessing a boom concerning the so-called *scientific* study of consciousness: the number of books, articles and meetings on the subject has increased exponentially over the last few years (Hameroff et al. 1996, 1997; http://www.phil.vt.edu/ASSC/). Why this current outburst after all the years of silence, when consciousness was an impolite topic even within cognitive science, the discipline whose vocation was to study mind? (Varela 1996b).

In a popular formulation, David Chalmers (1995:201) points out that the study of human consciousness underlines the really "hard problem", that is, the *experience* associated with cognitive or mental events:

> Sometimes terms such as "phenomenal consciousness" and "qualia" are also used here, but I find it more natural to speak of "conscious experience" or simply "experience".

After reviewing some popular functionalist explanations about cognition, Chalmers qualifies the remaining challenge as some necessary "extra ingredient". The choice of the term is already revealing, for Chalmers seems to assume from the outset that the only avenue to bridge the gap between functional cognitive mechanisms and experience is to add some new theoretical principle. As we argue here, it seems that another fundamental alternative is to change the entire framework within which the issue is viewed!

In any case, "[t]he moral of all this is that *you can't explain conscious experience on the cheap*" (Chalmers 1995:208; his italics). We entirely agree but the price to pay is heavier than most people (Chalmers included) are willing to concede. Again the central difficulty is that experience is "not an explanatory posit, but an explanandum in its own right, and so it is not a candidate for [reductive] elimination" (Chalmers 1995:209). What is needed, he concludes, is a form of non-reductive explanation. Here again we concur, but one of our tasks will be to detail how different our options are from most of the cognitive science community.

To be sure, after the peak of dominance of behaviorism there had to be a conservative phase before cognitive science felt that it had some ground under its feet. More important perhaps was the style of the dominant philosophy of mind in the USA (where the initial *elan* of cognitive science took place in the 60s), which is intrinsically suspicious of subjective experience. Within this framework, significant developments in cognitive science have been accomplished almost exclusively within a cognitivist-computationalist or a connectionist perspective. Especially under connectionism one could discern a truly revolutionary idea of transitions and bridges between levels of explanation, better understood as a philosophy of emergence: how local rules can give rise to global properties or objects in a reciprocal causality. This gave new meaning to the traditional mind/body interface, which, in the form of cognitive processes as computationalist or connectionists schemes, made an array of specific cognitive phenomena (vision, motion and associative memory are prime examples) solvable in principle (if not solved). These developments, at the same time, created the very background for the "hard problem", since they made consciousness appear as if devoid of any causal relevance. This is well illustrated in Ray Jackendoff's pioneering book, in which the "phenomenological mind" (i.e. consciousness *qua* experience) is seen as projection from a "computational mind" (i.e. cognitive mechanisms) where all causality takes place. Thus the only conclusion he can come to is that consciousness "is not good for anything" (Jackendoff 1987:26).

Further, in parallel developments, new techniques for large-scale analysis of brain activity and neuropsychology have for the first time allowed us to ask direct experimental questions concerning complex cognitive correlates in action, such as mental imagery and emotions (Picton & Stuss 1994; Ponner & Raichle 1994; Gazzaniga 1997). The experiments involving such non-invasive on-line measurements are particularly interesting since they have led researchers to confront such questions as: can a subject's report be taken at face value? What are verbal reports expressions of? These are basically experiential questions that already imply significant demands on the methodology under which accounts of human experience have to be approached in empirical research.

One day the intellectual history of the peculiar twists and turn of the problem of cognitive science and consciousness will be done thoroughly. But it has a *déjà-vu* aura to it, reminding us of many swings of the pendulum in the past history of science, between rejection and total fascination with the scientific discussions about conscious experience. This can hardly be otherwise, since any science of cognition and mind must, sooner or later, come to grips with the basic condition that we have no idea how the mental or the cognitive can be separated from our own experience. As John Searle has aptly remarked in his own contribution to the boom, if there is a phase favoring strictly materialist theories of mind:

> [the philosopher] encounters difficulties. It always seems that he is leaving something out ... [and] underlying the technical objections is a much deeper objection ... [that] can be put quite simply: The theory in question has left out the mind; it has left out some essential feature of the mind, such as consciousness or qualia or semantic content ... [Thus] if we were to think of the philosophy of mind as a single individual we would say of that person that he is compulsive neurotic, and his neurosis takes the form of repeating the same pattern of behavior over and over (Searle 1992:30–31).

We concur with the diagnosis: clearly we need some radical measures to compensate for this compulsive behavior. That is partly what this book does: setting the basis for a method to break the vicious circle of the attempts to "fix" it with yet another abstract, theoretical model.

A three-way sketch

In order to focus our position more clearly the reader should now imagine this intellectual area as containing three positions, from right to left (Varela 1996b). We do not intend to provide an all-encompassing chart of the various viewpoints, but an occasion to place our work in this context of some who have published extensive arguments addressed to cognitive science (generally in book form) over the last few years. A warning: this is a chart of naturalistic approaches, that is, positions that each in their own way provide a workable link to current research on cognitive science. This excludes at least two streams of popular discussion. On the one hand views that take a traditional dualistic stance (*à la* J. C. Eccles). On the other hand calls for new foundations from the quantum mechanics proponents. These views seem extreme and we concentrate on those that are based on current neuroscience and cognitive science in some explicit manner.

Let us begin with the position on the far right, where we have put the very vocal trend best represented by P. Churchland (Churchland & Sejnowski 1992), F. Crick and Ch. Koch (Crick & Koch 1990), close to the spontaneous philosophy of many colleagues in neuroscience, and appropriately labeled as neuroreductionism or eliminitivism. As is well-known, this view seeks to solve the hard problem by eliminating the pole of experience in favor of some form of neurobiological account which will do the job of generating an experiential account. Or as Crick puts it with characteristic bluntness: "You are nothing but a pack of neurons" (Crick 1994:2), and elsewhere: "No longer need one spend time [enduring] the tedium of philosophers perpetually disagreeing with each other. Consciousness is now largely a scientific problem" (Crick 1996:486).

In the middle position we have place for a variety of positions that can be broadly labeled as functionalists, and identified by Chalmers as being the most popular ecology of ideas active today (Chalmers 1995:204–209). Functionalism has been drastically preferred in cognitive science over the last 20 years, with the strategy to replace the link between cognition and consciousness (the most immediate one in western philosophical tradition) with the link between cognition and its corresponding functional or intentional states. In the best of cases the problem of consciousness is assimilated with that of "qualia" for some particular features of mental states. Thus the notion of experience becomes forcefully assimilated with that of cognitive behavior, propositional attitude, or functional role.

These views include a number of well-developed proposals including R. Jackendoff's (1987) "projective mechanism", B. Baars' (1997) "global workspace", D. Dennett's (1991) "multiple drafts", W. Calvin's "darwinian machines" (1990), or G. Edelman's (1989) "neural darwinism". The basic move in these proposals is quite similar. First, start from the modular items of cognitive capacities (i.e. the "soft" problems). Second, construct a theoretical framework to put them together in a way that their unity amounts to an account of experience. The strategy to bridge this emergent unity and experience itself varies, but it is typically left vague since the entire approach relies almost entirely on a third-person or externalistic approach to obtain data and to validate the theory. This position seems the most popular one in the current literature, and it represents an important segment of researchers in cognitive science. This popularity rests, it seems, on the acceptance of the reality of experience and mental life while keeping the methods and ideas within the known framework of empirical science.

Finally, to the far left in our imaginary map, we place the trend that interests us the most for our purposes here, and which can be roughly described as giving an *explicit* and central role to first-person accounts and to the irreducible nature of experience, while at the same time refusing either a dualistic concession or a pessimistic surrender to the question, as is the case for the mysterianists. This is in line with the identification of where the "hard" problem lies. As are the other general orientations, the group gathered here is a motley one, with odd bedfellows such as G. Lakoff and M. Johnson's (1987) approach to cognitive semantics, J. Searle's (1994) ideas on ontological irreducibility, G. Globus (1995) "post-modern" brain, O. Flanagan's (1992) "reflective equilibrium", and B. Baars's "theatre of consciousness".

What is interesting about this diverse group, within which we rank ourselves to a limited degree, is that even though we share a concern for first-hand experience as basic fact to incorporate in the future of the discipline, the differences are patent in the manner in which experience is taken into account. The phenomenological approach is grounded on a peculiar move to *explore* experience which is at the center of our work here.

Irreducibility: The basic ground

Hopefully, this sufficiently clarifies the context for our ideas within the current scene in cognitive science. After placing ourselves squarely in the left sector, we now get closer as to why the topic of this book is of relevance to a cognitive scientist. The main point is the need to find an explicit *circulation* between first and third person accounts, which amounts to a phenomenological position in fertile dialogue with cognitive science.

A phenomenological orientation starts from the *irreducible* nature of conscious experience. Lived experience is where we start from and where all must link back to, like a guiding thread. From such a phenomenological standpoint conscious experience is quite at variance with that of a mental content as it figures in the anglo-american philosophy of mind. In the best of cases the problem of consciousness is assimilated with that of "qualia", for some particular features of mental states. The notion of the mental becomes sneakily assimilated with that of cognitive behavior, propositional attitude, or functional role. But even cognitivist philosophers such as Ned Block (1996: 456–459) have began to re-introduce the distinction between the cognitive manifestations of consciousness and phenomenal consciousness in the sense of experience. But most authors are disinclined to focus on a principled distinction between mental life and experience, or manifest some suspicion about its status.

The tension between these two orientations appears in a rather dramatic fashion in Dennett's work. Sometimes he speaks as if he is talking about "mental states" when, in fact, he is referring to "conscious" states. For example, in Part II, curiously entitled "An empirical theory of mind", he explains his approach to consciousness as such:

> There is no such phenomenon as really seeming – over and above the phenomenon of judging in one way or another that something is the case ... But what about the *actual* phenomenology? There is no such thing (Dennett 1991: 364–365).

Isn't it a curious stance to accept that there is such a thing as qualia since he seeks an account of their appearance, but in fact there really isn't? But we are not surprised since Dennett has already concluded with little effort (15 lines in a 550-page book) that Phenomenology has failed. He remarks:

> Like other attempts to strip away interpretation and reveal the basic facts of consciousness to rigorous observation, such as the Impressionistic movements in the arts [*sic*] and the Introspectionist psychologies of Wundt, Titchener and others, Phenomenology has failed to find a single settled method that everyone could agree upon (Dennett 1991: 44).

This passage is revealing: Dennett mixes apples and oranges by putting Impressionism and Introspectionism in the same bag; he confuses Introspectionism with Phenomenology which it is most definitely not; and he finally draws his conclusion from the absence of some idyllic universal agreement that would validate the whole. Well, we do not demand "that everyone could agree" upon, say, Darwinism, to make it a remarkably useful research program. And certainly *some* people do agree on the established possibility of a disciplined examination of human experience. In a book that is in many other respects so *savant* and insightful, this display of ignorance concerning Phenomenology is quite telling. It is a symptom that says a lot about the dominant (and largely unexamined) basis of the current consciousness literature.

Let us go back to a related key point that must be brought to the fore, clearly made by Searle:

> (...) much of the bankruptcy of most work in the philosophy of mind ... over the past fifty years ... has come from a persistent failure to recognize and come to terms with the fact that the ontology of the mental is an irreducibly first-person ontology ... There is, in short, no way for us to picture subjectivity as part of our world view because, so to speak, the subjectivity in question is the picturing (Searle 1995:95, 98).

Where we part company with Searle's defense of the irreducibility of consciousness is in his inability to come to any conclusion about how to solve the epistemological issue concerning the study of consciousness (we will come back to his arguments below).

This is not unlike the limbo in Jackendoff's views, who in his own manner also claims the irreducibility of consciousness but when it comes to method is tellingly silent. He does claim that insights into experience act as constraints for a computational theory of mind, but follows with no methodological recommendations except "the hope that the disagreements about phenomenology can be settled in an atmosphere of mutual trust" (Jackendoff 1987:275). Mutual trust indeed! What is needed is a strict *method* and that is where both the difficulty and the revolutionary potential of the topic lie.

Following this line of thought it would appear that the development of new techniques in cerebral imaging have a paradoxical effect on how the psycho-phenomenological level is taken into account. The possibility of finely correlating an intellectual activity and the traces of it in brain structures could be seen as the triumph of the neurological level thanks to these new instruments. Nonetheless it is interesting to correlate the brain activity not just with the psychological level as defined by behavior, but also with the cognitive activity as the subject himself describes it in first-person terms. In this way brain activity can be related to a subtle, more functional level than the behaviorist approach permits.

Case studies

It seems useful at this point to sketch a few domains of experience and mental life to illustrate more concretely *how* a circulation naturally appears between the cognitive study of a cognitive capacity and its experiential dimension. Needless to say, these case studies do not constitute proofs of what we are saying, nor do they preclude the examination of other examples the reader may be more interested in. Moreover, in recent years there has been a number of different studies where, while remaining well-grounded in the scientific tradition of cognitive neuroscience, the part played by the lived experience was progressively more important to the extent that it begins to enter inescapably into the picture apart from any interest in first-person accounts. The following are illustrative cases touching both on large and more local issues.

The evocation of these cases study tries to provide a concrete background to discuss further a central concern that motivates taking into serious account the pragmatics of exploring human experience in the current situation of cognitive science. On the one hand we have a process of emergence with well defined cognitive-neurobiological attributes. On the other, a phenomenological description which links directly to our lived experience.

Large issues

Attention can be understood as one of the basic mechanisms for consciousness (Posner 1994). In recent years studies of electrical recordings and more specifically of functional brain imaging have led to the identification of networks and pathways that provide a useful background for distinguishing conscious from non-conscious cognitive events. Three such attentional networks can be distinguished involving orienting to sensory stimulation, activating patterns from memory, and maintaining an alert state. These results indicate that attentional mechanisms are a distinct set of processes in the brain which are neither located in a few neurons, nor is it merely the ensemble of the brain in operation. At the same time it is clear that the phenomenal distinctions between these forms of attention require detailed structural invariants of the varieties in which attention manifests to the subject (A first step in made by Steinbock & Depraz, forthcoming). A systematic study of the structures and strategies of attention is still a largely open task. But how is one to make the neural mechanisms relevant to consciousness unless such experiential counterparts can be sufficiently discriminated, recognized and trained?

Present-Time consciousness. Temporality is inseparable from all experience, and at various horizons of duration from present nowness to an entire life-span. One level of study is precisely the experience of immediate time, the structure of nowness as such, or in James' happy phrase "the specious present". This has been a traditional theme in phenomenological studies, describing a basic three-part structure of the present with its constitutive threads into past and future horizons, the so-called protentions and retentions (Husserl 1966; McInerney; Gallagher 1998). In fact, these structural invariants are not compatible with the point-continuum representation of linear time we have inherited from physics. But they do link naturally to a body of conclusions in cognitive neuroscience indicating that there is a minimal time required for the emergence of neural events that correlate to a cognitive act (Dennett & Kinsbourne 1992). This non-compressible time framework can be analyzed as a manifestation of the long-range neuronal integration in the brain linked to a widespread synchrony (Singer 1993; Varela 1995; Varela et al. 2001; Thompson & Varela 2001). This link illuminates both the nature of phenomenological invariants *via* a dynamical reconstruction which underlies them, as well as giving to the process of synchrony a tangible experiential content (Varela 1999b; and Depraz & Varela 2002b).

Body image and voluntary motion. The nature of will as expressed in the initiation of a voluntary action is inseparable from consciousness and its examination. Recent studies give an important role to neural correlates which precede and prepare voluntary action, and the role of imagination in the constitution of a voluntary act (Libet 1985; Jeannerod 1994). Yet voluntary action is pre-eminently a lived experience which has been well discussed in Phenomenology most specifically in the role of embodiment as lived body (*chair, corps propre*) and in the tight relation between lived body and its world (*Leibhaftigkeit*). Pain, for instance, is one of the most interesting "qualia" which reveals this dimension of embodiment most vividly, and its phenomenological study yields surprising insights both in body-image and its relation to neurophysiological correlates. Here again, a phenomenological analysis of voluntary action and embodiment is essential but only partially developed so far (Leder 1991; Rizzolatti et al. 1997: 190–191; Depraz 2001b).

Local Issues

Perceptual filling-in as used in visual science involves the spontaneous completing of a percept so that the appearance (i.e. a visual contour) is distinct from the physical correlate (i.e. discontinuous borders, as in the case of the popular illusory contours). The questions can be studied even at the cellular level, but raise more questions concerning experiential distinction of the appearance. In fact the neuronal data on filling-in seem to correlate well with what phenomenology had concluded some time ago: there is an important difference between "seeing as", visual appearance, and "seeing that", a visual judgment (Pessoa et al. 1998). This is the opposite conclusion from Dennett's for whom consciousness is "all tell and no show". These are issues that can only be solved with the concerted convergence of external and first-hand accounts.

Fringe and center. Interestingly for us here a number of studies have gone back to consider some traditional phenomenological issues such as the two-part structure of the field of consciousness between a center and a fringe or, in Husserlian terms, between the object given in flesh and bone, its inner profiles, and, more broadly, its inner and outer horizons. This mostly has come from the influence of William James and then of Aron Gurwitsch, but carried into modern laboratory protocols. In these studies the crucial experience to explore and target for refinement is the feeling of "rightness", here standing for a summary of cognitive integration representing the degree of harmony between conscious content and its parallel unconscious background (Mangan 1993).

Emotion. These past years have seen significant advances in the understanding of the brain correlates of emotions; the separation between reasoning and emotions is rapidly disappearing. Evidence points to the importance of specific structures such as the amygdala, the lateralization of the process, and to the role of arousal in emotional memory, both from examination of experimental protocols and from brain imaging. Yet these studies are entirely based on verbal protocols, and the questions of the competence for emotional distinction and the patterns of relations between mood, emotion and reasons need to be addressed explicitly at this stage of research (Damasio 1995; Davidson & Sutton 1994; Varela & Depraz 1999).

Many advocates of this general analysis of the current state of cognitive research would nevertheless agree that some foundational issues still stand in need of clarification. Chief among them is the problem of the relation of cognitive science to phenomenological *data*, which has, over the last few years, generated a growing number of publications. At the core of the problem is the concern that cognitive science somehow fails to account for such data, either because of its explanatory perspective, whether computational or connectionist, or because of its methodological commitments. In other words the argument is that cognitive science does not constitute a full theory of cognition, in the sense that its most general tenets do not apply to a certain range of mental phenomena. In the felicitous wording of Thomas Nagel, the worry is that cognitive science suffers from an "explanatory gap" vis a vis *a certain part of its own field* (Nagel 1974).

Perhaps the main contribution to cognitive science as a research domain of the present book, is the advancement of actual methods of phenomenological investigation for the purposes of the research itself, a topic completely absent from current discussion in any systematic manner, a first step in that direction having been made by Varela and Shear (1999).

The notion of phenomenological data

The notion of phenomenological data itself merits a brief discussion here given its role in the present book. In the relevant literature the explanatory gap argument is variously put in terms of subjectivity, consciousness, qualia or experience. It is important to disentangle these different concepts and see how they relate with that of phenomenological data.

In spite of the variety of the terminology being used, a sort of consensus seems to have emerged around the idea that Thomas Nagel's expression "what it is like to be" succeeds in capturing what is essentially at stake. Although the adequacy of this expression might be differently appreciated, it seems therefore appropriate to start with an elucidation of what it is meant to designate.

Clearly "what it is like to be" a bat or a human being refers to how things (everything) look when being a bat or a human being. In other words it is just another way of talking about what philosophers have called phenomenality since the Presocratics. A phenomenon, in the most original sense of the word, is an appearance and therefore something relational. By very definition an appearance is indeed what something is for something else; it is a *being for* by opposition to a *being in itself*, to what something is independent of its apprehension by another entity endowed with apprehensive abilities.

Phenomenality certainly is a crucial fact for the entire domain of living beings. It is, for instance, plausible that an organism with a sonar system like the bat does not perceive what an organism equipped with a visual system like man can perceive: the external world looks different to both. It is similar, although to much a lesser extent, for two individuals belonging to the same species.

Notice that phenomena fall into the two standard categories: internal and external. Broadly speaking, the notion of internal phenomena refers to how things happening in a subject look to that subject itself: it is clear for instance that feelings or judgements are not apprehended as located in the perceptual space where we locate our immediate environment. External phenomena, on the other hand, do have such a localization: when I see a house I see it outside of "myself". But according to the previous definition, these still count as subjective in the sense that they are what external things look like to a subject. As a matter of fact external phenomena usually are the prime examples mentioned when denouncing the insufficiencies of cognitive science with respect to "what it is like to be" elements.

Finally, when it is defined in this way, phenomenality does not differ in any substantial way from subjectivity, if by subjectivity we mean the subjective side of things, the way things are from a first-person point of view. Accordingly, it also sounds fair to say that what advocates of the explanatory gap argument complain about is that Cognitive Science is a theory of the cognitive mind leaving no less than phenomenality or subjectivity out, either because it does not attempt at accounting for it or because it fails to do so.

However these two notions stand in need of further refinement to really capture the point at stake. And this is where the notion of consciousness needs to step in. The progress of psychology as well as the development of psychoanalysis have made familiar the idea that something might happen for a subject, and in that sense be subjective, but nevertheless not be accessible to this subject. We naturally describe such a case by saying that the subject is not conscious of the phenomenon in question. A distinction must therefore be introduced between conscious and unconscious phenomena, or again between conscious and sub-personal subjectivity. The notion of consciousness itself is clearly meant to first and foremost designate the fact that the subject knows about, is informed about, or, in other words, still is aware of, the phenomenon. The definition of consciousness as awareness accommodates perfectly well the distinction between external and internal phenomena: the division between internal and external consciousness, or between object-consciousness and self-consciousness, is indeed one of the oldest in the philosophy. It can be argued further that awareness, both in its internal and external form, is analyzable in terms of reflexivity, although this is a point of controversy (Zahavi 1998; Depraz 2001a).

It might be tempting however to conflate the two concepts of phenomenon and conscious subjectivity. But the notion of unconscious or subpersonal phenomenon is clearly needed: there are for instance numerous aspects of external things which we perceive without being aware of them. What the idea is being reproached with is its failure to explain why and how the internal mechanisms of cognition as it specifies them result in the internal and external phenomenon we are aware of. And these phenomena are precisely what the notion itself of phenomenological data captures and will hereafter designate.

It should be said that if this notion of phenomenological data seems quite close to that of experience as used in this book, it is somewhat different from the concept of qualia as it is mainly used in the relevant literature, although the two terms are often used interchangeably (Shoemaker 1975). By quale or qualitative aspect of mental event, analytic philosophers and psychologists usually mean a feature of what we are conscious of which is subjective to the point of being absolutely unique, as well as ineffable and incommunicable. Some authors actually find qualia so ineffable as to believe that the concept of qualia itself is not definable and can only be clarified by means of some sort of ostensive definition. Even if one agrees that there are qualia to be usefully defined, it is clear that they do not by far exhaust the range of phenomenological data: the two concepts can be considered as synonymous only under the condition that the notion of qualia be considerably extended to cover the full range of subjective conscious data. Flanagan (1992, Chapter IV) has for example recommended such an extensive use of the term.

Mutual enlightenment

What is the motivation then, for cognitive science, to enter into the terrain of a disciplined exploration of human experience? The answer by now is clear: because it cannot progress to encompass the entire scope of mental phenomena without such decisive extension.

Fortunately the relevance of phenomenology to cognitive science has gained considerable visibility recently, so our developments here come at a fertile time. The point is to imagine what could be called a "mutual enlightenment" (Gallagher 1997) or a "neuro-phenomenology" (Varela 1996b, 1997), that is, an explicit articulation between the first and third person perspective. In *Naturalizing Phenomenology*, Petitot, Varela, Roy and Pachoud recently discussed the pros and cons of these issues with a number of contributions (Petitot et al. 1999). In its most traditional form, the mind-body problem refers to the long and complex history of attempts to link the mental-cognitive and the brain-bodily domains. These kinds of *linking propositions* belong more to the traditional eliminitivist or reductionist approach in a neuroscientific garb. The scope of the neurobiology-phenomenology relation broached here is quite different. The concern is made more precise by the perspective of mental phenomena and lived cognition which *grounds* phenomenology, which provides its empirical embodiment. Phenomenological description can only provide evidence and analysis within the bounds of the phenomenological method. If one wants to develop an explanation appealing to sub-personal levels, the question is how phenomenological description will figure in or will provide constraints to this causal description. Needless to say we exclude here the extremes of phenomenology being explained away, (a variant of eliminativism), or declared incommensurable (a dualist stance). So far, beyond these two extremes there seem to be two live options (Gallagher 1997; Varela 1996/1997).

One approach is that this link as an *isomorphic* one. In other words: the cognitive neuroscientist needs to take into account the phenomenological evidence in order to properly identify the right explanatory mechanisms on the neural and subpersonal levels. This is a reasonable and productive option that has several variants depending on the degree or force of constraint that one allows phenomenology to have. In the reverse direction, phenomenology is rendered more intelligible because it receives a causal explanation underlying the appearances analyzed and a natural link to the bodily phenomena. But this isomorphic option makes the implicit assumption of national boundaries: the job of phenomenology is to provide descriptions relevant to first-person phenomena. The job of natural science is to provide explanatory accounts in third person. Both accounts are joined by a shared logical and epistemic accountability. But is this really possible or even productive? Is this not another form of psycho-neural identity theory with a phenomenological garb? This book can also be read as a long argument against such an identity-theory. Phenomenology is more than a garb: it permeates the intrinsic nature of the phenomenon to be studied and needs to be taken into account as such. Isomorphisms, even subtle ones, will not break the gridlock of the explanatory gap.

The second alternative is what we can call the hypothesis of *mutual circulation through generative constraints*. This is the spirit in which this book is written, even if we do not pursue any empirical domain in great detail. (A first step is made by Lutz et al. 2002.) The point here is that phenomenological analysis not only provides descriptions but it also provides *evidence,* and produces phenomenological data, not otherwise available. This is *crucially* dependent on the fact that experience can be, in fact, examined in a disciplined manner with a method we call in this book *reflective reduction* as a reflecting act proper and elaborated in detail in Part I.

We now need to consider some of the other motivations for doing so. In this Section, our focus has been rather local: the cognitive neurosciences of today. Our intent was to see how the issues concerning human experience appear intrinsically in the dynamics of research itself and not by a purely logical argument. The consciousness boom in all its variety, attests to it, and in that sense this book fits squarely in the middle of this current debate. In the second Section of this Chapter we now turn to the related, but historically autonomous discipline of psychology, whose vocation is the scientific study of human mind.

4.2. Psychology and subjective experience: Introspection (P. Vermersch)

A historical perspective on psychology and subjectivity

Psychology appears to be the scientific discipline whose task it is to study subjective experience. But it has a double face: the first, intimate, private, corresponding to the first person point of view, makes it possible, thanks to verbalization, to gain access to the subjective dimension (mine, or that of an other with the data in the second person); the second, public, behavioural, taking its stand in the third person point of view, not only makes it possible to confirm the first but also to conduct research on behalf of those who are not, or are no longer, capable of speaking for themselves.

Scientific psychology started out in the 19th century by employing evidence derived from the first person point of view, in other words, by assuming the need for introspection as a privileged mode of obtaining data. But at the same time two methodological concerns made themselves known: control over variables and the possibility of making measurements. The early work of psycho-physics easily satisfied these conditions since it is easy to control parameters dealing with the emission of a stimulus and its response in terms of perception/non-perception or differentiation/non-differentiation, i.e. on the one hand, with the subjective dimension reduced to an elementary discrimination or with measurement posed in terms of stimuli.

The question which then becomes more pressing bears on the possibility of extending these methodological requirements to the so-called higher forms of behaviour: imagination, memory, reasoning. Wundt, the mythical founder of experimental psychology refused to accept the possibility of studying these more complex forms of behaviour since these methodological conditions could not be properly met (Dantziger 1990). But, in crossing this frontier in his study of memory, Ebbinghaus, in 1891 (Ebbinghaus 1885/1913/1964), played an extremely innovative role (Giorgi 1985). With a view to creating control conditions for the task assigned to his subjects he was the first to invent standardised experimental material: instead of offering words or phrases to be memorised, he used meaningless trigrammes whose associative value would (in principle) be the same for everyone and which, in consequence, ought not to introduce any bias linked to meaning. The order in which these trigrammes were presented, the degree to which they were reinstated or recognised made it possible to quantify in terms of frequency. This represented considerable methodological progress in the direction of control over the experimental set-up. At the same time this gain at the level of control brought with it a loss of information bearing upon learning acts or acts linked to any recall or recognition that the subject might be able to describe as soon as he became conscious of them. Even today a virulent debate continues concerning the advantages of the conditions of laboratory control and the disadvantages engendered by the fact that these forms of behaviour are studies under conditions which are meaningless to the subject (Neisser 1982; Cohen 1989). Exaggerated importance has often been accorded to the strict behaviourism of Watson. In fact, even if psychologists haven't placed first person evidence in the background they never gave up the study of mental images, reasoning, consciousness. Yet a permanent gulf has opened up between the quantitative data and its psychological significance. The question which has often been overlooked is that of the link between quantification and the behaviour it is supposed to translate. The question of establishing a more precise relation between mental action and its quantification is still relevant and only by taking into account the first person point of view does it become possible to assemble the elements of an answer, at least in cases where these elements are accessible to the subject.

This section aims to show how, by following up the development of the methodology of introspection, psychology, as a scientific discipline, has tried to account for subjective experience. It is not a matter of defending introspection at all costs, nor of making introspection the emblem of our own procedure. The guiding theme of this chapter is that it is possible to come to terms with almost all the sensible questions which could be raised as obstacles to the possibility of mobilizing the point of view of subjective experience in a regulated fashion.

The initial evidence and the first critiques

The evidence from the first person point of view
If one wants to understand the status of the emerging science of psychology at the beginning of the 19th century one has to recognize that the appeal to introspection in "the intimate sense", to apperception, was a call to study what did not fall under the heading of common sense but necessitated an already highly erudite attitude concerning the life of consciousness, thought processes, images, affective life. These phenomena could no longer be studied in a purely

speculative way, as the philosophers had done, but on the basis of observation and in the context of the natural sciences.

This point of view was upheld from the very beginnings of psychology, for example, by Maine de Biran (Maine de Biran 1807/1932), recognized as being the first author to merit the title of psychologist (Voutsinas 1964; Moore 1970), by placing internal events in the foreground and making use of the self's own familiarity with itself. The first-person point of view dominates. Not only is what appears to the consciousness of the one who experiences it accounted for but, in addition, the examination is limited to the observer himself. This procedure should not be dismissed as naive, even if it lacks any intersubjective control. Maine de Biran is well aware of the facilitating role that effort can play in the observation of intellectual activities. He looks at the experience of reading and shows how, at the very moment when we become aware that we have not understood a passage and consequently go over it again (Montebello 1994), we can note this awareness of our own acts of thought.

This initial insistence on introspection is to be found again, with striking variations, among several founders of 19th century psychology. Brentano in 1874 exerted a considerable influence over Husserl and on the development of phenomenological psychology, as we will see in more detail in Chapter 6, as did Wundt in 1874. As the famous declaration of W. James in 1890 puts it when he described the method of psychology: "introspective observation is what we have to rely on first and foremost and always." (James 1890: 185) An echo of this sentiment is to be found in a statement by Binet: "the act by means of which we directly perceive what happens in us, our thoughts, our memories, our emotions". And: "The new movement which has opened up over the last few years and to which I, together with several of my students, have contributed with all the strength at my disposal (...) consists in according a much larger place to introspection (...)" (Binet 1903). It is a matter of showing how "the experimental study of the higher forms of thought can be done with enough precision and control to be of scientific value" (Binet 1903: 2).

The primacy accorded initially to introspective methodology might appear very naïve today. But actually what is naïve is thinking this to be so. One has to understand that this introspection was already the product of a difficult proce-dure based upon the transition to a properly reflexive attitude. This first step is not in the least elementary. There is nothing naïve about suspending the natu-ral attitude, which consists in remaining engrossed in the perceptual spectacle, for example, with a view to grasping how it is set up.

In addition, these authors were not blind devotees committed to one method alone. All of them, including the oldest, were aware of the physiology of the time and its possible relation with the mental. They were also well informed about the need for indirect methods to study infants, the insane, animals, those who do not dispose of language.

The first critiques, impossibility in principle.
From the beginning of the century, two attitudes are adopted: the first aims at adapting introspection to the requirements of experimental method. It is therefore a matter of giving it a place in the scientific practise of psychology – and culminates at the beginning of the 20th century. The second, particularly well illustrated by the founder of positivism, A. Comte, refuses to accept even the very possibility of introspection. These critical objections are not nearly as decisive as their author supposes but they keep on recurring, right up to the present day. It is therefore interesting to spend some time analysing them and evaluating the contribution they might bring to our methodological reflection.

Introspection is impossible in principle because there can be no self-duplication.
This criticism stems from A. Comte; it is reformulated in a rather similar way by Searle (1992). It is transmitted *via* a simplistic aphorism which runs: "it is impossible to be on the balcony and in the street at the same time". So introspection is impossible in principle:

> The thinking individual can not be divided in two, one part of which would reason while the other would watch it reasoning. The observed organ and the observing organ being the same in this case, how could the observation take place? This so-called psychological method is therefore radically worthless in principle (Comte 1830/1975:34).

Let us first take note of the form of this criticism. What it affirms is not something empirical but logical and so it is affirmed *a priori*: "the thinking individual can not be divided in two". As with most of the criticisms we shall encounter, the critical point bears not upon the existence of an experience which has to be taken account of, no matter what conception of it one might adopt, but on a definition with regard to which we seek to show that it can not be applied, thereby leaving the question of the experience itself unanswered. A. Comte never raises the question of the nature of the cognitive activity which allows us (which allows him even while writing) to take note of his thoughts, to re-apprehend them, to correct them, to evaluate them; instead he sets up a conceptual mechanism designed to show that all this is not possible. Setting aside the psychological gulf that this opens up between the one who writes these lines and his own intimate experience (which contradicts the former), how does this help us with our research?

For his own part, Searle tries to save our mental health by affirming that one has to distinguish between common sense and science. Introspection does not exist in the scientific sense but, on the contrary, we do as a matter of fact examine our own thoughts and feelings in the course of our daily lives. He tries to get us to accept the idea that "the irreducibility of consciousness is merely a consequence of the pragmatics of our definitional practices" (Searle 1992:122); and that is why, although the irreducibility of consciousness remains a "legitimate argument", "it does not have any very serious consequences". In fact:

> The very fact of subjectivity, which we were trying to observe, makes such an observation impossible. Why? Because where conscious subjectivity is concerned there is no distinction between the observation and the thing observed. (...) Any introspection I have of my own conscious state is itself that conscious state (Searle 1992:118).

The mind is not in possession of a correct method for observing itself and so we are left with a logically clear conclusion but one which leaves us in a methodological limbo.

We must examine the distinction between this "introspection which does not exist and which is impossible" and "the examination of one's own thoughts and feelings" in the light of A. Comte formulations. Can one establish this kind of distinction without referring to the contents of one's own intimate experience, without describing the cognitive acts by means of which we accede to them? Can one criticize introspection without making use of the first person point of view? In order to be quite certain of its impossibility, would we not have to make use of introspection?

Even while admitting that there is an interest in this schizoid critique, the criterion employed by Comte is that of the impossibility of a spatial and material differentiation (he is referring to Phrénel's neurological localisations) between the sensorial organ and what is perceived. We find the same critique with Searle. If introspection is understood strictly in accordance with the mode of a perceptual act, a material distinction has to be drawn between what is examined and the one who examines and, since this criterion can not be met, introspection can not exist. It might however be objected that we now know that when the subject evokes a mental image or the acoustic image of a sound he mobilizes the same primary sensorial zones as when he carries out the corresponding perceptual acts. This demonstrates that one has no need of the mediation of a sensorial organ to gain access to remembered sensorial data which might furnish the material for statements characterized precisely by the quasi-sensorial dimension of that to which the subject gains access.

If an apperceptive activity of this kind does indeed exist, it does not have to be based upon sensorial organs of a homoncular kind. But I know that:

> [...] the moving flux of thought contains not simply words and images, visual or other, but other elements as well, which are neither verbal nor imaged. This is how, sometimes, a thought suddenly comes to me 'in a flash' and in a form which has nothing to do with words or images. (Comte 1830/1975:181).

How do I become conscious of such information? What does Comte call the cognitive activity which enables him to take note of it? Simply condemning our right to use the term introspection hardly makes a positive contribution to the question.

One might well ask whether the distinction between an act and the object of the act can only be arrived at by a sort of material separation. There are two distinct objects, the eye and the object seen – and they are spatially separated. The object can also be placed further away from the eye, which confirms that they are distinguishable. Comte, like Searle, emphazised the *intangible* character of this criterion. We propose instead to use a pragmatic criterion of differentiation, based on possibilities of substitution.

First of all, and with a view to abandoning denominations in terms of "mental states", which tend to mix up all forms of mental activity, it is worthwhile distinguishing between the mental act and the content or object of this act. This is moreover a distinction which one finds in Husserl's phenomenology, where one encounters the distinction between noesis and noema. An act can be distinguished from its content if I can, with regard to one and the same act, substitute different contents without changing the nature of this type of act. I direct my attention toward the content of what I have just perceived, then toward the way in which this content was evoked by me, for example, toward the means employed to evoke it (I talk to myself about it, I visualize it, I recover what I felt about it); then I compare it with another and older image related to the same content. At different moments my apperceptive (introspective) activity bears successively on different contents, or different aspects of the same content. Can the mental act which engages our attention be distinguished from other mental acts? By applying the same criterion of substitution one can, with regard to one and the same object, move from a perceptual act to a memory and move from these acts to the way in which they are brought into play. So I can apply an apperceptive act to another act with a view to getting to know the aspects available for experience – which may not necessarily cover the totality of the act, since there may be sub-personal aspects which do not give rise to any experience as such. One of the simplest ways of bringing to light this apperceptive activity consists in grasping it across that activity which consists in improving, regulating, exercising another mental activity, one which can only appear to me in the course of its unfolding (regarding that part which I am able to apprehend), and through its results, in a mental fashion. I am trying to learn a poem by heart. How do I organise this learning activity, how do I supervise the way in which I take it in, in which I take it up in different ways, with a different quality of attention, for example? The possibility of working with myself, on myself, brings to light this apperceptive activity, the activity by means of which I can inform myself regarding my own mental activity and modify it.

That there might be a distinctive way of articulating one's own subjectively conscious activity seems to be relatively easy to establish. There is no need to look for a hypothetical duplication whose very impossibility would make it possible for me to refuse the first person point of view.

Any attempt to refer to one's own lived experience would modify it and it would therefore be impossible to get to know it. The second argument consists in saying that in principle the practice of introspection deforms what is observed and so modifies the object of attention, which means that we cannot take account of it without it immediately eluding us by virtue of the fact that it gets transformed.

The first unanimous response devoted to this difficulty (James, Binet, etc.) consisted in invoking the possibility of retrospection. However, this solution created a new problem, that of the faillibility of memory. In addition, this first reply carries with it the embarrassing implication of admitting the difficulty by conceding, at least implicitly, that the critique is justified and that the best one can do is to get around the problem by embracing a methodology where the observation of the present is replaced by an observation of the presentification of the past.

However, becoming aware of one's emotions, especially if in certain cases this diminishes their intensity, is no guarantee of a fool-proof result. If such had been the case, one would already have found the perfect solution to the problem of controlling emotions and most psychologists would be nominally unemployed. Moreover, techniques of meditation aimed at emotion, as in Buddhist pragmatics and in Vedantic philosophy, offer indications relative to the possibility of attending to the birth of the emotional reaction without modifying it. Internal observation is brought into play, is improved. In short, rather

than limiting oneself to an affirmation of principle, it appears more interesting, and more scientific, to check on how emotional states are or are not
transformed, in accordance with what factors, and to what degree etc.

But the central argument is the following: it is not possible to describe
modifications of subjective experience without gaining access to this experience. How to do so without the methodology of introspection? In fact, if I
say that the fact of observing my internal states modifies them, it can legitimately be asked of me how I know this. How am I going to evaluate it? In
accordance with what criteria? And how might it be possible to reply to these
questions without passing by way of an observation of one's internal states?
This point keeps on recurring. Every critique of introspection itself employs a
naive reference to introspection in order to criticize what it supposes to be its
limitations.

It nevertheless remains the case that the influence of observation on what
is observed is a significant epistemological problem which can even be extended to all the sciences. And in consequence, the critique can be inverted:
if it is correctly established, the influence of internal observation will, in the
final analysis, offer supplementary information on the limits of the stability
of states, of acts, of contents envisaged through introspection. In that respect,
Piaget (1968: 186) already pointed out this idea that the critique directed towards introspection could be seen as a means whereby introspection can be
better understood: in the same way, "perceptual illusions" inform us about the
properties of perceptual activity.

The first improvements: Experimental introspection

Experimental introspection
The beginning of the 20th century sees the rapid expansion of the utilisation
of the methodology of introspection, which is now scientific, since it is called
'systematic introspection' or 'experimental introspection'. Of primary importance at that time was the procedure required to integrate data in the first-
and second-person into a controlled environment and within a structure composed of a number of complementary measures. Three centers dominated the
scene: in Paris, the school of Binet and his pupils (Avanzini 1974); in the United
States, at the University of Cornell, Titchener (along with his disciples: Jacob-
son, Okabe, Clarke), educated in Germany under Wundt, whose work he translated into English (Leahey 1987: 203); finally, the group of German researchers
known as the Würzburg School, who published a great deal over a ten year
period from 1901 (Mayer and Orth) to 1912 (Külpe).

The will to establish a methodologically rigorous context capable of attesting to the scientific character of the research makes itself known, verbally, through the way in which the research is demonstrated, but also in act. In fact, since the beginning of the 19th century we have moved from an exclusively first person point of view, where researcher and subject are confused, where the only subject present is the researcher, to a 'second person' point of view, where descriptions of subjective experience are gathered on the basis of a selection from a group.

This marks the beginning of a period where the collection of data acquires a relative autonomy with regard to the researcher himself. When the researcher refers to his own experiences, (which is often to be found in the Titchener's school), his experience, (precisely flagged as being his own), remains one among other acquisitions. The subjective experience in question is more carefully delimited, contrary to the early research which envisaged the experience of effort (but not in any specific occurrence) or the examination of the current of consciousness in general. Now we have specifically proposed tasks, which circumscribe, in time and with reference to the object, the very experience which is thematized. This orientation towards the realization of definite tasks represents a genuine revolution, one which brings this research within the purview of what is now known as the experimental set-up and its control. The tasks are the same for everyone, they are carried out under identical conditions and with definite results. In addition, the definition of these tasks leads the researchers to introduce dependent variables, by playing with the relation between one task and another, relations which, with regard to the analysis of results, make it possible to draw inferences bearing upon the disparity in the success rate between tasks and subjects. Researchers are attentive to the problems of description (Titchener, in particular, talked a great deal about this: English 1921), from the point of view of the neutrality of the descriptive terms employed, of the attention paid to the description of subjective experience itself and not of the reality evoked. We already find the beginnings of a concern with the de-composition of the description into small components, with a view to facilitating its formulation. But we are still far from any precise awareness of the demands of description and of its non-inductive orientation with the help of a more sophisticated maintenance technique.

Some of the difficulties raised by this description and by the problems of attention to subjective experience, are overcome if one works with subjects *trained* for this kind of experience. Yet this in turn gives rise to its own potential difficulties. If the subjects have been trained they might, at the same time, have been deformed, that is, 'adapted' to the hypotheses of the observer.

This question has already been encountered in the first Part of this book. Is a certain expertise even desirable for research? If yes, by whom should it have been developed? The subject himself, with a view to improving his means of access to, and description of subjective experience, and/or the researcher, with a view to improving his capacity to guide and to accompany the subject (in a non-inductive manner) in the course of the latter's attempt to accede to, and to describe, his experience?

An example of experimental work
Let us take a specific example in order to better understand how these different improvements are put into effect: the research of H. J. Watt. He decided to study "directed evocation" and, for that, he invented a group of six tasks (Watt 1905; Burloud 1927; Humphrey 1951). We will make no attempt here to go into his formulation of the hypotheses nor the internal coherence of the theoretical frameworks of the period, but will simply examine the form of the experience. Here are the principal elements of the experimental procedure:

a. On the one hand, we find a list of key words, on the other, six instructions: find a super-ordinate, a subordinate concept, a concept relating the whole to the parts, the parts to the whole, a concept of co-ordination or a concept of part to part. By varying the tasks it becomes possible to make comparisons. What has been improved since has been the setting up of the list of words with imagery values etc. When one wants to use verbal material stemming from what one knows in advance to be a given population, how is one going to master their inductive value a priori and from the standpoint of familiarity with it etc.

b. The key words are for the most part substantives, never going beyond three syllables. No description of the instructions is given, in the strict sense of that word, nor of the procedure by means of which the key word was arrived at, but, from the instructions, one is given to understand that it was drawn from a written text.

c. The sample is homogeneous. It is composed of professors and doctors of philosophy. They are six in number but each subject is subjected to fifteen series of tests taken at the rate of two a day on average, each one devoted to one of the tasks (the experimental procedure could have been better prepared from the standpoint of their ordering), as a result of which one is provided in total with thousands of elementary pieces of evidence.

d. For each item (induction) the researcher disposes of the resulting performance (the reply thereby induced) and of the possibility of classifying it with regard to its type and successfulness relative to the instructions as also, in a more qualitative way, to the type of relation between the key word and the induced response. On the other hand, the time taken to develop a response, i.e., the time separating the presentation of the key word from the response, is made available to him. Finally the written transcription of the description of the subjective experience lived out by the subject in the realisation of his task is also made available to him. This description is itself split up into four moments which the subject is invited to describe: the preparation, that is, the period before the presentation of the key word, the appearance of the key word, the analysis of the key word and the response itself.

In this way, for each item of the task, three series of independent pieces of evidence are generated (the result, the time, the subsequent description) as well as those possibilities of analysis and inference which make it possible to generate such rich data. Here one finds all the ingredients of a scientific research project which respects the rules of experimental method. These data were gathered in 1902 and published in 1905. So we are in possession of an experimental program, a control of the experimental procedure, a collection of independent and complementary evidence. If a critique of introspection is justified, it cannot be with regard to the methodology. In fact, as we shall see, for the most part, problems concerning the correct interpretation of the data have been confused with a critique of its method of collection.

What we want to emphasize with this example is that, from the very beginning of the century, the methodological criteria for research based on introspection were 'standard' with regard to the requirements of the experimental method and that researchers did not restrict themselves to working on the data alone, but also exploited traces and observables. One could take other examples from the research of the Würzburg school or from other work, such as that done by Binet. If one wants to criticize this research it cannot be in the name of a confused amalgamation attempting to justify the belief that the research was not rigorous, that a century ago researchers only worked in an approximate fashion, which explains why the results obtained were 'reputed' to be untrustworthy. But who has read carefully through the research protocols of this period? Of course, one might be tempted to say that the experimental method was rigorous 'in spite of' the fact that it was based upon introspective data!

When one examines in detail the data gathered by different researchers of the Würzburg school on the basis of the protocols that these authors submit with their interpretations, what is remarkable is that the verbalization data are extremely consistent. It would be perfectly possible to mix up the protocols, to the point at which they became indistinguishable each from the other, leaving aside the clues offered by the difference between the tasks. But if one compares them with the data obtained by Binet, or with that obtained by the students of Titchener, they are, as regards their structure, entirely comparable. Certain attempts made recently, in a non-published work carried out by Vermersch with GREX (1996), to re-take the tasks of that period have produced evidence that is more detailed but does not differ in any fundamental way. In this sense one might say that it seems rather easy to replicate the results. But naturally not if you go about it as did Lyons who, with a view to reproducing an experiment by one of Titchener's students, Okabe, claims not to have been able to obtain any data at all, since the subjects did not understand their instructions. (Lyons 1986:21). By contrast, what really did present a problem was the fact that the evidence went against the hypotheses formulated initially, leaving researchers confronted with a major problem of interpretation which forced them against the current of their expectations. But it should be emphasized that the debate bore upon the problem of contradictory evidence, not upon the inability to reproduce the data, or upon the trustworthiness of this data. If one had to reject all the research leading to results which appeared contradictory, scientific research would lose some of its most precious discoveries!

Our reading goes against the generally expressed views regarding the fallible, insufficient, contradictory character of these studies. But the problem lies not in the methodology but in the fact that the data were too "strong" for the period. Researchers did not have access to the theoretical frameworks necessary to think them through. From their point of view they represented "modern psychology", new psychology, psychology that was scientific because it was experimental. For the first time the higher forms of behaviour were tackled in an empirical fashion. Their attempts were noteworthy but determined by their past history: the idea that thought is a conscious, rational activity and that it was enough to simply ask "observers" (the name for experimental subjects at that time) to describe what was taking place in order to get information. But the first conclusion to be reached and reproduced in a clear fashion was that the subject is not necessarily conscious of all the steps in the elaboration of his cognitive activity and that there are periods of silence with regard to which the observers have nothing to contribute in terms of contents of consciousness, even though they may very well have felt that their activity had been guided in some way. These results could be re-interpreted by saying that they had brought to light the unconscious sub-personal dimension of intellectual activity. They also brought forward evidence relating to that with regard to which the subject is nevertheless conscious in his own intellectual activity (something that tended to be forgotten). How could the researchers of that period have integrated this kind of data? It is not at all surprising that this should have given rise to innumerable contradictory debates amongst the laboratories functioning at the time. But the disagreement bore upon the interpretation of the results, not upon the gathering of the data, which can be reproduced without difficulty. At that time, they could do no more than take up a position for or against associationism and the sensualism associated with it. The whole of psychology still had to be opened up. Researchers at the beginning of the century did not have available to them all the theoretical, empirical and practical advances developed later in the fields of problem resolution, child psychology, differential psychology or comparative psychology. It is interesting to note that this research did not immediately lead to anything even though it had a global impact at the time. The interpretation that can be made of this is precisely that, initially, each and every new initiative could only give rise to the same results and that a detour was required to get back to these results from the standpoint of their applications.

With the work of the Würzburg school and that of Binet, we witness the birth of a long tradition of research which continues to the present day and which consists in studying cognitive functioning through *problem solving*. Their point of departure was the desire to study the "higher functions", in opposition to the partisans of study of the elementary acts (this takes up again the opposition of Külpe and Wundt), as also a program which was highly innovative for the time, that of defining the tasks and problems with a view to studying intellectual functions directed towards a finished result. The subject has a goal (in any case, one is proposed by the instructions) and has to look for a result, propose a response, all of which makes it possible to relate what the subject did, what he said he did, and the properties of his final response, or even of his intermediary responses when traces and observables are available.

An objection emerged progressively with the progress of empirical research in experimental psychology and in neuro-physiology and, in an even more remarkable way, with the arrival of contemporary Cognitive Science. To the extent that it is empirically founded, we introduce it here rather than in the context of the objections, to which it could equally well be attached.

Introspection is useless because the mechanisms and the essential properties of cognitive functioning cannot be brought to light in subjective experience. To put it otherwise, don't ask of the subject what he can not be expected to know. In fact, the premise of this objection is legitimate. A large number of facts studied by psychologists are not accessible to first-person experience and can only be brought to light with the aid of a particular apparatus and/or statistical techniques of inference. Such a dimension reappears today in cognitive science under the heading of the sub-personal level, and corresponds to the neuro-dynamical evidence which underlies the mental level. This is the reason why these objections are frequently to be found amongst neuro-scientists of cognition whose vocation it is to deal with this sub-personal level more than with anything else.

But the fault in the reasoning consists in concluding that, because certain facts are inaccessible to consciousness, everything which is accessible to consciousness is scientifically uninteresting *a priori*. This reasoning is both absurd in itself and utterly unjustified. The evaluative mistake consists probably in the fact that it seems to go without saying that what is most interesting scientifically is what arises out of the 'deepest' and 'most essential' mechanisms, so that one does not even have to consider the legitimacy of positing a plurality of levels of analysis nor their eventual causal disconnection. Trying to establish, as does Kosslyn, that there exists an amodal propositional stock underlying images touches upon a level which is not phenomenological but clearly neuro-biological. Describing the properties of images through the study of the parameters of the results obtained from tasks with mental rotation, as does Shepard (Kosslyn 1994; Shepard & Cooper 1992), touches upon another aspect which is also inaccessible to subjective experience since it can only be established by statistical inference. By contrast, bringing to light the mental acts by means of which a pianist provides himself with an imaged representation of the score or of the keyboard helps shed light on what is done by those who do not adopt this procedure. Again, teaching someone how to provide himself with visual images when he does not do so is also well adapted to a phenomenological mode of access and corresponds to a level of analysis quite distinct from the two preceding ones. Shepard could have duplicated the results he obtained from verbalisations bearing on the subjective experience of acts put into operation by the subject by trying to work with mental rotations. A reading of his more autobiographical work (Shepard 1990) would lead one to believe that, like many others, it was his aim to remain within the orthodoxy of "methodological correctness".

In fact, not only is what the subject can be conscious of in his own subjective experience scientifically interesting but, in addition, with regard to what he is not directly conscious of, it remains interesting to ask what the subject is phenomenologically conscious of at that very moment, and what relation there might be between his experience and what the researcher might describe as being what 'really' took place. In other words, our position vis a vis this frequent criticism is very simple: introspection and phenomenological data possess their own level of access and of description. Not only does this not exclude, in any way, the sub-personal level, it actually opens up the question of their structural relation. If one deviates from this methodologically simple axis one is easily led, yet again, either to a dualism or to one form or another of reductionism of the kind analyzed in Chapter 4.1.

Assessing the positions

Introspection, as a methodology, often becomes the object of justifications and of defence, as for example with Burloud. The manuals and treatises of the time generally adopt a balanced position, one which admits this method on condition that it is not the only one employed. Dumas' great treatise on psychology, dating from 1924, expresses this point of view rather well in a conclusion composed by the editor himself (Dumas 1923–1924: 1123).

> We don't have to insist upon the importance and the need for introspective psychology. Even though stimulus-response psychology thinks it can do without introspection, no one disputes that, for every other form of psychology, introspection is indispensable. One may criticise the bearing of the introspective method, point out its difficulties, have reservations about the type of certainty attached to it, show that it deforms the very mechanisms it seeks to attain when it does not simply cook them up ready made for the convenience of its explanations or the triumph of its preconceived ideas etc., but, even when one has assembled all these criticisms, one is still obliged to admit that none of them is decisive and that the difficulties pointed out only demand that certain precautions be taken.

In spite of this the place officially reserved for introspection will decline. One of the most remarkable of later attempts to utilise the method is that of Sartre in 1940, and precisely with regard to the question of the relation between image and thought in the context of the young philosopher's early attempt to found a phenomenological psychology. In doing so, he shows much finesse and interest in first person analyses relating to his own cognitive activity but makes no use either of the second-person point of view or of the constraints of experimental procedure.

It is equally interesting to cite Guillaume's thoughts in his manual of psychology of 1932, to the extent that he shows in a dispassionate way the complementarity of introspective methods and the gathering of data on the basis of a simple example dealt with in a paragraph entitled "Introspection and Language" (Figure 9). Learn the table of figures included here in such a way as to know them by heart.

12	8	9
4	21	6
7	15	11

Figure 9.

Certain people will perhaps find, on watching themselves carefully, that, while reciting, they do, in a certain sense, read off from an imaginary table, make use of a visual representation. Others are guided by an auditory memory, as if they were reproducing a heard melody. The first have a simultaneous image of a whole in which each figure has its place; the second hear mentally a succession of syllables. What can we learn from the descriptions due to the introspective method? The results do not seem essentially different from those that could have been furnished by an objective method. Try asking people who have learnt the table of figures to no longer observe themselves and describe what they observe but rather recite the lines either in a vertical or a horizontal direction. (...) These variations are very difficult for those who employ the auditory method, who are unable to do much more than write things down in the order in which they have been learnt; they present fewer difficulties for the one who is able to evoke a visual table. (...) These examples show that the subjective method, to the extent that, in order to be effective, it is restricted to verbal expression, is not essentially different from the objective method and that we are talking about disciplines stemming from the same science. We will see that both methods have contributed to the development of psychology. If the purely objective technique tends to prevail in animal, infantile and pathological psychology, both procedures are employed concurrently in relation to most questions stemming from normal human psychology. One should never neglect to throw light upon an experience by soliciting the subject's introspection; it will help in the understanding of objective results and will often make it possible to dispense with laborious control experiments (Guillaume 1942: 11–12).

This example shows that there should not be any antagonism between different approaches; it shows the limits that the objective method encounters in determining how the subject gets along. In effect, complementary requirements can bring to light the use of different modes of encoding information (simultaneous/successive), without for all that making it clear whether, for example, the successive stems from the verbalization of the unfolding of the figures or whether it is not more a matter of each figure being placed according to a particular trajectory; whether the verbalization of the unfolding of the figures is done by using a pattern or not, puts the emphasis on a rhythm or not etc. Any comparison between these two approaches also shows that the interpretation of the objective data could not be done without referring to the content of subjective experience. Finally, this study is exemplary in the sense that neither of the two methods yields the sense of the data. In and of themselves, neither can provide the theoretical context for interpreting the data.

Strategies of circumvention

Replacing introspection with verbalization
Studies of problem solving begin to get ever more numerous and indeed become the dominant paradigm of the study of cognition. At the same time, references to introspection start to disappear. Discussions of method now bear upon the assembling of verbalizations, that is, upon the products of introspection. Verbalization begins to replace attention to the introspective act through which it becomes possible to become conscious of experience. From 1934, with Claparède (1934) we find the instruction, destined to become famous, of "thinking aloud". This tendency can equally be seen as just another decisive critique of introspection, namely, that *introspection brings us no original data*.

In a well-known article which generated extensive debate, Nisbett and Wilson (1977) tried to prove experimentally that there could be no such thing as introspection but only the expression of subject's naive theories. This is one of the few pieces of research which actually attempted to produce empirical evidence on introspection. In experiments of a psycho-social kind where one seeks to influence the decision-making process of subjects, the authors show that verbalizations do not reflect the reality of what took place, (that the subjects were influenced and changed their points of view or their assessments), and that, if one asks external observers to make predictions about what the subjects are going to verbalize, there is not much difference between what they say and what the subjects say. Conclusion: strictly speaking, there is no such thing as introspection.

A great deal of criticism has been directed at the extreme conclusions of these authors, but no fundamental criticism has ever been formulated. But if one wants to use introspection one must at least seek out data compatible with the possibility of an experimental access making it possible for the subject to generate descriptive verbalizations. However, authors only ask questions about the form of the "why", questions which, in effect, amount to a demand for causal explanations. They do not ask their subjects to describe what has taken place *for them*, given the nature of their mode of access to these events, but simply why they did or said this or that. The methodology of introspection cannot require of the subject that he be a psychologist or the theoretican of his own cognitive processes. But introspection can seek to ascertain the descriptive elements which make up the actual lived experience of the subject, whether these elements have already been, or are simply capable of being, brought to consciousness.

The methodological mistake made by these authors as regards the difficulty of not demanding of their subjects that they reply directly and in the same terms as those in which the researcher seeks to conceptualize the objects of his research, is very instructive. The subject who undergoes introspection at best only gains access to a description of the different aspects of his experience. It is up to the researcher to draw inferences regarding the verbalizations he has been able to gather, and this in the context of a second-person methodology. If the research bears upon the inferences which the subject might be able to draw regarding the causes of his behaviour then either the researcher has to ask him about them directly, entering the realm of "folk psychology", studying the beliefs and naive theories of the subject; or else he simply asks for a description of what took place for the subject, the history of his experience, in the hopes that, if the subject has been led to draw inferences, they will appear either directly as verbalizations, or indirectly, *from* verbalizations. As a mode of gathering data, introspection cannot go further than describing, gathering phenomenological data. Otherwise it ceases to be introspection and becomes an enquiry into the beliefs and the spontaneous theories of the subject.

Introspection has disappeared. The only thing that is now brought to light are verbalizations, the products of introspection. The latter are public, objective; they have to do with a piece of behaviour so they are methodologically correct, scientific, even if an essential part of what takes place for the subject when one asks him to describe how he proceeded has been lost. And so innumerable questionnaires are now produced in which intimate questions are put to the subject without anyone being in the least bit interested in knowing how the subject is able to reply to these questions. Is there only one way to do this? As Boring remarks in 1953: introspection survives *under another name:* "verbal reports".

The most remarkable case – a reference for an entire generation of cognitive psychologists – is that of Ericsson and Simon (1984/1993), whose book *Protocol Analysis* enjoyed huge success. Strategically, the authors have to justify their proposal to avoid being critiqued as introspectionists. They have to show that one is entitled to use the descriptive verbalizations of the subject with-out, for all that, falling into "non-scientific" introspection. They go so far as to quote Watson with a view to establishing that it is "scientifically correct" to gather such data. On the basis of a very large number of experimental results they argue that the simultaneous verbalization of the activity in progress does not modify the processes under study and that the contemporary character of this putting into words eliminates most of the risks of deformation, of forget-ting, of the kind of rationalisation that an *a posteriori* verbalization might occa-sion. In talking of "verbal encode" of "simultaneous verbalization" they make us forget that, to produce these verbalizations, the subject has to gain access to something. If he is going to describe his mental operations, the content of his representation, he has to put into effect some particular cognitive act. This careful restriction of the methodology to the concomitant verbalization alone, without any taking into account of the subjective act which produces it, which feeds it, makes the experimental relation intersubjectively weak. A simple ini-tial instruction to "speak out loud" suffices, without any relational dimension, without any genuine interview techniques, to sustain the mediation needed for the realization of introspection.

This way of making introspection disappear under verbalizations has had a number of damaging consequences:

–   Not accounting for the question of access and the problems associated with verbalization as a subjective act have covered over the need for tech-niques of mediation, essentially the interview techniques needed for going still further. The work of Ericsson and Simon, even in its revised edition (1993), never addresses the question of interview techniques; it starts from the erroneous presupposition that the fact of posing questions amounts to inducing the content of the response. As a whole, and until very re-cently, there has been no teaching of interview techniques for cognitive psychologists.
–   As a general rule, one can say that, for more than fifty years, we have seen no development, no improvement, the emergence of no expertise as a result of the taboo imposed upon the theme of introspection.

Replacing introspection by psychometric scales
The study of the subjective dimension of intellectual functioning has also been pursued independently of introspection, by means of the artificial technique stemming from the psycho-metric approach. Rather than carefully questioning a subject, it is possible to produce tests composed of numerous sub-problems

and to distribute them to large populations. This multiplication of data makes it possible to extract invariants by using statistical methods alone. This has functioned well for sixty years but, with this method, the individual is submerged in the medium of the group without it being possible to account for the sources of variation due, for example, to intra-individual differences. The only way of refining this analysis is to begin by examining one description, by subject and by item, before gathering these descriptions together in the analysis of groups. It is amusing to see that one is then inevitably brought back to the study of individual performance on a task by task basis, precisely what differential psychology sought to avoid. And the 'miracle' method which makes it possible to obtain a high degree of coherence in the results consists in asking the subject how he went about his task. One does not ask him to introspect, simply to verbalize! As Marquer notices (1995:113): "These results have led us to propose a new approach to cognitive strategies. With each block of trials the experimenter asks the subject to explain how (s)he has proceeded, with an interview technique which minimises the effect of factors which might in any way diminish the validity of the verbalisations."

Data relative to the first person point of view have not had any impact

One of the most ferocious criticisms which psychologists, as well as cognitive scientists, levelled against introspection or, more generally, against first-person data, consists in affirming that work from this point of view did not lead anywhere, and did not bring with it data which made any difference to anything. Such an argument is a good one. It has to make us wonder about the interest of pushing things further at the risk of finding oneself in the uncomfortable position of trying to be right, where everyone, and not the least important ones, seem to have been proved wrong by history. One can assess the bearing of this argument retrospectively by trying to understand why this research has been discontinued.

The most radical calling into question of the interest in first-person methodology might well be derived from the history of this research-program itself. One gets the impression that they all suddenly disappeared from the university scene. But one might have thought that, however powerful the criticism stemming from behaviourism (or other fashionable trends of the day) might have been, they would have been continued, even discretely and by virtue of their results alone, if there had been anything interesting to be found in the work based on the methodology of introspection. To the extent that they seem to have produced nothing that endured, perhaps we could simply continue to

ignore them! Fraisse who was at the time the French figure most committed
to the scientific and institutional defence of experimental psychology, wrote in
a basic manual for students in psychology: "Titchener, the student of Wundt,
who represents in America and as a result of his 35 years of teaching at Cornell, a psychology founded systematically upon introspection will – by virtue
of the very vacuousness of his great work – contribute to underlining the basic
errors of this psychology" (Fraisse & Piaget 1963:20). In the first instance, one
could look for historical explanations for this absence of continuity. First, the
three schools disappeared with their founders: Külpe leaves for Berlin in 1909
and dies in 1915 and no more of this work emerges from Würzburg; Titchener
dies in 1927 (Leahey 1987) without leaving a successor; Binet (1857–1911),
with a reputation for getting interested in countless things (Avanzini 1974),
has nothing more to say, and gets involved with other work, in particular his
scale for measuring intelligence. And yet, the latter enjoyed a continued development, first with Burloud's (1927–1938) research, then with de La Garanderie (1969), his pupil, who produced a number of works of a pedagogical
kind. To all this one should add that the disappearance of introspection coincides with difficulties in European history which interrupted a number of lines
of thought.

All work in this field is brought to a close with World War I, the first publications which connect with the past only emerging in 1921. It is the same thing
with regard to the rise of fascism: the emigration of German psychology, silence
on the part of Russian and Italian psychology then the break due to the second
World War. At the end of this troubled period, the taking into account of subjective experience is once again conducted within the framework of a clinical
approach and, quite often, in a theoretical framework inspired by existential-
ism, which emphasises the meaning of experience through a description of acts
as such. But even this kind of historical perspective still appears insufficient to
account for the quasi disappearance of introspection. Why did the latter not
make a come back in the 1950s?

Here is one of the most vigorous criticisms ever addressed of the work
of Titchener (Boring 1953:174). The latter recounts in particular an anecdote
where J. W. Baird, a student of Titchener and the author of a methodological
manuel on introspection (which it would be very interesting to find) (English
1921:404), gave a demonstration of the introspective style of questioning at
the American Psychological Association in 1913. He describes the general reaction as incomprehension with regard to the interest in descriptions perceived as
constituting "(...) a dull taxinomic account of sensory events which, since they
suggest almost no functional value for the organism, are peculiarly uninter-

esting to the American scientific temper". In particular, reference was made to kinaesthetic sensations during the unfolding of the task with which one could do nothing. While a visual image can support a piece of reasoning, can be described in terms of the properties of the task, the presence of a kinaesthetic sensation seems not to warrant any interest relative to intellectual functioning. It is precisely with regard to this sensorial dimension that the most extreme lack of understanding will be displayed. The psychology of thought processes at the beginning of this century hoped, through an extension of sensualism, to be in a position to determine cognitive functioning by way of the conscious imagery supposed to accompany all thinking. The non-imagistic dimension of thinking is brought to light, its operative dimension (in Piagetian terms), its finalized dimension. The study of problem solving will look into the logical laws linking the stages of reasoning, structured by the content of the reasoning process. In this framework, the sensorial dimension of the thought process, set aside initially as a superseded hypothesis, is later on entirely forgotten by research programs.

This anecdote is eloquent to the extent that it really does put us on the track of what was lacking at that time, and which forms an essential dimension of our entire presentation, namely, the importance of numerous practical fields regulated by a know-how. In other words, the real problem is that of the concrete *sense* of the descriptive data available to introspection. The critique no longer bears upon the method of gathering the data but on their *interest*, on their functionality. The question which then arises is that of the function of those psychological elements which derive from phenomenological consciousness, namely, those which the subject is able to experience.

Our principal concern is to uncover the meaning of this research and the reasons why this meaning could only make itself known outside the University. It certainly did produce results but outside the standard scientific institutions. In fact, it is its practitioners (teachers, special education teachers, speech therapists, etc.) who make it meaningful, who take into account the sensorial manner in which a content of thought, a mental act, is experienced as being used. Such an opening up in the direction of the dimension of a *praxis*, over and beyond scientific theorising, is *crucial* for us. Chapter 5 is devoted to this dimension.

Improvements on the way

Introspection as a source of empirical data

As a source of phenomenological data introspection furnishes first- and second-person descriptive verbalizations of what can appear to the subject within the limits of what has already been, or what could be, brought to consciousness. As it was stated recently (Howe 1991:25): "(...) if there is an argument against the use of introspection, it has yet to be found". In this sense, introspection does not pose any more problems than any other data or, what comes down to the same thing, just as many. No more than any other data, these verbalizations are not taken to be true *a priori* – that they are the subject's verbalizations of his own experience does not make them any more certain *a priori*. As much as anything else, they will be subjected to critical evaluation and, in particular, inserted into a research program which can be correlated with other series of independent data (traces, observables, time). The play of experimental variables, like the choice of samples, plays its usual role, whether in an experimental, or in an observational context.

This point of view is not new; one finds it regularly expressed by authors who know nothing of the ferocious cricitism to which introspection has been subjected (Radford 1974:245–250). In his polemical work of 1968, aimed at philosophical psychology, Piaget explains:

> On the other hand, there remains the problem of introspection and it is on this point that we approach the essential difference between scientific and philosophical psychology. But this difference has nothing to do, as one might be led to believe, with the use of introspection as such. (...) Even when he engages in introspection, the scientific psychologist looks for controls, which latter has nothing to do with objectivism (since consciousness is the issue) but with objectivity (Piaget 1968:168, 192).

Moreover, this point of view had already been upheld by psychologists of a scientific turn of mind from the beginning of the XXth century as we have tried to show above with reference to the work of the Würzburg school, Binet, Titchener and his students. Improvement has been confused with the general evolution of the methodology of research, even if procedures for the treatment of verbalization data which will make it easier to make use of it are yet to be found (Ericsson & Simon 1984/1993).

Even if psychology has the formidable privilege of working on a double-faced object (since it belongs to those disciplines which have for object of study, a subject), there still remains the question of the right way to conceive of the relation between the first-person point of view and a third-person point of view based on traces and observables. We already drew attention to the nature of the reciprocal constraints holding between the first- and second-person in the Part I. But the difficulties with which we are confronted are not resolved by simply being suppressed. As a result of having tried to ignore data in the first-person, we have tried above all to develop competences and a wealth of experience which would have made it possible for us to deploy a rigorous methodology which could be used to form researchers. Now that psychology is more certain of its status as a fully fledged science, perhaps it might be possible to stop being afraid of introspection and to start trying to uphold the phenomenological point of view with a view to relating it to the other evidence. The whole history of research shows that, sooner or later, one has to refine the qualitative typology of the data furnished by the subject, at least to try to do so, with a view to a better integration of the sources of inter- and intra-individual variation (Marquer 1995).

Introspection as act

But this point of view only clears the ground. We still have to address the question of introspection as a cognitive act effectively put into operation by a singular subject. What does the fact of considering introspection as an act consist in? We first have to get past a misleading truism, as if the simple fact of calling a mental operation an act exhausted all that could be said about it. In so doing, we are immediately brought up against the by now well known problem of didactics and psychology, namely, the implicit character of the procedural dimension. Describing the structure of an act requires that we describe its temporal unfolding at different levels of granularity (Vermersch 1994), the linking up of sub-goals, the succession of stages and, at the heart of each stage, elementary actions, together with their ways of being brought into operation and registering information, then the micro-operations, etc.

But to proceed with such a description it is not only necessary to practice introspection (one certainly has to refer to lived experience) but, also to envisage the act itself as a subjective experience, something that has never been done by psychologists making use of introspection.

Only Titchener (1912: 500, 506, 507) posed the question of the description of the practice of introspection, giving no satisfactory response: "Experimental introspection, we have said, is a procedure that can be formulated; the introspecting psychologist can tell what he does and how he does it." After conducting a review of the publications of the Würzburg school, then his own and those of his students, the conclusions he reached were rather meager: "it is evident that these accounts are meagre; it is evident, too, that they contain an unsifted mixture of fact and theory, of exposition and valuation" and a little later on: "One gets the impression, indeed, that the experimenters, or at least the earlier of them, took the introspective method for granted: they were setting a straightforward task, which the trained observer was competent to perform." In the final analysis, the harvest is disappointing, something he will try to mitigate by pleading the novelty of this procedure and the need to improve it. But the unanswered question remains: how is one to know in what the practice of introspection consists?

In all the literature relating to introspection we have not come across a more lucid and clear position than that expressed by Titchener. However, in the article we have cited, he never saw that he was only making use of second-hand information. In all that he relates, what is taken into account is the third-person statements of experimenters. There is no reference to the first-person descriptions of the practice of introspection. What was lacking was an awareness of what had to be done to correctly carry through a first-person study of the act of introspection: using as an instrument what one hoped to study by bringing into play a supplementary stage (Piguet 1995; Misrahi 1996); *being present to introspection itself with a view to identifying its structural dynamic.* Such is precisely the major challenge of this present work, as it has been set out in detail in the first Part.

Conclusion

To say that it is currently cognitive psychology that brings the methodologically most pertinent response to the question of access to subjective experience is quite contradictory. On the one hand, historically, the latter has opened up a path made up of numerous steps which it is useful to examine in detail. On the other hand, no scientific discipline has gone to greater lengths to reject any accounting for the first person point of view. It has not proved difficult to enumerate an impressive array of such criticisms (Vermersch 1999), and we were not able to tackle all of these critiques in this chapter.

The chapter has been written from a psychological point of view. One might even wonder whether the study of subjective experience, utilizing a first-person point of view, will not in the end be adopted by almost all scientists except psychologists, who will probably be the last to be convinced of its utility, assuming that they will be convinced of it one day! Witness to this today is the contemporary development of certain disciplines at the heart of the near-sciences of cognition, less bogged down by the setbacks that introspection has encountered in the history of psychology.

Introspection is difficult, it is technical, it demands an apprenticeship, requires the progressive development of a genuine expertise. The greatest difficulty lies in the fact that this technicality is masked, that it can pass unnoticed due to the apparent ease with which it is possible to obtain a minimum of information about our states of mind, our thought processes, our emotions. However, such an impression of facility disappears as soon as one is in a position to furnish a true description of it and to gain access to it in a sufficiently stable and precise way. But just as looking at a garden gives one no gardening or botanical competence, so our familiar contact with that with which we are intimately acquainted does not give us the competence of a phenomenologist or psychologist. Piaget has brought this to our attention in a quite remarkable way (Piaget 1953:82–86): knowledge of the "interior" world is no more given to us than is that of the world of objects. In both cases we are faced with a construction on the basis of an interaction between the subject and the world, between the subject and itself.

CHAPTER 5

Concerning practice

5.1. Introduction: Practice is the privileged site for grasping experience

From this point of view, this chapter forms a turning point within the location of the various motivations which govern our interest in subjective experience. After a conjectural framing of the question through situating the topic of awareness in the cognitive sciences and a methodological framing with the stages of the development of introspective psychology in Chapter 4, we now direct our attention towards experience at the level of its *praxis*, which immediately takes us to the heart of the method privileged in this work: to describe the process of becoming aware from its very enaction, to describe it as it is carried out. This second practical motivation is consequently the one which causes us to now adopt the particular approach taken up here.

In the previous Chapter we thus developed a number of the important motivations that now lead to a more careful examination of this pragmatic realm. In order to do so, a few details concerning the conceptual underpinning are necessary. We specify first how such pragmatics appear in the light of cognitive science, then turn to the different philosophical underpinnings of the practical dimension, and finally take into account the point of view of the psychological applied disciplines.

5.2. Embodied practices in cognitive science

We will start our discussion by underlining the difference between *know-how and know-that*, the difference between skill or spontaneous coping (*savoir-faire*) and voluntary knowledge or rational judgments. In this context of the cognitive sciences, "intentional" has the meaning of a voluntary and rational *a priori*, in the quasi-Kantian sense of the motives and reasons for action posed as preconditions to this one resulting in a reflexive deliberation, and not the phenomenological sense. The latter does not intrinsically imply a voluntary or rational signification, but simply corresponds to an act of aiming at the objects of the world, to a movement of directing or orienting oneself towards them, to the point that, as we will see later, the question of the intentionality of action or practical intentionality can reshape in phenomenology the dimension of savoir-faire (of *know-how*), which appears to be, ever since the cognitive sciences, a contradiction in terms.

A relative neglect in understanding immediate coping is also manifest within the very sciences that are dedicated to mind and knowing: the cognitive sciences. But, recently, there are strong indications that the cognitive sciences are slowly growing in the conviction that the traditional picture of mind as a form of computation is upside down and that a radical paradigmatic or epistemic shift is rapidly developing. In that respect, the inspiration for this crucial observation comes mostly from a modern re-evaluation of the central role of sensori-motor coordination in cognition (Maturana & Varela 1992, and Varela 1996a). At the center of this emerging view is the conviction that the proper units of knowledge are primarily concrete, *embodied*, lived; that knowledge is about situatedness; and that the uniqueness of knowledge, its historicity and context, is not a "shadow" that occludes the brighter pattern to be captured in its true essence, an abstract configuration. What is concrete is not a step towards something else: it is the way itself and it is where we are (Steels & Brooks 1993).

In fact, all along, there have been a number of pioneering lines of work holding to the persistent intuition that cognition needs to be understood in terms of how significance arises out of the autonomous totality which is the organism. A good example is Jean Piaget, who offered a basic clue as to how to transform this intuition into good research: to study the constitution of a perceptual object grounded in ontogeny, how children shape their world through sensori-motor actions. What Piaget introduced in a way that can never be forgotten, is that cognition – even in what seems its high level expressions – is grounded in the concrete activity of the whole organism, that is in sensori-motor immediate coupling. The world is not something that is given to us: it is something we engage in by how we move, touch, breathe and eat.

This is what can be called *cognition as enaction* since enaction connotes this bringing-forth by concrete handling (Varela et al. 1991). In a nutshell, the enactive approach underscores the importance of two interrelated points: (1) that perception consists of perceptually guided action, (2) that cognitive structures emerge from the recurrent sensory-motor patterns that enable action to be perceptually guided.

Let us begin with the notion of a perceptually guided action. For the dominant computationalist tradition, the point of departure for understanding perception is typically abstract: the information-processing problem of recovering pre-given properties of the world. In contrast, the point of departure for the enactive approach is the study of how the perceiver guides his actions in local situations. Since these local situations constantly change as a result of the perceiver's activity, the reference point for understanding perception is no longer a pre-given, perceiver-independent world, but rather the sensory-motor structure of the cognitive agent, the way in which the nervous system links sensory and motor surface; to determine the common principles or lawful linkages between sensory and motor systems that explain how action can be *perceptually guided* in a *perceiver-dependent* world.

In the enactive approach reality is not a given: it is perceiver-dependent, not because it 'constructs' it at whim, but because what *counts* as a relevant world is inseparable from the structure and history of coupling of the perceiver. Thus cognition consists not of representations, but of *embodied action*. Correlatively, we can say that the world we know is not pre-given; it is, rather, *enacted* through our history of structural coupling, and the temporal hinges that articulate enaction are rooted in the number of alternative copings that are activated in every situation. These alternatives are the source of both common sense and creativity in cognition. What all living cognitive beings seem to have in common is knowledge that is always a know-how constituted on the basis of the concrete; what we call the general and the abstract are aggregates of readiness-for-action.

In other words, cognitive science is waking up to the simple fact that just *being there*, in immediate coping, is far from being simple or merely a matter of "reflexes". It is in fact the real "hard work", since it took the longest evolutionary time to develop such basic abilities; voluntary and rational analysis during breakdowns developed only recently and very rapidly in evolutionary measures. This point of view is also developing vigorously in modern robotics and the new research trend of artificial life, which cannot detain us further here (Varela et al. 1991; Bourgine & Varela 1992).

Immediate coping stands in contrast to deliberation and analysis, but we do not mean to negate entirely the role and importance of these latter. The point is to see them in their distinct roles and relative relevance. This distinction was recognized very clearly by Dewey in *Human Nature and Conduct*, from whom we borrow the distinction between *know-how* and *know-that*:

> We may be said to *know how* by means of our habits (...) We walk and read aloud, we get off and on street cars, we dress and undress, and do a thousand useful acts without thinking of them. We know something, namely, how to do

> them (...) (If) we choose to call (this) knowledge then other things also called knowledge, knowledge *of* and *about* things, knowledge *that* things are thus and so, knowledge that involve reflection and conscious appreciation, remains of a different sort (Dewey 1922: 177).

The main point raised is that both philosophers and scientists concerned with mind have grossly overlooked the importance and the central role of the immediacy of practices, skills and their pervasiveness. We should try and impress on ourselves what an enormous part of our lives – working, moving, talking, eating – manifest in know-how. And, concomitantly, what a small part of our lives is spent in deliberate, rational analysis which is symptomatic of knowing-that.

Now, we acquire our behavior in regards to our immediate present in much the same way as all other modes of behavior: they become transparent to us as we grow up in society. This is because learning is, as we know, circular: we learn what we are supposed to be in order to be accepted as learners, and thus most of our mental and active life is of the immediate coping kind which is transparent and stable, acquired by history. We do not see that we do not see, and this is why so few people paid attention to it, until phenomenology and pragmatism, cognitive psychology of an applied bent, and the new trends in cognitive science just outlined have brought it to the fore.

To approach experience in this manner thus supposes a consideration of all human activity while having in mind the following observation: practice makes an activity initiate by the simple fact that the activity takes place. Practice understood in this sense is not specifically bound to the execution of a physical action. Doing algebraic calculations is a practice: it is not enough to master mathematical knowledge, but it is necessary to organize the draft, to find the adequate way of writing them, to avoid errors while writing. In doing such calculations, one not only develops this mathematical knowledge, one deploys as well a practical skill which conditions success and efficiency. In all mental action, we have become accustomed to valuing knowledge that defines its content or objective, but all these actions are at the same time the site of a practice, and can only be incarnated, can only be authentically assimilated with such a practice. In this sense, one can justifiably speak of a "theoretical practice".

5.3. A diverse philosophical background: Practical reason, pragmatism, praxis and habitus

It is precisely such a practice of theory that philosophy has theorized, while striving to apprehend it, not as a representation, but as a *praxis,* i.e. in its immanent logic. We have too often considered philosophy through the distorting glasses of theory and reflection, while forgetting that an entire tradition, from Aristotle to Wittgenstein and to K. O. Apel in passing by Marx and James, endeavored to make a place for practice and action. Phenomenology itself has been burdened by its Husserlian foundation; Heidegger perpetuated such a theoretical shortcoming coming from the perceptive paradigm of the founder while emphasizing pure thought as opposed to practical efficacy. Nevertheless, Phenomenology has also essentially assumed the task of conferring meaning and status to the practical dimension in all its specificity. To be convinced of this, it suffices to think of the careers of Merleau-Ponty, Sartre and Ricoeur, or of the appropriation of phenomenology by the movement of Schutzean sociology, itself further developed in an original way by E. Goffman and H. Garfinkel in particular.

It is true that the enthusiastic attachment of modernity to the figure of Kant and to the critical Rationalism he embodied could make us temporarily forget the importance of this tradition of "practical philosophy". Indeed, even when the author of the *Critique of Theoretical Reason* takes "practical reason" for a topic in the *Critique of Practical Reason,* it is to insist on the fact that the moral law is in me as a transcendental a priori objectively founded, and which governs as such all my actions. Practice, for Kant, is pure or is not: it refers to a morality of duty and of freedom of the will, a morality for which I act always out of pure respect for the moral law in me; I obey under the obediance of a commandment which precedes me and exceeds me; a categorical imperative, which is unconditioned because it is independent of all material finality (Philips 1981).

But is this a genuine analysis of human action, if to act is always to have preliminary consciousness, in this case moral, of a goal in sight? Also, doesn't one act – most often – to overcome a situation, in urgency, independently of all (moral) preliminary representation of his action? Kant himself understood this very well, when he wrote, to overcome this gap, *The Foundation for the Metaphysics of Morals,* then *Anthropology from a Pragmatic Point of View.* Here action is measured in its validity not by the standard of the purity of its apriori principle, but with respect to the usefulness of the means implemented. Kant thus distinguishes, within the framework which he names "conditional or hypothetical imperatives," between technical imperatives which entail skillful-ness (I apply such a means in view of such an end) and pragmatic imperatives, which refer – in terms of a number of rules of prudence – to well-being.

When one insists on the practical rooting of cognition, it is consequently the Kantian pragmatic, even the technical side, to which it is appropriate to refer. The latter opened and re-opened the way for all analyses of action (*pragma* in Greek). Drawing its origin from the Aristotelian theory of deliberation (*bouleusis*) and of prudence, this practical intellect (*phronesis*) (Aubenque 1963/1986), was re-taken by Peirce, James and Wittgenstein, to cite only the most well-known philosophers.

Essentially, the dividing line between the two traditions in question, intellectualist on the one hand, pragmatist on the other, is the following: does the criterion of validity of action lie in its representation, whether it is a matter of morality, of rationality or of intention, or in its particular efficacy, whether it is a matter of the means of implementation, of the results attained or even of its immanent dynamic itself?

If one starts from the inaugural, Aristotelian analysis on this point in the *Nichomachean Ethics* (Book III) for example, one finds the structural distinction between know-that and know-how, which was treated above in reference to Dewey: the carpenter or the doctor practice is a know-how, i.e. they utilize the appropriate means in view of a determined end, the tools in view of construction, the remedies in view of a cure. In each case, unlike the necessity revealed in the a priori knowledge of geometry, the know-how of each of them belongs to a skillful and prudent management of the contingency of particular circumstances, a certain art of seizing, in situation, the opportune moment (the *Kairos*) – what materials are employed for such a structure, how to respond to the demand of a patient? – independent of all possible predetermination in terms of the project. Clearly, the truth of the action is measured here by its utility and by its efficacy, which merges purely and simply with its good and its virtue. It is again Aristotle who proposes the first clear distinction between *praxis* and *theoria/gnosis* on the one hand, and *poiesis* on the other. Only *praxis* corresponds to an immanent activity which contains in itself its own end (Aristote, I 1, 1094 a 4–9; VI 5, 1140 a 2).

Such a common emphasis put by Marxists and Pragmatists on the logic immanent in action follows from this Aristotelian horizon. The logic in question draws its sole knowledge from the concrete and immediate testing that everyone knows before such and such a situation, and which it is appropriate to face no matter what preliminary knowledge one has. In regards to such a capacity to mobilize resources for the proof of a situation that is new each time, one could mention, in the field of political action, the incisive analyses of Machiavelli in *The Prince*, which offer us, in terms of strategies and tactics for the conservation of power, a remarkably precocious illustration of teaching drawn from practical and technical procedures appropriate for this practical knowledge. We can also think, in a more literary style, of the memoirs of Cardinal de Retz.

Without going into the details of the Marxist concept of *praxis*, which has a surprising complexity linked to its different interpretations throughout the long history of Marxism, one can say that *praxis* corresponds to human activity, the material and social transformations of nature and of society, by which the very processes of knowledge and of theorization come under a practical appropriation by the world and by the self. Thus, with Marx, the myth of a purely contemplative or representational knowledge definitively disappears, for the simple reason that all theory has as its very dynamic a basis in practice, even in the notion of a theoretical practice (Althusser 1963; Desanti 1975).

The pragmatist tradition is evidently the second philosophical origin of this promotion of practice as the privileged site of the grasping of subjective experience. Here again, the richness of its development since Peirce prohibits one from offering an exhaustive account of it. It will suffice to indicate the point of its crystallization in the domain of the empirical sciences and the personal battle it has waged against all speculative metaphysical temptation. In other words, a concept will be true or valid if it possesses a practical effect, if it can be verified in a determined activity. Without entering into the debates which have tended to oppose the pragmatists against one another, we will make wide usage of the term, following R. Rorty, which refers to the Peirce-James tradition, a usage which consists in "eliminating the contrast of the Greeks between contemplation and action, between the fact of representing the world and the fact of struggling with the problem it poses to us." (Rorty 1971/1979, 1982)

These different philosophical horizons all converge in their insistence on the necessity of drawing the validity of knowledge straight from its implementation in practice. It is from this orientation that we want to get our footing now in phenomenology. In fact, beyond the intellectualist tendency, present namely in Husserl, to insist on the logical or perceptual acts, there is a group of subsequent phenomenologists who emphasized themes of a more emotional color (the young Sartre), or oriented towards the sensible ("the flesh" in Merleau-Ponty), the affective (M. Henry), or the historical (Ricœur). In short, they are concerned with "de-theorizing" phenomenology as a rigorous science, without, nonetheless, reducing its initial rigor.

Yet this common will to make phenomenology a more incarnated approach does not contribute to strengthening its methodology, nor to situating the level of its implementation, namely by describing the practical realization of its cardinal method, reduction (Depraz 1999a). The more concrete descriptions that one finds in Sartre as well as in Merleau-Ponty are still deployed in an *immanent* manner, and thus do not account explicitly for the singular power of finesse and the subtlety of the writing itself. Otherwise, and still more problematically, the experience in question is apprehended on a strictly speculative level (Fink, or in other aspects, M. Henry), or purely and simply retracted in favor of hermeneutical exegesis (Ricoeur).

To be sure, if one examines more closely some of the phenomenological perspectives just mentioned, one discovers that these same authors have strived to give due attention to this practical aspect of phenomenology: think of the phenomenological work of B. Waldenfels in the wake of Merleau-Ponty (Waldenfels 1980), of the monumental work by M. Henry on the young Marx (Henry 1976), or again of the article by P. Ricoeur attempting a fruitful confrontation between the Marx of *German Ideology* and the late Husserl of the *Krisis*, and revealing, as it concerns the relationship between the Husserlian life-world and Marxist praxis, the following analogy: substruction of Husserlian ideality is to practical and sensible experience what Marxist ideology is to concrete, material reality (Ricoeur 1997).

Husserlian phenomenology itself, as it developed in the 1920s with the so called "genetic" phase, reveals unsuspected dimensions from the point of view of the conversion of phenomenology to practice: on the individual level, with the evidence of *habitus* (Husserl 1966) and of the recovery of corporeity (*Leib*) as originary practice (*Urpraxis*) (Husserl 1973a); on the intersubjective level with the insistence on the practical behavior anchored in the world of micro-sociality (Husserl 1973b: no.9, 10); or on the historical level with emphasis on generative sedimentation (Husserl 1993; Steinbock 1995).

However, once again, the question one is led to ask oneself is that of the actual practice of phenomenology. There is a difference between making a place for practice, *praxis* as a major theme in phenomenology (it is already commendable, no doubt, in relation to being entrenched in logic or theory) on the one hand, and *effectively practicing* the reduction, and discovering the experiential means to describe it on the other hand.

5.4. The "handle" of cognition: The psychological view of knowing-how and coping with

In that respect, we must not confuse practice with language (Livet 1997): to speak or to write about the phenomenological reduction is not to actually practice it, but to practice the fact of thinking about a concept. That is certainly also a practice, but one that is distinct from the fact of performing experientially a reduction. Thinking the fact that an addition is possible, speaking of this addition, are different practices from actually adding. Therefore, with each action, the question arises of knowing which is its practical dimension, with what the subject is in actual interaction, what forms it within the exchange.

What is even more important is the fact that this practical dimension develops in an essentially pre-reflective manner, in the sense that action is an autonomous knowledge that is for the most part transparent: there is no intrinsic necessity between to know how to do something, to know I know how to do it.

From the point of view of methodology, it is thus essential to consider human experience as it is *actually embodied*, which has nothing to do with the fact of thinking about experience or of knowing how to talk about experience. Concretely, this means that we approach reflecting upon experience and the description of this reflection starting with a singular lived moment, from the engagement in a task, in a finalized situation. But it also means being attentive to how the wording is carried out in direct relation to the singular lived moment in question. This could be done with the help of what can be technically called a guidance toward "a position of embodied speech" (Vermersch 1994).

The subject uses his own cognition in a competent manner, without being a *savant cogniticien*: he knows how to *handle* it, what to do with it, how to use it perfectly, therefore the image of "the handle of cognition", which stresses the user-aspect of cognition, the fact that I know how to cope with my cognition. No one has learned to give himself a mental image, to recall a past moment, to think, even if some occasions to practice these activities have been available, and some similar goals have been proposed and encouraged in the cultural and educational spheres. We deploy basic mental operations in action without explicitly learning how to do so, much less learning to set in motion a movement or to retain it. There is a basic level of competence in the use of our bodies or of our cognitive capacities, with regard to which we are experts in competent action. These are habits, the traces of human practice which constitute our immediate and everyday experience.

Now this efficiency is not based on a reflective, conceptualized or formalized knowledge. It is even a bit scandalous that we can do all this without the assistance of the cognitive sciences or of philosophy! What in fact do we know of this competence? We know a number of things that we can infer from the products of theoretical and cognitive activity, but this does not give us knowledge on action, or knowledge of action. We know a number of things about the procedures implemented, expressed in the language of the task, starting with the traces and observable aspects of the action. But this doesn't provide information on action as it is lived, initiated, guided by the subject and describable in the sphere of a first-person point of view.

Now, experimental psychologists, excluding attempts made at the beginning of the century, have abstained from investigating such matters. In addition to the methodological difficulties involved in accessing these data in a reliable manner, inferred data used to have an indisputable greater scientific tenor. But this means abandoning all information regarding the way the subject implements his cognition in action as he describes it from his own point of view.

Of course, this direction of work meets with difficulties which have not been analyzed yet in other works. The first is how to distinguish between that which is "conscientisé" (has become conscious) and that which is "conscientisable" (able to become conscious). In other words, it is necessary to take into account that it is not sufficient to ask questions in order to have answers, that it is not enough to simply ask for descriptions to obtain them in a complete, precise and detailed form. Access to the data in first-person conflicts with the demands of helping the being-able-to-become-conscious to become conscious of itself, and from there to express itself and even to put itself in words. The second difficulty is to make a relevant use of the descriptive categories, which give access to a descriptive language, starting from what the subject is describing in his own words. Now, it seems to us, in a large measure, that these categories will emerge from the very practices which utilize this first-person information. For, and we will return to this later, teachers, social workers, coaches and psychotherapists have all "naturally" researched this subjective information from a first-person point of view.

What is a user's competence? From the point of view of specialized knowledge, it is minimal. If I compare my competence in using my television's remote control to the competence required for the comprehension of the function of the infrared transmission of the remote control, there is a huge gap between the two spheres of competence. If I compare that which I know how to do in my head to produce for myself a mental image of an object to the mountain of knowledge on machinery and the laws of mental images, the difference is considerable.

Hence, our metaphor: the psycho-phenomenological level allows us to describe "the handle of cognition", whereby the subject can "hold" or "catch" his cognitive instruments in action. The neuro-dynamical level is "the blade" or the active part of the tool, but without the handle, there is no tool. In a different way, the handle proves as important as the tool: at the very least there is a close inter-dependence if there is to be an efficacy.

Whatever may be this divergence in terms of the user's knowledge in relation to expert knowledge:

1. the user's knowledge persists in its validity: it is with this competence that we think and act;
2. it persists in its intrinsic necessity: without this competence, how would I think with "my head"; no learned knowledge can substitute itself for the fact that it is I who act;
3. it persists in the pertinence and the necessity to study it and to take account of it.

The essence of the argument rests on the rehabilitation of user-competence apart from the emphasis placed on theoretical knowledge, or relative to the mechanisms of the cognitive neuro-dynamical type, however interesting these may be. This user-competence arises from the level of the *experience* of the subject; its approach is difficult because it is primarily a competence in *action*, it exists in a large part on the pre-reflective level, and it is necessary to take precautions, to use techniques in order for the subject, who nonetheless does not stop using it, to be able to speak of it. It does not mean that subjects have a sheer instrumental relation to their own experience and cognition (as in instrumental reason as *techné*), because mental experience is both the instrument (the means) and the result (the goal). So in the last instance, there is no point to make a distinction between the handle and the blade: to know how to handle one's cognition, to know how to work with it is a global holistic competence.

By working with the "handle of cognition", practitioners obtain effective results. They are creators and users of basic techniques to account for subjective experience. If this pertinence, this necessity of the competence of the subject as being a user of its cognition is valid, then one must find confirmation of it in the practices which seek to modify, or "remedy" this functioning.

This is an approach to the argument by validation of the pertinence of the "handle". Hence, if a child who makes spelling mistakes describes to me the way in which he represents a word to himself when he evokes it in the form of sounds, i.e. when he names it interiorly, it is a matter of a phenomenological datum which the child alone can directly access. What confirms this description are the types of errors he commits. This process of relating acoustic representation of the word to foreseeable linked consequences, (particularly in French), to homophonies, to double letters, to accented letters, to muted "e's" etc., leads to confusions of the type *"c'est"* ("it is")/*"sait"* ("knows") for example. One thus obtains a first level of validation of the phenomenological description through the verification with the foreseeable behavorial traces (errors of the homophonous type). But it is possible to remedy this spelling difficulty by proposing to the child that he uses a more functional evocative coding with regard to the task to be accomplished: in this case, he should try to represent to himself the linguistic signifier (certain children easily present images to themselves starting with words, but these are images created by the signified, which are of no help to anyone in the task of spelling a word correctly). It is possible to teach him to present to himself the image of the linguistic signifier as an effective strategy (Dilts 1990). A second phase of validation of the phenomenological description opens up with this remedial work, its effects, the success or failure of the proposed exercises. Since, if the difficulty was real, and thus the initial phenomenological description exact, then the verbalizations of the processes employed by the child will evolve with the remedial work, and the behavorial traces will evolve as well.

The remedial work will then deal with the apprenticeship of the fact of presenting to oneself a visual image. In doing this we remain on the level of psycho-phenomenological work and obtain an effective change if there are no other obstacles to the change. In the research on the memorization of scores by pianists, we find this same diagnostic level confirmed by the efficacy of the subsequent remedial work (Vermersch 1993; Vermersch & Arbeau 1996).

The methodological implications of these distinctions are important, since if one does not take them into account, one makes gross errors of evaluation. If I ask a subject a question in order to find out what he knows of his experience, following the formulation that I utilize or the sphere of communication that I deploy, the subject can confine himself to a "I don't know" or to some general comments which would seem to supply the proof that it is useless to question him and in general to make him verbalize it. Now, the sole thing that one proves this way is the incompetence of the person who asks the question regarding technique of conversation and comprehension of the conditions to be observed to help a subject to verbalize that which is not yet apprehended, but could be: the domain of the pre-reflective. This pushes us to clarify our vocabulary with regard to consciousness and to the personal and subpersonal domains.

5.5. Practitioners validate and enrich this level of analysis

Historically, it would be more true to reality to proceed in the opposite direction from the argument of validation. One can observe that practitioners are the only ones to have explored this phenomenology of cognition, because to act, to be effective, they have seen themselves as "constrained" by the very direction of their practice in taking account of it. Since the beginning of the century a change has occurred, the consequences and extent of which have not yet been determined. This change bears on the appearance of the professions of *relation*: psychoanalysts, psychotherapists, specialists in manager coaching, coaches, trainers. If in the past confessors, spiritual advisors, sages, elders, healers or sorcerers used to respond to the need for support, accompaniment, purification, help in changing, we have seen a growing new class of professionals arise in the 20th century whose practice is measured in terms of a demand that doesn't cease to grow.

The fundamental characteristic of these professionals is that they are practitioners: they use techniques, they diagnose problems and attempt to solve them on bases that are pragmatic, not theoretical or scientific, since the science on which they would need to ground their practices does not yet exist. It has scarcely been 20 years since these sub-disciplines have been in the process of birth and institutional recognition. A good number of these professions develop outside of the University curriculum; others receive theoretical education based on the basic disciplines, but form themselves practically with training techniques, in internships where the reference to University knowledge is secondary and perhaps even radically irrelevant (Argyris & Schön 1976; Schön 1983; Schön 1990). Finally, in professions highly structured by a long university education, practitioners are obliged to develop techniques which are related to these same studies.

This is a situation without precedent from a historical point of view. For 50 years thousands of professionals have been trying to invent new guides, new observables, new techniques of modification, new forms to help in change on the level of cognitive activities, beliefs, emotions. All work directly with human experience, with subjectivity, *developing that which one might call a psycho-phenomenological practice*. This represents an immense resource of non-thematized knowledge pertinent for the objective which concerns us in this text.

In several fields there has been a huge increase in creativity:

1. In the field of *education*, in particular in the area of remedial work to academic failure (De la Garanderie 1965, 1969, 1989, 1990).
2. In the field of *psychotherapy*, envisaged as a problem of communication and of help to change, as it was developped by Bateson, Pearls, Erikson, Satir, the Palo Alto school, Grinder et Bandler and the creation of PNL.

The common characteristic of these fields is that the knowledge developed is directly confronted with reality through the problems of application. This gigantic effort of creation and of invention still goes unnoticed because it is done by practitioners who write little or do not concern themselves with explicitly stating the theories behind their practices. Furthermore, all these practices are "enclosed" in less public situations (private offices, work-groups of obscure internships). We can only give here an idea of the reservoir of knowledge that these practices contain with regard to subjective experience.

In these contexts, the distinctions and methods utilized are all subordinate to a criterion of efficacy: what can produce a diagnostic differentiation to allow one to distinguish the choices of intervention in a pertinent manner is what we conserve as a distinction. A purely pragmatic criterion of efficacy is substituted for a criterion of verifiability or of evidence. It is one of the explanations evoked above from the fact that the first introspective data did not have practical effects, that the researchers who updated this data did not know what to do with them. Inversely, it is perhaps the fact that what underlies Buddhist phenomenology is a practice which seeks to bring internal changes that has helped it to form itself and to endure.

CHAPTER 6

The philosophical challenge

With this chapter, we confront the properly philosophical implications of this return to subjective experience, an experience obtained by means of an explicit self-awareness. Objects and the world are themselves properly given to me only to the extent that I become conscious of myself.

The philosophical movement which will be accorded a privileged place here will be phenomenology in its Husserlian and post-Husserlian versions. This movement stresses just such a return to the internal, direct and intuitive experience of the subject, to his own awareness and makes the latter a condition for access to external experience which is given with the freshness of its ontological naturalness. In addition, Phenomenology promotes a descriptive investigation of the different acts of consciousness by means of which I stand in relation to the world. In that respect, perception remains the paradigmatic instance of such acts, but is supported by memory, imagination and empathy, the so-called intuitive or cognitive acts, or else, will, desire, affection, intuitive acts of a more pragmatic kind, and finally, judgment, predication, categorization or more broadly, expression, which are all acts of signification.

This is the reason why each of us has drawn from Phenomenology the concepts providing the general orientation for the present work, which can be summed up as follows: the practical and procedural description of the phenomenon of awareness, grasped from the standpoint of its internal dynamics, as has been shown in the first Part.

The first section of this chapter is devoted to retracing the philosophical genealogy of the concept of experience up to the point at which it is effectively taken over by Phenomenology, and this within limits laid down before any theorizing. In the second section, the primary method of Phenomenology, the reduction, is taken up but in a new way, that is, with an orientation to its practical applications. In fact, the reductive operation will be presented as the theoretical analogue of that 'becoming aware' described in its procedural effectuation in the first Part, just as the reflective act is its psychological analogue, or mindfulness/awareness its meditative analogue. All three thereby constitute so many partial initiatives which, developed further, will make possible a complete description of the structural dynamic of this process of becoming aware.

The reduction harbours limits which are, above all, linked to its primarily theoretical dimension. What is at stake with the philosophical contribution to the challenge represented by the present work is therefore two-fold: 1) to provide a conceptual anchorage capable of furnishing a methodologically solid underpinning to the phenomena described; 2) to exceed that theoretical limitation inherent in phenomenology as it was historically constituted, by proposing a dynamic schema of conscious awareness which might be ontologically more adequate to the attention we pay to our daily affairs, to ourselves and therefore, in consequence, to the attention we pay to the world around us.

6.1. The place of experience in philosophy

> Everyone thinks they understand what is meant by the term "experience" (*Erfahrung*). It is a term fundamental to philosophy but it is, at the same time, a word drawn from familiar, everyday language and which fits into its vocabulary, a word which even those who know nothing about philosophy think they understand (Landgrebe 1982:58).

This is the way an article by Ludwig Landgrebe, devoted to the "Phenomenological concept of experience", begins. On the one hand, the author indicates that experience is the object of an immediate, spontaneous, in short natural, pre-comprehension, so that one could almost, or so it seems, save oneself the trouble of bothering with a theoretical explanation for it. On the other hand, this pre-comprehension is itself embroiled in the belief it leads to, which is nothing like genuine knowledge. "Everyone *thinks* they understand what is meant by the term *experience*", (our underlining) Landgrebe affirms from the very outset. And it is for this reason that the notion of experience calls for a specific investigation dedicated precisely to the elucidation of its meaning.

All of the above is well understood by Phenomenology, which has made of the return to experience its first principle, its regulative principle, even its criterion of truth. This aspiration is inspired by a recognition of the impoverishment of the meaning of experience in the course of the modern epoch. This is linked to the too-narrowly scientific inflection with which it has been endowed, *grosso modo* of a physicalist or causalist kind, and to a correlative forgetfulness of its vital and practical roots. In *Krisis,* Husserl therefore ties down experience to what he calls the "life-world". This return to experience, to which we will come back in some detail later since what is at stake is the so-called return 'to the things themselves', is nonetheless not a simple 'appeal to experience', which always looks more or less like a pious vow (Depraz 1995: 4–5).

This is where, even if only in a preliminary way, it is worthwhile raising a few questions: by making of experience the phenomenological criterion, one would be rapidly brought to confer upon it an *authority* such that one would be in a position to pass judgement upon what is or is not phenomenological. Here we run the risk of embracing a 'dogmatism' of experience, the risk of appealing to it as that very instance which would function as a final court of appeal in questions of truth and objectivity, whereas in fact, what is to be found is nothing more than a claim on behalf of the private experience of each individual. "Experience speaks for itself", "if it's your experience", "I've experienced it", pass for irrefutable testimony which one can only accept and respect. As ultimate arguments advanced by the phenomenologist, this type of testimony gives rise to doubts about the capacity of experience (to what experience?) to function as a primary criterion for the elaboration of a theory. This is why this term has to be clarified in and for itself, that is, made the object of a *critical* investigation.

The situation of Phenomenology with regard to the history of philosophy

Without taking account of all the different meanings which this notion has covered, the following initial idea can be registered: that with experience there is something like an encounter between a subject and a reality which transcends him and which, by its novelty, creates surprise. From this we may conclude that experience is, for the subject, both active, in so far as it represents a formative *trial*, in the sense of an attempt at knowledge of what is encountered, and passive in as much as it is a trial in the sense of an *ordeal*. In that respect, *experiri* in Latin means "trial" in the sense of "ordeal" just as much as "trial" in the sense of "attempt", and "test" is another word for expressing the meaning of the french "épreuve". Depending on the emphasis, the activity is either a quest for experiential data suitable for knowledge, or a receiving of the fruits of such an action, in a more passive way.

This last approach certainly characterises the meaning conferred upon experience by the English philosophers of the 18th and 19th centuries.

> Let us suppose the mind to be, as we say, white paper, void of all characters, without any ideas: – How comes it to be furnished? (...) Whence has it all the materials of reason and knowledge? To this I answer in one word, from EXPERIENCE (Hume 1748, Book II, Chap. 1, §2).

The mind is receptive; the data of experience are impressed upon it. This gives empiricist thinking an impressively fundamental orientation. For Locke, the subject, void of all apriori determination, receives, passively, the sensory data, which constitute the genetically unique source of all knowledge, since *sensation* and *reflection* are for this philosopher the two types of simple givens on the basis of which alone ideas can be formed. Hume will also assign a dual source to knowledge but, in this case, the difference between impression and idea (Hume 1739-40/1962: 62–66) is one of gradation rather than polarity. Besides, he starts from the principle of an original connection between ideas. Experience is always relational and, in the first instance, associative, and this is the case whether it is a matter of resemblance or continuity (Hume 1748: 58–59). *Knowledge of what is singular is then knowledge of an original link.* From this conception of experience, phenomenology will take up, on the one hand the Lockian notion of a genesis of internal experience, on the other, the human notion of *belief,* synonymous with belief in the existence of a *world (Weltglaube)* constitutive of the natural attitude and of its *habits/customs,* reformulated across universal laws of association and of the sedimentation of the habitus (Husserl 1962: 29, 286; Berger 1939; Landgrebe 1963; Murphy 1980).

However, in the Second *Logical Investigation,* Husserl will call into question Locke's artificially dualist disassociation of sensation and reflection and his obsession with ultimately simple givens, in short, his "naive naturalisation of consciousness" (Husserl 1956/1959: 100, and 1954: §22). He criticizes Hume for his generalised scepticism, what he calls his "fictionalism" (Husserl 1954; §23). Well before the twenties, and going back to the time of *Logical Investigations,* he questions the "abstractness" of empirical theories, and especially those of Hume, who claims to refuse any general representation, favouring the singular individual, while, in reality, he is reverting to a sort of atomisation of experience. It is on this basis that Husserl is able to question the psychologism of Mill, Spencer or Sigwart, then, and along similar lines, the sensualism of B. Erdmann and even the associationism of A. Meinong (Husserl 1970). In place of a reduction of experience to atomist impressions and to an association of particular unities, Husserl proposes modes of consciousness, *acts* in the sense of intentional lived experiences. It is the mode of consciousness, the so-called act, the *manner* in which the object is given to me rather than its content, which makes it possible to establish the difference between an abstract generality and an equally abstract atomic individual (Husserl 1970: 187; Depraz 1994).

With regard to this decisive anchorage of the phenomenological problematic in historical empiricism, the limits which Kant assigns to experience seem to impose a severe constraint upon the field of investigation. The possibility of experience is brought back to the realisation of those apriori forms of intuition which are space and time applied to matter, that is, to the diversity of sensation. This process whereby experience is rationalised in laws which are, in the final analysis, those of understanding, therefore leaves little room for the thematic analysis of a perceptual activity reflecting back onto itself as a function of its encounter with the contingent. Besides, in the Analogies of Experience of *The Critique of Pure Reason*, this properly perceptual level remains relatively undetermined with Kant, sometimes being assimilated to sensation, at other times reabsorbed into the concept in a Cartesian fashion.

Even the elaboration of a "reflective" judgement which is opposed to any determinative judgement upheld by understanding remains incomplete. The faculty of judging is defined as the power of finding, of bringing out, the universal *for, and on the basis of,* the particular, which constitutes the true meaning of the singular; this is not, therefore, a simple determination of the particular by the universal. However, the *reflective* character of judgement confers a motor role on experience. Experience is no longer a simple instrument destined to determine the concept; it produces on the basis of itself the reflection of a particular experience upon itself, that is to say, it gives rise to the very form of this experience. This simple "power of reflection in accordance with its own proper subjective laws" lets it be known that there where a reflective judgement is to be found, there is also a first sketch of the synthesis between the activity of the understanding as it appropriates, *goes out to look for the data*, and the passivity of the reflective judgement which *receives* the singular and gets in-formed about it upon contact with it.

However, with Kant primarily, but also with empiricism, the question arises of trying to grasp what it means *for a philosopher* to pay attention to experience. Over and beyond our taking the latter for the source of our knowledge, is it a matter of our reflecting upon it, of our taking it for a theme? Can one get back to experience without being immediately deflected from it with a view to developing one's own theory about it? How can one engage in a discourse which is not a discourse *about* experience but a discourse *of* experience?

Hegel, in promising us a *logic of experience* in his *Phenomenology of Spirit* and in his *Logic,* claimed to have abolished the theorising abstraction of all discourse about experience. Through his dialectic he sought to reinstate a concrete logic, to render philosophical discursivity immanent in the very course of experience. The immediate is therefore to be seen as always already taken up in a mediation which is originally exhibited in the sensible quality of experience. It goes without saying that the opportunity of refusing the dialectic credit with regard to experience has not been lost, given the speculative logic which it puts into operation elsewhere. One is also entitled to question the effective possibility of a "philosophy of experience" (in the sense of the subjective genitive: experience taken as the philosophical act par excellence and not of the objective genitive: experience taken as the theme of reflection for philosophy), or even to conclude that, for the philosopher, and with regard to his paying attention to experience, there can only be one *philosophical* experience, that is, one which is originally conceptual. If taking experience as one's guide is to make of it an object (among others) of investigation, what has one gained at bottom? How can one provide oneself with a genuine access to experience which does not make it disappear under its theorisation but which is, and remains, at the same time a philosophical access?

In this regard one might consider Phenomenology to be just a new form of conceptualisation of experience, one which operates by shedding light on the *act* and on the *mode* of consciousness, i.e., through the refusal to apprehend experience as the simple association of particular sensible concepts. I can only experience that which is given to me which I can access through an act of consciousness; experience is thus the meeting place for an act of consciousness directed towards an object and of an object as it presents itself to consciousness. Phenomenology thematises access to experience as an access to the act of consciousness and to the mode of being given of the object – act and mode having precisely the value of describing and of taking account of this access itself – but it does this by making use of concepts. Are these concepts also reflected? This question poses the problem of an access to experience through the concept. Even as phenomenology, is philosophy actually able to do anything else, and if so how? So the problem is not so much that of the use made of concepts as that of a *regulated usage*, that is to say, the reflected usage of a given conceptuality. In his own context of psychological and psychiatric investigation, Gendlin (1962) raised, with his notion of "felt-meaning", this same question of the possibility of a logic of experience which remains conceptual even while integrating the sensible, felt and anti-predicative course of experience.

Access to experience as a return to the "things themselves"

Gaining access to experience phenomenologically means getting back to it without any of the baggage of theorisation, which thrives on a multitude of unperceived presuppositions. In this context the return to experience means, precisely, a return to the things themselves. As Husserl put it in a well-known passage:

Meanings which are animated only by remote and imprecise, therefore in-
authentic, intuitions can not satisfy us. We want to get back to the "things
themselves" (Husserl 1970: II, 1, 209).

Or, as Landgrebe will put it in his own way:

(...) we need to acquire a concept of experience which comprehends in itself all the moments which confer a sense upon the term experience in everyday discourse and which have been set aside by philosophy. In consequence,
we have to develop a phenomenological concept of experience which allows
us to capture in abrieviated fashion the 'thing itself' envisaged by the word
(Landgrebe 1982: 59).

In this regard those contemporaries of Husserl who were W. James in the
United States (especially with his *Principles of Psychology*), and H. Bergson in
France, for example with his celebrated *Essai sur les données immédiates de la
conscience* but also with *Matière et Mémoire* converge at a deep level upon this
requirement. Husserl (1970: II, 1, 209) knew about the work of James (Landgrebe 1982: 66; Cobb-Stevens 1974); and the agreement with the Bergsonian
problematic is striking (Patocka 1992, Chap. VII).

But we should try to get a little clearer about the meaning of this expression
under the German syntagm "Zurück zu den Sachen selbst". The most prevalent
misunderstanding is that which consists in identifying these things to which
one returns, these *Sachen*, with *physical* or ontic *res*, with transcendent realities.
That is, realities external to consciousness, which in German would be called
"*Ding*" – what Husserl himself then calls the field of *Reales*. Interpreting this
return to the things themselves as a return to *Dinge*, comes down to clearing the
table of all those criticisms, in philosophy of science and technology, directed
towards an objectivist and realist interpretation of scientific activity (Latour
1987; Stengers 1994), already anticipated in Bachelard's critique of "chosisme":

In the unknown world of the atom, could there possibly be a sort of fusion
between being and act, between wave and corpuscle? Should we talk about
complementary aspects or complementary realities? Might it not have to do
with a deeper cooperation between object and movement, of a complex en-
ergy where what is and what becomes converge? Finally, since these ambiguous
phenomena never designate our things, it is a major philosophical problem to
determine whether they designate things at all. Hence a complete overthrow-
ing of all realist principles with regard to the syntax of the infinitely small
[...] So it can no longer be the thing which directly instructs us, as empirical
orthodoxy once proclaimed (Bachelard 1931/1970).

By contrast with the *Ding*, the *Sache* is to be understood as the object or the business of thinking, the problem or the theme of reflection. So the Husserlian critique of empiricism becomes a refusal of all positivity which is not conjointly reappropriated from the standpoint of an act of consciousness. Returning to things themselves is a matter of paying attention to the object inasmuch as it is a subjective meaning, or an entity originally envisaged through an act of consciousness. It is also, and correlatively, a matter of refusing to leave the last word to doctrinal discussions of a historical or hermeneutic kind with a view to emphasising the "things themselves" as problems for thought (Husserl 1970 I: XIII; 1960: 254).

The specific quality of phenomenological experience in relation to naively scientific experience corresponds to this determination on the part of the acting subject to take charge of his relation to things. As a result of his action, things acquire the status of units of sense for him. To be sure, Husserl also recognises the value of empiricism, even of positivism, in its respect for things themselves (Husserl 1982: 35), but he sees them as erring by their restriction of experience to *sensory* experience. Gaining access to the object by the only legitimate approach, that of the lived acts of consciousness which thematize it, implies therefore a conversion of the meaning of experience into an experience lived out (*Erlebnis*) in the first-person and no longer into an experiment (*Experiment*) in the third person. In contrast to the latter, which places the accent upon the objective, external construction of the real, the former underlines the rootedness of the object in the intimate and intuitive lived experience of consciousness.

Nevertheless, this phenomenological concept of experience has to be completed. By holding on to the internal (private) lived experience alone, one runs the risk of falling back into the trap of subjectivism. With a view to ensuring the objectivity of experience, that is, its universality and necessity, consciousness needs, in addition to its immanental lived character, to be endowed with an intentional character that links it to the external world. Consciousness is consciousness of something, is essentially what Husserl says in §14 of *Cartesian Meditations,* thereby indicating that it is intentionality, this correlation of conscious lived experience with the object envisaged, which makes up the fundamental character of phenomenological consciousness.

Husserl analyses this correlation on the basis of two central concepts. The noema is the meaning *(Sinn)* belonging to the object while the noesis corresponds to the constitutive pole, a subjective, lived experience. So, the concern with the noetico-noematic structure of consciousness makes of the object a subjective meaning for consciousness and relates the immanent and intimate lived experience of consciousness to the external world. Intentionality is this correlation of lived conscious experience and the object envisaged which dismantles the traps of subjectivism as well as those of objectivism. Experience, in the phenomenological sense, thus invokes both the *Erlebnis* (immanent lived experience) and the *Erfahrung* (experiential apprehension of the object). It is, in a strict sense, the connection of intentional lived experiences which co-ordinates consciousness and the world (Husserl 1974:62).

In this sense the object is given "in flesh and blood" *(leibhaft)*, which means that it is given in itself *(selbstgegeben)* at the very moment when it is given to consciousness. Apprehended by consciousness, it is embodied in it and by it. This means that when I perceive the plum tree in the garden, it is indeed *it itself* that I see, its ripe fruit that I am aware of and, at the same time, *I myself* am enjoying its visual and olfactory sensations. If the embodied givenness of the object is a givenness through and for subjective consciousness, one is far removed from that risk of realism which might *a priori* be implied by the notion of *Leibhaftigkeit,* nor does one fall into the trap of an idealism for which subjectivity is often held responsible.

Phenomenological experience is neither empirical nor constructed: It is eidetic

What is first required of an experience whose description is phenomenological is something which is both simple and restrictive: in conformity with the need to concretely re-activate any such singular experience and not to be satisfied with merely talking about it, no statement must ever be pronounced whose content is not sustained by an effective *practice.* In other words, we are committed to a vow of poverty as far as argumentative and interpretative panache are concerned. But this requirement would be insufficient if it were not followed up with a second: to constantly control the process of conceptualization, i.e., the elaboration of categories designed to take account of the experience of the reflecting subject by referring to this experience. So, if not abandoned altogether, hermeneutical exegetics must at least receive highly regulated treatment.

Let us be more exact. With a view to complying with this refusal of any conceptual packaging, two critical strategies are required:

1. Control of the use of the referential contents which preside over the description by reflecting upon their status. The description of the lived experience of an act integrates material which comes to it from a diversity of

horizons and which functions in the descriptive elaboration. Its use should be filtered with a view to making it work better rather than letting them operate it in raw form.

2. careful work at the articulation of the relation between description and construction. It would, in fact, be an illusion to suppose that a description without any constructive dimension were possible. Rather than allowing speculation to creep back in surreptitiously, it would be better to channel it by enabling the description to produce rules on its own. This is what is at stake in an *eidetic* description.

The first point concerns the status of examples or of those more general aids which are brought to bear whenever one attempts to describe the lived experience of an act. The latter can be textual reference (doctrinal, literary, scientific), intersubjective references (to a common good and so on) or private references (anecdotal, ideological). Textual references apparently enjoy historical and philosophical guarantees; intersubjective references rely on the existence of a consensus and enjoy the self-evidence of a prejudice; private references are forbidden but used implicitly as a borderline argument whenever the textual argument is wanting (Vermersch 1997).

A text is always that into which its author deposits his experience, an experience which has been formalised with the conceptual tools at his disposal. It is useful to bring to light the fruit of this experience above and beyond the normalization to which it has been subjected. Studying a text in and for itself (its arguments, its way of rendering explicit the development of its style etc.) is interesting in itself and may even contribute to an elucidation of the experiential foundation in question, but must not be allowed to obscure the descriptive analysis of the experience. Dominant philosophical concerns, largely hermeneutical, tend to push the experiential analysis into the background, even to make it disappear altogether in favour of the analysis of the text which is simply its support. The doctrinal corpus then appears as the sole reference, the only criterion of truth, and philosophico-hermeneutical logic, the paradigm for phenomenological discursivity.

When the phenomenological philosopher wants to free himself from textual constraint or finds that such a constraint makes it impossible for him to nourish an affirmation which he believes important, he throws caution to the winds and plunges right into the treasure of his intimate experience, seeking to draw from it the ultimate argument which will convince, or at least arouse in other philosophers a sceptical respect mixed with grudging admiration for the audacity of the adventurer. From reference to reference one moves from one

extreme to the other, from textual incarceration to an experiential licentious-
ness which knows no bounds. And this is what provokes the return in force
of those prejudices artificially channelled by textual practice, personal or ideological (political, religious, familial) prejudices, in any case prejudices which
have nothing to do with philosophy. Sometimes these prejudices are not seen
as such simply because they are shared by the entire philosophical community,
and so we may speak of an epochal prejudice or of a conception of the world.
Heidegger has shown that these are quite unphilosophical – even though they
always have supporters. This intersubjective reference is the most insidious, the
least discernible because, to one degree or another, we are all taken in by such
prejudices (Heidegger 1949). From 1911, Husserl, in his critique of Dilthey,
took issue with any relativising apprehension of philosophy as a conception of
the world (*Weltanschauung*), a term which one also finds, as a synonym for
Weltbild, in Heidegger's lecture of 1938.

So we want to make a strong claim about what is meant by the word "experience". Unlike most phenomenologists who rely on experience as being a
"given", something standard that is taken for granted and accessible to everybody quite spontaneously, we insist that a truly phenomenological experience
has to be trained and cultivated. In his *Tonpsychologie* for example, C. Stumpf
very early stressed the necessity of a *training* in order to get genuine access
to one's own experience. In that respect, examples must be well-chosen and
reflected upon.

In his method of exemplification, Husserl does not succeed in avoiding
this very kind of crude usage of references. Even if he is suspicious of the doctrinal approach of certain authors and has little to do with hermeneutics, even
though, as do certain of his predecessors, he looks for problems and questions
rather than textual coherence or historical exactness, his choice of examples is
hardly ever subject to critical examination. He remains dependent on his personal tastes and those of his age without ever reflecting upon – this is the least
one might have expected – what is, in the final analysis, an irreducible depen-
dence. Among those which are left unreflected on ("let us take the example of
a thing!") we find examples which are so general that they evoke nothing at all
(the table, the tree etc.) (Husserl 1982: 73–74) and those which are derived from
a received education (the portrait in the gallery at Dresden, Dürer's engraving:
"the knight, death and the devil", the red and/or green ball, spherical and/or
dented, the Gretel of the marvellous story which bears her name, Goethe's
Faust and Raphael's Madonna etc.) (Husserl 1982: 211, 212; 1939: §21a, §40,
§65); the example does no more than illustrate a proposal which stood in no
need of it rather than being inherently linked to it.

One of two things follows: either the phenomenological description is so conceptual that it leads back to a philosophy of experience which talks about it without ever re-activating it, and this with the help of examples which are nothing more than purely illustrative pretexts; or it is so concrete that it can do without examples or at least only use them as exemplary cases. In the latter case, the example would no longer be one example among others, but would be *exemplary* in itself, that is, would guide the entire analysis.

In consequence, a phenomenological experience is committed to what Husserl calls a "pure description", neither a factual, nor an *apriori* but an eidetic description, which, as he notices remarkably like Stumpf before him, requires a *training*:

> The evidence can only be verified by someone who has acquired, through an appropriate training, the capacity to effect a pure description in accordance with the anti-natural habit of reflection (Husserl 1970: II, 1; 1982: §71).

So it is worth distinguishing between a non-phenomenological construction and a construction dictated by descriptive regulation itself (Fink 2000: §8). It is not possible to do justice to every object with a description regulated by intuition since certain objects presuppose an intuition followed up and prolonged by symbolic modalities. It is not a matter of refusing the symbolic or signifying register but of regulating it, that is, analysing its departure from the norm represented by a relation based upon intuitive givenness. In so doing one short-circuits the naive duality between description and construction and so brings to light the different gradations separating pure description (a myth) and speculative construction (just as unreal) by setting out the inductive mediations. In that respect, Merleau-Ponty (1977) will take over for himself Husserl's eidetic procedure by according to it its full concrete significance and in showing how it rejoins a well understood inductive procedure.

But Merleau-Ponty's later critique of Husserlian essentialism (1964: 145–152), which is *a fortiori* also a critique of the "logico-eidetic" (Richir 1988: 169–216), carried out in the name of a carnal concreteness or of an archaic and brute dimension of experience, is even more mistaken. To accuse phenomenology of being a new platonism or a refined form of logicism, comes down, in both cases, to misunderstanding one essential fact. Eidetic singularity unites universality and concreteness. In other words, the individual and the essential (in the vocabulary of the Sixth Logical Investigation in 1901) or else fact and essence – that which follows 1913 (Husserl 1970, 1982) – are not opposed to each other but entertain a double and correlative relation. The first is the sensible foundation of the other in the order of appearance, the second is the apriori condition of the first in the order of constitution.

To refuse the eidetic in the name of that overseeing of experience which it supposedly brings with it or of the formal disembodiment which it implies, is to be mistaken about the constitutive role of the categorial essence in the description of experience. As if one could get rid of it. It is no good trying vainly to develop a "cohesion without concepts" or even an "eidetics without concepts". Rather one has *to regulate the use* of concepts and *eide*. Moreover, the youthful author of *The Phenomenology of Perception* was not wrong when he indicated:

> [...] when we try to comprehend in direct reflection and without the help of the varied associations of inductive thought, what a perceived movement or a circle are, we can elucidate this singular fact only by varying it somewhat through the agency of the imagination, and then fastening our thought upon the invariable element of this mental experience. We can get through to the individual only by this hybrid procedure of finding an example, that is, by stripping it of its facticity. Thus it is questionable whether thought can ever quite cease to be inductive, and whether it can assimilate any experience to the point of taking up and appropriating its whole texture (Merleau-Ponty 1945/1962:63).

Here we see Merleau-Ponty recognizing the relevance of the eidetic but rejecting the exemplary as a negation of contingent singularity. The example is simultaneously singular (unique, non repeatable) and universal (exemplary, paradigmatic). Its double status is homogeneous with that of the *eidos*. Functioning as a guide and not just illustrating in a derivative way, it gives rise to a universality which retains its singular contingence. The latter nourishes the former, guarantees its concreteness, the former confers the necessary objectivity, the criterion of scientificity.

But, with Husserl, does the example fulfill this function of real ideality in an unequivocal way, or does it not rather remain an "ideal reality", or even worse, a totally contingent reality, extrinsic to any theoretical affirmation? The status of the *eidos* rests upon that of the example. What is at stake is of importance. But it is impossible to offer an unequivocal reply to this question. Certain examples look like simple illustrative pretexts. Others serve as genuine descriptive themes, melting pots of categorial elaboration (Husserl 1973a:n.18a, b; 1966:§33; 1939:§21, §40; Depraz 1996a), even if they can never constitute absolute points of departure, as Muralt (1958) contends. From the start they are inscribed within a pre-existing categorialization. This categorialization is, in turn, subject to modifications imposed by the exemplary. It is itself affected by the regulatory function of the examples.

So one might say that it is in this double movement of a categorial inscription which is indifferent to the contingent fact and of an exemplary affection which is constitutive of it that the true meaning of an eidetic phenomenology is worked out. Certain residual traces of this meaning are to be found in Husserlian manuscripts from the thirties, notably, under the heading of an eidetics of facticity. There, the *eidos* is not purely and simply indifferent to the fact but receives its limiting variability and its concrete flavour from it (Husserl 1973c: n.22; Lobo 2000). It is just such an eidetics reviewed by the constitutive power of the exemplary fact, that is to say, freed from any idealising slag, that it has been our task to present in the first Part of this work by instituting a permanent to and fro between exemplary cases and structural stages of the process of becoming aware.

The transcendental character of experience: Phenomenology as "transcendental empiricism"

At this stage we have come to this point: eidetic construction derives its phenomenological legitimacy from the fact that it draws the rules of its lawfulness from the factical domain and gets modified thereby in line with any variation in the facts. But an essential dimension of experience has not yet been taken into account, one which can be designated by the expression "transcendental experience".

A certain number of precautions need to be taken in a preliminary way to dispel persisting misunderstandings. Well before the contemporary epoch, a "theological" use had been made of the term "transcendental", a use inspired by a kind of neo-platonism and, more generally, by the so-called medieval "transcendentals": the One, the True, the Good. In this context "transcendental" possesses a meaning quite close to "transcendent". Any reality rising above human finitude inscribed in time and space is transcendent/al. But already with Kant the transcendental dimension is no longer understood as that which is over and beyond, separated from us and inaccessible to our perceptual consciousness. It refers to the egoic form of apperception and, more precisely, to the conditions of the possibility of any experience, that is, to the *apriori* forms of knowledge, both categorial and intuitive. The transcendental is what structures spatio-temporal experience in terms of categories and intuitions without ever being given as a spatio-temporal phenomenon.

Of course, pleading for the "transcendentality of experience" is a gesture which is first inspired by critical philosophy. However, it turns out to be anti-Kantian. In fact, for the author of *The Critique of Pure Reason* a "transcendental experience" is a contradiction in terms. Experience is strictly "phenomenal" limited to its situation in space and time. Husserlian phenomenology only retakes the Kantian transcendental prerequisite after having thought through the exact modalities of its phenomenalization. There is not, on the one hand, a non-phenomenal transcendentality and, on the other, a non-transcendental empiricity. It is not a matter of proceeding towards a "transcendentalization" of the empirical on the basis of a transcendental domain shut up in itself nor, at the other extreme, of declaring the fact to be irreducibly mundane. This would be to maintain an *artificial duality* between the transcendental and the empirical. At bottom, the problem is that of the (1) purity of the transcendental or (2) of its necessary involvement with the facts.

One can thus distinguish two versions of transcendental phenomenology which correspond to two successive phases of Husserl's development:

1. The first goes back to the idealist conversion of phenomenology around 1913 and *Ideen I*. The phenomenologist adopts an attitude called transcendental as soon as he operates a radical reduction which leads him to call in question the existence of the world itself. He turns away from the latter, cuts himself off from the natural attitude in which we are for the most part absorbed and so comes to posit himself, *qua* ego, as the sole source of meaning-giving. Phenomenology is then synonymous with "transcendental idealism"; since egoic consciousness alone is apodictic and, as such, founds the possibility of a world which remains always merely presumptive.

2. The second phase of transcendental phenomenology, which coincides with what has been called "genetic phenomenology" in the twenties (Husserl 1966, 1954), can be regarded as a "return to the world". The natural/mundane and the transcendental attitudes are not opposed to each other as the impure to the pure, and the phenomenologist is more concerned with understanding the genesis of the second out of the first. I only detach myself from the world to be better able to grasp its meaning for me, that is to say, to be better able to settle myself in it. With regard to this phenomenology of a secondary and reflective restoration of the sensible world one can then talk about a "transcendental empiricism" (Szilasi 1959; and Depraz 2000, 2001b) to the extent that, while retaining distinct functions (since one is meaning-giving while the other forms the motivating impulse

for meaning), subjectivity and world, are closely correlated with each other. The transcendentality of subjective experience proceeds precisely from this non-reversible co-ordination of consciousness and the world.

While the intentional and eidetic character of phenomenological experience meets the requirements of an introspective psychology concerned with a descriptive and regulated categorisation, the transcendental dimension brings into play evidence which goes beyond the frame of a scientific psycho-phenomenology and so raises the question of the *ontological* bearing of subjective experience, that is, of the mode of insertion of the subject in the world. Although the ontological underpinnings of the dynamic of becoming aware are not at the centre of this work it will nevertheless be necessary to re-insert the methodology proposed in the first Part into the context of the transcendental ontology which forms its more expansive horizon. So the section which follows, devoted to the "ways of the reduction", will review the philosophical version of the method of becoming aware, namely, the reduction, and fit it into the more encompassing ontological order of transcendental experience.

6.2. The ways of the reduction

The ethos *of the reduction*

The issue we will handle here forms an orthogonal complement to the previous issue. The problem to be dealt with is no longer the context and the place of experience in the history of philosophy; nor the way in which it has been developed within the phenomenological tradition. Now, we are going to tackle the central theme of this book: the *practical procedure* that needs to be put in place at the heart of the eidetic and transcendental phenomenological analyses. As we have already indicated, this problem is entirely rooted in the group of cognitive and pragmatic techniques introduced by Husserl under the heading of the reduction. This question has undergone considerable development and further differentiation by Husserl himself, in the course of the last years of his life, and by numerous philosophers who followed him. But we must not lose sight of the fact that, basically, what matters to us is the practical structure of the reduction. Thus, a detailed presentation of the ways of the reduction is necessary at this stage.

As an operation by means of which my view of the world is transformed until what I envisage is not another world but the world in *another* way, the reduction is a conversion of my attitude with regard to the world. Beginning as naive or natural, my attitude becomes philosophical or phenomenological, adjectives which designate, in a specific way, this change in my way of viewing the world. It is no longer an object which can be taken for granted and in which I am immersed, absorbed in its habitual routines, but is literally an ob-ject, i.e., a reality standing in op-position to me, which is a problem for me because what is enigmatic about it resists my grasp. The reduction is the movement of discovery involving a process of questioning which bears upon what surrounds me (Bernet 1994: 15–36).

In so far as it involves a change of attitude, the reduction also presupposes a habitual *ethos*, in the sense of a comportment, a behaviour, in short, a *praxis* and its transformation into an anti-natural *ethos*. We will try to come to terms with this kind of anti-natural ethic by trying to grasp the problematic character of its non-motivation in relation to the everyday world, that is to say, its status as purely self-motivated. How then does one prepare for the reduction? What does carrying out the reduction mean if it has been preceded by no previous exercise of it, no prior disposition towards it? Are the "ways of the reduction" just so many prior dispositions towards the exercise of it, and what are the practical repercussions of such dispositions for the philosophising subject? What are the implications for his existential situation? Can one point out one, or even several, corporeal, physical or even spiritual techniques which might be mobilized in the very carrying out of the reduction, techniques which Husserl, though we can find some elements of such a concern (1959), might not have taken account of, given his lack of interest in communicating the unique knowledge of the reductive practice?

This phenomenological method is a discovery whose paternity is incontestably attributable to Husserl. He never stopped trying to refine it, to deepen it, by correcting and varying it, from the moment of its appearance in the years 1904–1907 to the end of a long period of intellectual maturation (Lavigne 1989). The reduction is born of an awareness of the dogmatism concealed in presupposed positions which go unquestioned. It is presented as the putting out of play *(Außer-Spiel-setzen)*, out of circuit *(Ausschaltung)*, or between brackets *(Einklammerung)* of the thetic character which fixes thought (Husserl 1970: II, 1, §7; 1982: §30–32).

The uniqueness of the operation which converts my relation to the world is ceaselessly affirmed and, at the same time, the passages in which it is presented appear astonishingly theoretical and general. If they are convincing as regards the *why* of its execution, they really do not allow us to understand *how* I am able to acquire this new state of mind opened up by the conversion of attitude. This deficiency seems all the more curious since phenomenology is defined by its insistence upon the *quomodo* of the givenness of phenomena, on their mode of givenness and not on their *quid,* on content. One might therefore have expected that a method that gives primacy to the "how" arising out of an unquestioned given would find this orientation reflected in its *mode* of operation.

Although Husserl did little to thematize just such a reflexive distance, he does develop different means to prepare the way for the reduction and talk about its structural characteristics, each of which, in its own way, does try to furnish us with an understanding of its functioning and possible methodological appropriation.

Ways in which the reduction is prepared

The first type of reflective return to the reduction which one encounters in Husserl's writings, and which can be employed by the phenomenologizing subject with a view to putting such a reduction into operation, is of a comparative order. One prepares oneself for the reduction by understanding how it approximates to (but also differs from) other forms of withdrawal thematised by other philosophers or in other disciplines than philosophy. By coming to terms with these varied structures of self-transformation one learns what they have in common with the reduction – and which makes it possible for them to provide a point of departure, according to Husserl. But one also learns in what they remain unsatisfactory, thereby making it necessary to adopt the properly phenomenological operation.

Reduction and Cartesian doubt

If Husserl elaborated his reduction in the wake of the Cartesian procedure of doubt, it was not out of any purely historical and doctrinal affiliation but because the experience transcribed in the first *Metaphysical Meditation* seemed to him a particularly powerful illustration of the attitude required to effect the reduction.

A reading of the experience of doubt that Descartes relates in the first Meditation reveals an existential modification of the doubting subject whose principal features are taken up by Husserl:

a.   its expression in the first person,
b.   its being accompanied by a situation of radical solitude,
c.   the taking into account of how prior existence was regulated by opinion and belief, in other words, by prejudices,

d. the break with the senses, that is, with the body.

These existential indications furnish the principal elements of the reduction (Husserl 1960):

a. the positing of an ego,
b. the exclusion of all alterity, therefore a solipsist position,
c. a structure of self-consciousness,
d. freedom from embodiment.

But, even if these dimensions preside over the experience of the reduction as pre-requisites, these dimensions are already committed, they bear witness to the fact that it is already operating in me, that is to say, they presuppose that the reductive work has already started. So there are no prior conditions which have to be met before beginning a reduction but rather factors which implicitly predispose the one who is going to put it into practice even *before* any explicit intention to do so.

   In Descartes' meditation, whose form Husserl borrows, certain arguments get added to the *tabula rasa* which methodical doubt makes possible. For example, the absolute determination to deceive myself, dreaming as a factor of illusion and hallucination, the figure of the "malin génie". The Cartesian experience of doubt is crystallised in fictions which are constructions or dramatisations of experience itself. Even if Husserl does not adopt hyperbolic doubt for his own purposes, the bracketing of the world which is the reduction leads to a staging of the ego as responsible for the constitution of the world.

   Through the reduction the ego makes its appearance (*tritt ... auf*) and produces itself as a transcendental ego observing the world as well as the natural ego which he is no longer limited to being (Husserl 1960: §15). The theatrical metaphor can shed light on the transformation of the self required by and accompanying the reduction. This means that the reduction implies a mode of life regulated by fiction and the imaginary dimension. It allows one to understand that the body is not so much negated as subjected to a metamorphosis and proportional to the transformation of the mind. While Cartesian doubt tends to reject any reference to the senses the reduction does no more than neutralise them – suspend them – in their capacity as bearer of illusions and of naiveté, and so give it back its transcendental intensity. To be sure, Husserl distances himself from Cartesian doubt, but it would be better to put off until later the examination of a certain number of massive objections to the Cartesian style of the reduction: its subjectivism, its solipsism, its disembodied tendencies.

Transcendental and psychological reduction: The structure of reflection
A second figure which prepares the way for the reduction – and not the least –
is to be found constantly running parallel to transcendental phenomenology.
Phenomenological psychology offers analyses analogous to those of transcendental phenomenology, so much so that the structure of reflection implied
by the psychological reduction is often taken by Husserl to provide the best
propadeutic to the transcendental reduction (Husserl 1962).

In fact, living an experience means putting it to an immanent trial or
test. This "living" (*Erleben*) necessarily remains unreflected or, at best, pre-
reflective. But when one reflectively recuperates such a trial, this reflection almost always takes place in the aftermath *(nachträglich)* of recollection (Brand
1955). The structure of reflection which is at the centre of the reduction in its
psychological form implies in consequence a *duplication* between the reflected
ego and the reflecting ego: this doubling might be seen as analogous to the
split opened up by the transcendental reduction between the natural ego and
the transcendental ego. Moreover, in this regard Husserl describes the experience of recollection and that of the imagination in an equivalent fashion as so
many experiences of the duplication of the ego into a present and a past ego,
or an effective and an imaginary ego. In this sense, reflective duplication plays
a paradigmatic role not only for obtaining access to the structure of the reduction but for the more general comprehension of acts of consciousness (Husserl
1956/1959, Lectures 40–41).

Nevertheless, if psychology furnishes a decisive impulse for the reduction
through its reflective thematic, it also conceals major difficulties and limitations. We will now review a certain number of objections that phenomenologists themselves have brought against reflection.

1. Husserl is the first to proceed towards a strong critique of reflective *duplication* just as soon as it creates *a spatializing split* between two egological entities at the heart of consciousness, that would make it impossible to think their
unitary reflective dynamic.

> How is it that we are able to employ the image of a split (*Spaltung*) which
> refers back to the disassociation of a unitary element (...) in the same way that
> the trunk of a tree, for example, in being split (*Gespaltensein*) does not yet
> necessarily mean that it is cut up into scattered pieces completely separated
> from each other? (Husserl 1956/1959:90)

In the same vein as Comte and more recently Searle about introspection (see
Chapter 4.2), Husserl notes the risk – Cartesian in origin – of the dualist sep-

aration proper to the reflective structure, and therefore insists in these pages upon the process of the becoming-conscious of an ego whose unity is thereby preserved.

2. Fink, in Husserl's wake, warns us of another risk inherent in reflection, that of infinite regression. This infinite regression must be brought to an end. Transcendental phenomenology limits this indefinite reflexivity through the hypothesis of a disinterested spectator. As a spectator, the transcendental ego is no longer caught up in the world. Its reflection is ultimate because it does nothing other than observe. There is therefore no need for the hypothesis of yet another agent which would in its turn come to reflect upon the work of observation performed by the spectator (Fink 2000: §3; Waldenfels 1997: 63–75).

3. As for Merleau-Ponty's critique of reflective analysis (1945/62) or philosophy (1969), it characterises the *"overview"* implied by the thinking of Husserl and Fink themselves as an *idealising attitude* which runs contrary to our embodied being-in-the-world. With Merleau-Ponty the unreflected has to be retrieved through a "radical reflection" or a reflection ("surreflexion") which follows up the very movement by which consciousness is engendered (1969: 61).

These three first critiques of the reflective schema point out its basic limits even while arguing for a dynamic, unitary, limited and incarnate reflexivity. On the other hand, the critiques which follow are much more radical in the way they contest the relevance of any reflexive dynamic of consciousness, the first because of its monism, the others, inversely, due to their attachment to alterity and difference.

4. Thus it is in the name of the auto-comprehension of factical existence by itself that Heidegger very early on will call in question (Heidegger 1927/1975: §9 a), b), §14 a), b), c); Dastur 1992: 44–49) the legitimacy of the reflective intentionality imputed to psychology. For reasons close to those of Merleau-Ponty, reflection will be rejected on account of the *residual duality of subject and object* which it retains, and its favouring of an ontological monism of existence.

5–6. By contrast, Levinas' critique starts from a completely different hypothesis: reflection as a return to self is a *movement of identity* which absorbs the alterity of the other and presents an obstacle for the movement without return which is implied by total abandonment to the other (Levinas 1988: 188–189);

this critique will be carried further by Derrida when he foregrounds the movement of difference as an unrecoverable displacement making the identity of consciousness with itself impossible to recover (Derrida 1967).

However, although all these critiques adopt Husserl as their target, not one of them takes into account the dynamic of that decentering of the self, of that alteration which brings to light the becoming aware at work in reflection, where the act of the reflecting ego is distinguished from that of the reflected ego (Husserl 1956/1959: 89), and that in so doing frees itself from the interconnected but unilateral critiques stemming from monism or difference (Depraz 1995: §23).

This is why, in the first Part of the present book, we decided to put into effect a "reflecting act", *alias* reduction as *praxis*, which simultaneously upholds just such a dynamic becoming-aware and, under the heading of accommodating or letting-go, does justice to the passive dimension essential to that becoming aware. Quite correctly, Levinas and Derrida speak of it in terms such as "abandonment" or the "unreclaimable", while on the contrary, Husserl certainly underestimated this dimension in his analysis of the reflective movement. By emphasising the reductive *praxis*, the procedural character of the reduction, we will be able to invoke both the particular dynamic of reflexivity and the dimension of letting-go which the process of becoming aware implicitly harbours.

The practice of the reduction and the platonic myth of the Cave

Finally, a third figure preparing the way for the reduction is available in the dramatised version proposed by Eugen Fink. Contrary to Husserl, whose entire attention was focused upon the scientific description and intellectual analysis of a relation to the world modified by a consciousness which itself undergoes modification, Fink studied the Husserl of the texts that were unedited, expressed therefore in a manner which is not readily communicable, since many of these texts are research manuscripts written for Husserl himself, with no view to publication. However, understanding the thinking of another is also making it intelligible to oneself. Fink had to deal with texts, even if he enjoyed the privilege of being able to discuss matters with Husserl on a daily basis over many years.

For Husserl's assistant, the reduction represents a "catastrophe" for the existing being that we are ourselves. It takes on the guise of a violent eruption which obliges the one who undergoes it to take leave of himself. At the same time, it means a liberation from the circle of worldly motivation within which I am imprisoned. The reduction is a liberation vis-a-vis what Fink calls *Weltbe-*

fangenheit, imprisonment in, or captivation by the world (Fink 1974:81, 122, 124).

Moreover, the latter tries to account for the affective tonality of the reduction which, for him, is its most essential dimension, by relating it to a founding philosophical myth, that of the Platonic cave. Just as in the case of the first comparative figure, the experience of Cartesian doubt, we here have to do with a fictive experience staged, or at any rate reconstituted, by Plato.

But the accent placed here on the existential and practical aspect of the reduction remains ambiguous. It is both an absolute constraint and a supreme liberty. I am at the same time both eminently passive with regard to it and at the highest point of my spontaneity and activity. From this point of view one understands why the Platonic figure of the prisoners in the cave appeared to Fink (1994; 177–198) more appropriate than the Cartesian doubt as a basis of comparison for the reductive operation. Here the accent is placed upon the concrete transformation, inclusive of the corporeal, implied by the reduction and not just upon the spiritual work which it also equally requires. These two aspects are of course complementary, to the extent that the spiritual liberation which the doubt allows presupposes a transformation of the body, just as the freedom from sensory chains implies a spiritual mutation. All the same, what is presupposed in one case is thematically set out in the other.

The features of the allegory of the cave which Fink isolates are in this regard exemplary.

a. The violence of the exit of the prisoner out of the opaque space of the cave, a violence linked to the constraint he was subjected to when blinded by an overly bright light.
b. The incomprehension of the other prisoners when he tries to communicate his painfully acquired knowledge of the shadow as shadow.
c. The absence of any worldly significance attached to this painfully acquired liberty.

All these points refer back to the self-affection inherent in the pain and suffering linked to the disturbance and then the expulsion from a comfortable and familiar situation. They find precise phenomenological expression in the terms retained by Fink to characterise the reduction (2000: §5, §10):

a. The absence of any natural motive for effecting the reduction.
b. The difficulty of conceiving of a transcendental style of language which would not belong entirely to the order of mundane communication.
c. The significance of a transcendental motivation for the reduction.

For Fink language and motivation are the two correlative elements of Husserlian alterity and corporality; it is with reference to these that the meaning of the reduction is developed. Language and alterity define a common front. Even the plurality of the modes of access to the reduction will have to integrate this plurality into the common front in the course of transforming it. Motivation and the body form a second front and we will try to evaluate the form of the phenomenological *ethos* which comprehends them.

While the Cartesian and Platonic figures bring to light the obstacles to be transformed (alterity and language; corporality and motivation), psychology yields – with associated difficulties – the reflective structure in which the reduction originates. If doubt is a pre-suspension which introduces the epoche, while the expulsion from the shadowy world of images yields an existential and practical inflection of the reduction which emphasizes the passive disposition of the subject, the service rendered by the figure of psychology is to make it possible to grasp, even in transformed form, the psychic structure which drives the reduction, namely, reflection. These three features should therefore be seen not so much in opposition to, as in liaison with, each other. Now we are going to examine the way in which Husserl re-introduces these three comparative figures into his presentation of the ways of the reduction.

Multiple access to the reductive attitude: The problematic of the ways

The preparatory steps to the reductive operation which make comparisons possible remain external to it. Their virtue is to propose different facets, each one being in itself unilateral but offering a noteworthy highlight which is in each instance quite distinctive. The three panels of the reductive triptych:

a. the anticipatory doubt of the suspensive *epoche,*
b. the preparatory reflexive structure, which emphasises the reductive activity,
c. the existential practice which brings to light the passive disposition,

can very readily be dealt with methodologically through what Husserl thematised under the heading of the three major ways of access to the reduction.

The preparation for the reduction *via* external comparison is therefore internalised, deepened by a reflection upon the method itself. But here again, as we shall see, this theorising about the method yields few elements bearing on the practice itself of the reduction. So, in this context, we will not set out these three paths in any detail (Kern 1962/1977; Landgrebe 1963), but only to the extent that they can tell us something about the reductive exercise itself.

If the Cartesian way deepens the experience of doubt, the psychological way confers a properly phenomenological meaning upon the reflective structure. As for the ontological way, based on the life-world, it formalises the dramatic version of the exit from the cave. More important still, these three paths are like the three panels of a triptych, each related to, without however being confused with, the others.

Among these three paths, only the first, the one inspired by Descartes, will take on a solipsistic appearance. The other two are intrinsically intersubjective, which will make it possible for us to call into question, from the first, the overly simple opposition between reduction and intersubjectivity – in much the same way that, with regard to introspection, we have already had to demonstrate the naivety of the thesis which sets up first-person experience (which remains subjective), against third-person experience.

The royal way

The Cartesian way places us in an existential situation of radical and absolute solitude. Given the importance of the double methodological constraint which conditions the realisation of this path, namely, indubitability and necessity (what Husserl calls apodicticity), only the subject's currently immanent lived experiences fail to succumb to this critical constraint, and by virtue of the fact that their truth is only hypothetical or presumptive, as is the case with the world and with others, but also with my own past or future (Husserl 1960: §9; 1954: §58).

The ego is delivered over to itself, without any other resource than itself. My view of worldly objects makes of them external realities, "transcendent", whose certainty is only relative. I could never draw from them any kind of anticipatory knowledge of the reduction. My experience of others presents them to me as both extremely close and irreducibly remote. I can only gain access to the other's psychic experiences in an indirect way and, moreover, only on the basis of my direct experience of a body whose sensible and motor structures appear similar to my own. But how can the simple knowledge of the body – if it is not equally a knowledge about the body stemming from another realm, the psyche or mentality – determine access to a reduction which itself cannot be exclusively corporeal?

But the knowledge at work in the lived experiences of the other is indirect since it rests solely on the access to the body of the other. Apprehended in this way, the other hardly seems capable of providing me with an effective knowledge concerning the mode of exercise of the reduction. Finally, references to my own past states of mind (anticipation of future states does not enable me to acquire the required knowledge), those in which I have already undertaken a reduction with a view to grasping anew the conditions controlling this operation, remain, according to Husserl (1956/1959, Lectures 39–40 and 49–50), extremely difficult. I can remember a given situation, a privileged situation in the course of which I got the feeling of having attained this state of suspension of the thesis of the world and of a certain detachment vis-à-vis my interests – the determining centre of the reductive conversion. Such situations are rare and are practically never perceived as such at the very moment when they are lived. One only gains access to them by remembering. I am in a foreign country (Sweden) and I observe behaviour which differs considerably from our own; or again, I am somewhere where I am ignorant of the language (Turkey) and my interest in what surrounds me is therefore suspended in the linguistic medium. On such occasions I can get an impression of the vanity, or at least of the relativity, of the acts and gestures which I see being unfolded before me.

Solipsism and dis-embodiment consequently appear as major limitations to the Cartesian way which the other two ways will have the advantage of overcoming, each in its own manner.

The genetic way of psychology

This descriptive initiation into a detachment vis-à-vis what one is for the most part (driven by a goal to be attained, caught up in an activity, living in the wish or desire for an impending fulfillment) already precipitates us into the frame of what Husserl thematized under the heading of the "psychological way". If the structure of memory seems to accommodate a reductive "knowledge", however difficult and infrequent rememoration might be, the situations in which it would be possible to utilise memory arouse a feeling of self-alienation by virtue of their very strangeness. We will therefore make use of the experience of that alteration of the self with regard to itself, constitutive of memory, however rarely this may be experienced in the moment in which it is lived – which therefore means that it is always lived out in a differed retrospection. Memory is the privileged cognitive organ of that radical experience of self-alteration which lies at the root of the reductive operation (Depraz 1995: §19).

Yet, no memory is pure. Often, a figurative element comes to complete an incomplete, even confused, remembering. I have in mind the image of a spatio-temporal situation in which I was able to live out this disjunction from myself linked to a feeling of strangeness provoked by certain features of the surrounding world. But this image is far from being complete because I was not attentive to the situation from beginning to end. At a given moment in time I was distracted by a familiar melody and I became, all of sudden, glued to myself. All our memories are interrupted in this way, discontinuous or fragmentary. I can re-establish a continuity or complete this truncated memory by prolonging it in the imagination. But contrary to memory which presupposes a continuous identity between my past and present self, imagination rests upon a structure of alteration such that this self tends to no longer coincide with itself (Husserl 1973a: n.8, n.10; 1973b: n.2, n.7; 1973c: n.6). Imagination introduces an extreme distortion into the identity of the self, to the point that it makes it possible to live the self-alteration constitutive of the reductive knowledge in the present – in one's imaginary present (Depraz 1995: §21). In this sense, the imagination actually produces the cognitive knowledge of the reduction rather than simply providing a medium for it, as memory does. Supplementing a deficient memory, fiction enables one to live, in the present, this altering break in the self which alone structures the conversion of attitude.

In this context of constitutive alteration, psychic consciousness is not necessarily solely egological, and it is certainly not solipsist. To be sure, each of us lives this alteration for him or herself, but a fictional account, no matter of what kind, narrative, painterly, poetic, musical, justifies the intersubjective distribution, through empathic connection, of something which was first of all lived out in an interior and solitary fashion by each. In and through fiction, we find both the production and exchange of the altering splits lived out in each, so many reductive acts lived out in this way on the intersubjective plane through a mutual *Einfühlung* as Husserl claims. This common ground is thenceforward the source of reciprocal enrichment since I can translate, transpose what the other gives me to see – thanks to the power of the imagination – into my own proper idiom, with a view to making it more fecund. In other words, I put myself in the place of the other in imagination *(Hineinphantasieren)* just as the other is capable of transposing himself to my place. This inter-empathy welded by the efficacy of the imaginative act therefore corresponds to an "intersubjective reduction" in the strong sense of that word (Husserl 1956/1959, Lecture 53; 1960: §34).

The generative way of the life-world

We are now quite close to what Husserl conceived of as the "way of the ontology of the life-world". The reductive criterion is no longer either the apodicticity of the Cartesian way or the inhibition of interests belonging to the way of psychology but the dismantling of idealizations which regulate our life as we try to theorise. In order to do this we must, on the basis of our everyday experience, get back to a lived experience which is no longer a mental construction. Reduction is henceforth neither suspending nor reflecting but undoing the element of construction or of idealisation which often inhabits our lived experience (Husserl 1954: §§34–41). In this sense the world of our sensitive and affective life furnishes the index of just such a reduction, which makes itself known as a liberation from presuppositions and as a shattering of accepted evidence.

This path goes in the very opposite direction from that taken by the suspensive Cartesian *epoche* and of psychological dis-interestedness. There, on the contrary, it is a matter of trying as hard as possible to stick to experience, to focus on it and to join with it with a view to intensifying it, that is, to unearthing from it all its potentialities, all its sedimented meaning. What brings us together is no longer the intersubjective community of reductive acts but the world itself, a store of *habitus* and sensations from which everyone draws the singularity of his experience. In fact, it is clear that I am not always held at a distance from myself, whether it is through the *epoche* or through a reflective distantiation. However, this absolute coincidence with oneself is a "secondary" coincidence. It is therefore not that habitual and naive feeling that one often has unconsciously sticking to oneself.

I have just learnt of the death of an intimate friend and am still under the shock of the loss of this cherished person. All the aims and desires of my daily existence are brutally interrupted by this sudden breach in the continuity of life. I am so "glued" to this misery that I no longer stick to this self of habitual routines. I then become vertiginously aware of the fragility of everyone's existence. And there arises out of this abysmal misery a self which is deeper than my natural self and whose depth is measured by my anguish in the face of the finitude of our being; it only nominally remains a self to the extent that it opens up upon a much larger sphere of my being where body and spirit are intimately tied up with each other. Another example: the occupations which feed daily life are suddenly thrust into the background by an unexpected event which transforms their sense into non-sense: the birth of a new baby, which overthrows the known order of values by placing the value of the new life before all the rest. This absolute value orients and organises the new life, to the point where the absence of the being in question inhibits enthusiasm, arouses boredom. It is the discovery of the vanity, even of the relativity of previous activities which provokes this profound boredom (Depraz & Mouillie 1993).

All these feelings or affective dispositions reveal an abyss there where daily life was stitched together by projected desires and ends. Heidegger is certainly the philosopher who best described these *Stimmungen* (especially anxiety and boredom) through which the vertiginous depth of existence is revealed (Heidegger 1984: §29; 1983; Courtine 1990; Marion 1990: 65–119). The ontological way through the life-world is the one which stays closest to Heidegger's affective thematic. The version of the reduction which it promotes is just as contrary to nature as the two others. All the same, its effort at liberation is the inverse of the former, in that it consists not in disengaging oneself from oneself by getting away from one's habitual being but in coinciding more completely with one's profound nature.

These three forms of reduction do not contradict each other. They form a spectrum across which the structure of alterity, already at work in the reductive process, is deployed. This spectrum reaches from the radical suspensive distancing of the self from itself, through the structure of reflective withdrawal, and on to the absolute affective coincidence of the self with itself. What they share is their anti-naturalness. This, one might say, is the distinctive mark of the reductive subject, its *ethos*.

The ethos of the reductive subject

The phenomenological ethic runs profoundly counter to nature. The reduction is not an exercise that the subject would operate willingly, of his own accord, and in a spontaneous fashion. Of his own accord, such a subject would remain with, or would return much more naturally to, the daily course of his familiar activities and of his most comfortable thinking.

Only the unforeseen eruption of alien elements, of unknown places, the discomfort due to the ignorance or the strangeness of a location, painful or upsetting events, could, or so it seems, provoke this remarkable conversion of attitude which is the reduction. This is how the advent of the reduction has been presented to us up to now, at least in the majority of cases, and which makes it appear as something motivated by external contexts, whether spatial or temporal (places, events etc.). Such a motivation remains external to the subject or, at least, its initial impulse corresponds to nothing like an auto-determination, even if later on something is made out of this exteriority, a feeling of strangeness or of suffering which represents the auto-affective interiorisation of it. A motivation of this kind therefore implies a sort of passivity on the part of the self-affected subject.

But this affective passivity, linked to a natural motivation external to the reduction, runs totally counter to certain of Husserls' statements which insist upon the internal motivation (of a transcendental order) which regulates its exercise. In this context the reduction would spring from a free act linked to a decision on my part. How are we to reconcile this claim to a natural motivation for the reduction (which brings with it a form of passivity on the part of the subject) with the affirmation of an absolute liberty in the exercise of the reductive act, which calls for a transparent and spontaneous consciousness? It is also possible to reconstrue this alternative in the more classical frame of the opposition between ethical action and moral judgment, which comes down to distinguishing between two forms of phenomenological ethics, one being pragmatic in character and rejoining the natural attitude to some degree, the other having a constraining character which runs counter to nature and implies the unusual effort of reflection and the transformation of the subject (Varela 1999a). But beyond this dual alternative, the question which presents itself for us here is that of the possibility of a transcendental ethics.

Fink tries to account for this difficulty with his formula for a circular motivation constitutive of the reductive operation (2000: §5).

1. I move in the realm of the evidence which surrounds without asking questions, pursuing my normal goals. In such a context, nothing forces me to turn the world into an enigma that might lead me to raise questions about its very possibility. From the standpoint of the natural attitude, no external motivation forces me in the direction of a reduction of what surrounds me with a view to calling it in question.
2. I am in a state of extreme lucidity: my consciousness has been aroused to the highest degree because, in the course of a walk, walking allowed me to sharpen my attention or, while writing, the very need to find the most precise and the most adequate formulation led me to a linguistic crystallisation.

In the one case as in the other – being enclosed in the natural attitude, the affirmation of an interior liberty – the *transition* from one attitude to the other remains unexplained. (1) the natural attitude imprisons us in the world and renders useless the exercise of a reduction, the need for which is not realized; (2) the affirmation of our freedom installs us from the first in the reduced attitude and gives rise to a motivation which can only proceed from an entirely lucid consciousness, but without enabling us to understand how we got there.

Fink insists upon the fact that this problem of a transition is a false problem, brought forth in order to demonstrate the circularity of the analysis. In reality, experience displays a continual *back and forth* between one attitude and the other. Schematically speaking, one might say that the Husserlian, ontological way gives rise to a polarisation of the reduction around an affective and worldly motivation, while the psychological way insists much more on an internal self-motivation. With regard to Husserl's followers, one might situate

Heidegger, and then Merleau-Ponty, on the side of a corporeal and worldly approach to the reduction, Fink and Sartre, on the side of a psychical and transcendental approach.

But in distinguishing these two contrasting approaches to the reduction, has one accounted for the necessary transition from one attitude to the other, for the profound change in our attitude which the reduction implies? If there is anything like a reductive *ethos*, it is precisely because the opposition of liberty and facticity, however intertwined they may be in the polarization in question, still remain naive with regard to the most intimate, and acute experience of the reduction. Whenever I walk or write, the attentiveness of my consciousness is not the simple fact of my free will. The countryside which unfolds before me, or the familiar place where I am living, are not just simple and contingent props, or pure contexts which, as such, remain extrinsic to my own self-awareness in *statu nascendi*. They cooperate with the latter.

How? The walking or the writing body frees itself from the *substantial* body thanks to the space of the walk or the room which is not an exterior, objective space but an intimate location inhabited by this body and which I inhabit *through* my body. This inhabiting, this incarnation alone, make possible a detachment vis-à-vis the body which opens the way to a spiritual disposition (reflective, transcendental) where the body finds itself incarnated in reflection. Pacified, as if absent, the body is no longer receptive to sensorial excitations, to emotional disturbances – the troubling distractions which mark our usual way of being in the world. But this does not mean that our body has been negated. Through the capacity for detachment, it becomes requalified, re-sensitized. If there is anything like an incarnation of the body through reflection, this incarnation is at the same time a more intense incarnation, that is to say, it arises in the context of a liberation from the naive objectification of the most commonplace corporeal regime.

So, when I am struck by some tragic event which affects me to the point of relativising every other activity, the motivation is only apparently natural and external. If affectivity is able to effect such a breach in the habitual course of my life, it is because it is situated on a plane which surpasses the natural and is committed to a transcendental incarnation. This pure affective coincidence of the self with itself is what defines an eminent detachment.

Aids to the reduction

In this way we are brought to call in question the vocabulary of *motivation*, a vocabulary which is quite incapable of characterising the type of predisposition for the reduction which we are looking for. In fact, the structure of motivation is aporetic to the extent that it remains dependent upon the factical and a-phenomenological duality of natural exteriority and transcendental interiority.

In making use of the term "aid" ("supports" in French), we are trying to define the framework, or the context, which makes the disclosure and the unfolding of the reduction possible. An aid is neither an apriori, nor a contingent condition. It makes its contribution to the reduction. Without it, the reduction could not take place and yet, even with the aid, there can be no apriori guarantee that a reduction will take place. In other words, an aid is not a mechanical trigger automatically releasing the reduction but it is not a circumstance which remains extrinsic to its accomplishment either. In this way we try to render intelligible the concrete genesis of the reductive activity which cannot be naively empirical since it is upheld by the transcendental meaning which inhabits it.

Moreover, such aids to the reduction are, in fact, "empirico-transcendental". They concretely structure the exercise of the reduction by participating in it in advance without, nonetheless, pre-determining it. It is by making available an effective exercise of the reduction at the transcendental level that a genuinely experiential dimension is conferred upon it. Describing the concrete aids to the transcendental reduction is a matter of identifying the material fulcrum hitherto missing between the transcendental and the natural attitude; the absence of this fulcrum would make of both of these pure abstractions.

It is therefore better not to allow ourselves to be limited by the idea that the transcendental structure constitutive of the appearing does not itself appear. If this reductive experience can itself be described, it is because it is given in act in its supportive structures; it is present across the very structure which regulates each phenomenal aid. Moreover, each requires a different mode of expression, specifically differentiated linguistic situations which, while remaining subject to the facticity of their mode of givenness, are nourished by the transcendental meaning. Corresponding to the three principal ways of access to the reduction we are going to finish up by distinguishing three empirico-transcendental means of carrying it out.

1. The first implies a situation of methodological solitude where the page is the only aid in the concretisation of experience. Writing manifests itself as the impulse, the motor of the explanation rather than remaining a simple product of it, a transcription after the event of the experience in question.

In other words, it is the act of writing that produces the description in the course of its own self-unfolding rather than the thought about the description which, prepared in advance, finds its derivative linguistic form later on.

2. The second way of proceeding is written into a context of thought and of life which is intersubjective from the start, a context where the privileged aid supporting the exercise is a regulated polyphony. As a matter of fact, the verbal exchange is always in the first instance bi-polar, in strict conformity with the dialogical situation, and it only proliferates in small steps. The paradigm for an aid of this kind is the general situation underlying teaching, where the teacher addresses a plurality of students, a potential polyphony but one which can only be realized by one student alone initially raising a question. Bi-lateral exchange then gives rise to other possible interventions. One might say that the intersubjective situation is intuitively "satisfied" when two students finish up by discussing something together without the mediation of the teacher. From an asymmetric relation one crosses over to a relation which falls under the head of mutuality. Introduced and set up by the teacher, both the theme and its description are progressively opened up to discussion by others, that is, filled out, corrected, modified.

3. Corresponding to the third procedure, we find an intensification of the first two. It rests upon the act of writing but re-invests it with a native plurality of writings. It corresponds to a writing situation in which there are several authors, as exemplified in the present work. Even while remaining alone in the act of writing and even while maintaining his or her individuality, each tries to co-operate with the others. In this case there is a mutual community, a community in which authorship is progressively developed in reciprocally adjusted acts of writing. The theme of the description can, at this stage, only be determined in common and on the basis of a prior sharing of the individual experiences.

Bearing and limits of phenomenological philosophy

Trying to grasp the concrete experience of becoming aware leads one to develop certain techniques designed to maintain an attention which is, in principle, fugitive and variable. It is indeed very difficult to remain attentive not only to a sensory, perceptual or affective experience but also to the sensation of this sensation, the perception of this perception, or again, the affection of this affection. These techniques are indivisibly both corporeal and spiritual. They transcend such an opposition, in itself still naive, and bring into play a practice, an exercise which must be situated outside the distinction of the voluntary and the involuntary. They are intended to ensure the persistence of a state which is not one of focalised concentration but is not one of dispersion either, since it opens up onto an aptitude for experience as such.

We are going to note three of these techniques which, between them, might reasonably be regarded as covering the entire thematic field. Over and beyond the methodological specificity and the historical origin of each of these, all of them are concerned with resisting a tempting conceptual detachment by scrutinizing the immanent genesis, in act, of consciousness *in statu nascendi*. If the psychology *via* debriefing interview, which foregrounds the description of the act of evocation, is a method historically based in the psychological tradition, the transformation which it effects with regard to classical psychology brings it into contact with phenomenology and its methodologically primary act, the reduction. In this respect, there is a certain complicity between the act of evocation favoured by the psychology in question and the Husserlian act of re-membering, itself a model for reflection under the guise of a higher-order perception.

In addition, the practice of evocation unfolds in the frame of an intersubjectively dialogical structure which recalls the intersubjectivity-in-act of the reduction. Finally, we know that phenomenology is born of a radicalization of intentional psychology. It is therefore legitimate to make comparisons between techniques derived from these two methodological fields. Finally, the methodological act which lies at the root of Husserlian phenomenology makes available an ontological radicality, empirico-transcendental in this instance, which can be profitably put to work by just such a psychological project aimed at re-founding, in a methodologically adequate way, the experience of becoming aware.

However, the transcendental power of the reduction conceals a difficulty, that of the bodily practice which obviously underlies it but which is never (hardly ever) rendered thematic. This is where the non-verbal forms constitutive of the debriefing interview as well as the technique of mindfulness at work in Tibetan Buddhism, succeed in enriching, in grounding in a practice what the theoretical radicality of phenomenology loses in practical rootedness. Bringing to light the bodily practice of letting-go as an aptitude for non-focused concentration thereby becomes the crucible for an experience of the birth of reductive consciousness which cannot be divested of its incarnate character. If Husserlian phenomenology appears the poorer in this context, the technique derived from Buddhist meditation brings the mind-body to the fore. Psychology and phenomenology have not sought to clarify their relations with the East, except for a few recent attempts (Kern 1988; Laycock 1994; Gupta 1998). Yet the richness of the methodological foundation of certain oriental practices provides an undeniable justification.

CHAPTER 7

Wisdom traditions and the ways of reduction

7.1. What do we mean by spiritual traditions?

In order to answer this question one only has to follow the main thrust of the previous Chapter concerning the phenomenology of human experience. In its existential dimension, the examination of human experience cannot but touch the wider dimension of the sense or meaning of human life. The quest for such meaning, rooted in experience itself, is what we refer to here as spiritual or wisdom traditions of humankind, which have been active throughout history in various cultural contexts, with more or less degrees of sophistication and capacity for transmission of their acquired observations and methods for future generations. These traditions have also examined the structure of experience by means of disciplined methods of the greatest sophistication, as we shall see below.

We wish to draw a rather sharp distinction between spiritual inquiry (in the above sense) and religion. We use this word to designate first the great monotheistic traditions of Abrahamic source: Judaism, Christianity and Islam, but also ideological and social formations which are not necessarily monotheistic. Hinduism has its religious formations (ranging from polytheistic to monotheistic and pantheistic forms) and indeed so does Buddhism: even though Buddhism can be described as a form of nontheism, certainly throughout its history and for the majority of its members it has had all the social trappings of religion. Although often amalgamated, the distinction between religion and spirituality is crucial here, for it is important to draw from extant methods and observations, but we have no intention to identify with a particular religious lineage. Hopefully this will not distract those readers who might look down with a frown at the use of the word spiritual in a work such as this. It would have been much safer not to do it, of course, and we are aware of the potential misunderstandings. However, to deny ourselves the rich sources and accumulated knowledge of these traditions of human phenomenology, would be a serious mistake, much like not availing ourselves of the data from people working in applied fields (who are called in French "praticiens") (Chapter

5), with the excuse that their disciplines are not "academically correct". So we choose to treat such *spiritual* traditions as non-religious wisdom traditions, by pointing to certain elements within the whole range of phenomena that make up elements that stand out for us because of our Western traditions of ethical philosophies (e. g., the Hellenistic ones) and because of the rise of Western secularism. So we distinguish between religion, on the one hand, and spirituality on the other, where both are to be found across the entire spectrum of world traditions.

Since our focus is directed towards the dynamics of the act of becoming aware, we have selected a small number of main traditions as useful sources, or more precisely as exemplary variations on the theme of accomplishing reduction. Two of them have already been mobilized in Part I, the Philokalia tradition and Tibetan Buddhism, along with some psychological techniques, already discussed above in Chapter 5. More explicitly these main traditions are:

1. The Philokalia tradition of Heart-praying, stemming from the eastern (primitively Greek and then Slavonic) Christianity, grounded on a number of exemplary individuals, mystical texts and practical instructions for human development.
2. The Jewish Kabala, as exemplified in the mystical experiments of Abraham Abulafia, and revived today in Mosche Idel's movement.
3. Some streams of the Sufi tradition, in particular the Naqshbandi lineage, which has kept alive a tradition of refined practices of various kinds.
4. Buddhism in its various forms as the most universally developed repository of mindfulness-based practices. They are widely different according to their lineage: Theravadin, Chinese Mahayana, Japanese Zen, or Tibetan, just to name a few.
5. Sankara's Advaita Vedanta, generally regarded as having best developed and systematized a main strand of Upanisadic thought.
6. Taoism as the indiginous Chinese wisdom tradition, interacting with Buddhism and thereby giving rise to Chan and Zen Buddhism. It is the most universally developed repository of practices working directly and actively with the vital energies of the lived body.

It is not possible to cover all of these methods, although each of them potentially contains an experiential search for awareness. Instead we have chosen to detail the method of mindfulness/awareness (*shamatha/vispashyana*) common to many Buddhist schools as the exemplary variation to be developed here, mainly because this tradition has kept alive the most accurate techniques of the act of becoming aware we are seeking.

We are dealing here with a non-occidental spiritual tradition, pragmatic and philosophical at the same time. The historical origin of this method of "mindfulness" comes from the Buddhist tradition cultivated in the East (India, China, Tibet, South-East Asia) where the very word "phenomenology" does not have any meaning. So, we have to conduct a dialogue between quite diverse traditions. In English, one speaks of "comparative philosophy", but this term has a negative connotation in French. (Loy 1991; Nishitani 1983). This does not pose insurmountable problems, but, clearly, such an exercise raises great interest and numerous dangers at the same time. What we sketch out here is therefore not a thesis, nor ideas to defend, but rather an open proposition, above all motivated by the general project of this work.

The presentation will include three parts. The first will be historical or contextual. The second will examine the point of view of practice, the central theme of our project. Finally, we will link back this presentation to the phenomenological tradition as presented above in Chapter 3, in order to give substance to our assertion that what is most relevant in the Buddhist tradition, as exemplar of spiritual traditions, is its own development of a "phenomenology of human experience".

7.2. The practice of mindfulness (shamatha): The historical context

Since we find ourselves in a transcultural context, we must sketch out the historical, geographical, and human background from which these ideas emerged. This will also allow us to situate ourselves by indicating the perspective in which we integrate these ideas. Otherwise, we would fall into the "orientalist" trap that amalgamates everything that comes from the Orient. It is true that the history of Buddhism in the Occident is full of misunderstandings (Fields 1984, 1993). It is evident that in the philosophical, scientific, and religious traditions of the East, there are as many distinctions to make as in our own tradition. We must consequently historically situate the completely singular theses concerning mindfulness that we want to develop.

The grounding

The method of mindfulness is historically connected to Siddhartha Gautama, the Buddha (566–486 BCE). Sakyamuni Buddha is the term used by later Buddhists to refer to the historical Buddha of our time, by comparison with the Buddhas of other times (e.g. the future: Maitreya). Sakyamuni means Prince of the Sakya clan. He was a revolutionary who instituted a radical break with respect to the tradition that he was born into, the Brahmanical thought of the Vedas and the Upanishads (Thich Nhat Hanh 1991). If this tradition itself presents a great diversity, we can nevertheless disclose a certain unity at the heart of this type of life and thought. Completely belonging to this tradition, Sakyamuni introduces a *gesture*, seen in that time as revolutionary from the start.

What is this revolutionary gesture? Although he belonged to a hermeneutic tradition, very anchored in the texts and the teachings of the written tradition, as was, for example, Judaism in the time of Jesus Christ (though the latter belonged to the priestly class, whereas the Buddha was part of the warrior class), the Buddha reversed this tradition in *a first-hand test of lived experience*. While recognizing the importance of reading and the understanding of sacred texts, he considered that one must go further, so far as to conclude that it is essential to found oneself on a movement of personal testing. Other than the example of Jesus Christ, this gesture is consonant with other foundational gestures, like that of Socrates at the moment of the foundation of philosophy. In that respect, it is interesting to note that Husserl, in one of the rare occurrences of his manuscripts where he mentions the historical Buddha (Ms. B. I 2/88–94 about "Socrates – Buddha"), analyzed precisely his revolutionary and instaurational attitude as a pre-phenomenological critical attitude, and that, beyond this, by comparing the attitude to the socratic attitude in terms of radicality (Schuhman 1988: 180; Husserl 1925: 125–126). What Sakyamuni's gesture demands is a recourse to direct experience, a return to the "things themselves". However, the revolutionary character of his gesture needs to be detailed further. First, the emphasis on personal experience was common to many seekers of the age. They were known as *samanas* and rejected the Vedic tradition, preferring to wander free of family ties, meditating and debating in the forest. The Upanishads grew out of this movement, and so did Buddhism. Indeed, the Buddha, when he renounced his life in the palace and set off to search for enlightenment in the forest, became a *samana*. Second, his revolutionary gesture is the Buddha's discovery of a new form of meditation insight (*vipashyana*) and his discernment of non-self (*anatta*) on the basis of that kind of meditation. In fact, this gesture on his part, the so-called middle way, is what radically differentiated the Buddha from the other samanas, the Upanishadic yogis in particular.

This gesture is not introduced in order to improve intellectual comprehension: it has an existential motivation. We will not understand anything important about the tradition of mindfulness/awareness if we remain in an intellectual apprehension of it, even if such a means of access is not excluded. The essential strength of such a tradition resides in a diagnosis that consists in *noting a non-knowing* in human life, which no doubt reminds us of the Heideggerian version of the access to the reduction. This is expressed in a traditional manner in all of the Schools of Buddhism by what are called the *Four Noble Truths*.

The first noble truth corresponds to the affirmation that human life is filled with difficulties, anxieties, suffering. *Dukkha*, the Sanscrit term used to designate this state of affairs, usually translated as "suffering", is in fact a very polysemic word. It does not just signify an immediate suffering engendered by hunger, pain, or sickness, but also an existential suffering, of an ontological type, which remarkably echoes the Heideggerian analysis of the paradigmatic *Stimmung* that is anxiety and its interpretation as existential reduction (Courtine 1990; Henry 1963). Different levels of suffering are distinguished as well, among them, the suffering of non-knowing. This is one of the sufferings most often evoked in the texts attributed to the Buddha. The first noble truth is thus an appeal to note that one can never escape from this suffering.

The second noble truth responds to the question of the origin of this suffering, which arises from craving for substantiality or permanence. The cause or origin in question corresponds to a specific misrecognition, that of the fluidity, impermanence, non-solidity, or the non-substantiality, of the experience of the self and of the exterior world. We will return to this, but we must note that this is the most original orientation of Sakyamuni that distinguishes the tradition of mindfulness from all the rest of the Indian traditions.

The third noble truth affirms that there is a way to overcome suffering, to treat the illness generated by it. Called the truth of the way, it is what allows one not to be disarmed when faced with *dukkha*: there is something that one can do in order to engage onself in an apprenticeship, in a *savoir-faire* capable of surpassing this misrecognition. In a perhaps parallel manner, the psychoanalytic tradition affirms that there is a truth of the way, because the misrecognition of the unconscious is a notation of something on which one can act (Epstein 1994).

The fourth noble truth is practical. Only a practice allows one to surpass this misrecognition. *This practice is the method of mindfulness*. It consists in affirming the reality of change: the apprenticeship can provide a stable *transformation* of human experience that accompanies the cessation of suffering. *Niroda* is literally the cessation of suffering, and it is also noted. It is there that the Buddha reveals himself in his different aspects, as thinker, as master who sets to work a certain tradition, and as exemplar. His logic is less de-monstrative than monstrative: he makes himself a model, a lived example.

In short, the historical Buddha has left us an extremely revolutionary and complex aid, in which an existential diagnostic, an intellectual deepening, the introduction of a methodology, and finally a gamble on the result are reunited; these are well expressed in the four noble truths.

The consolidation

It is useful to sketch the later evolution of the tradition inaugurated by Buddha, as well as the way in which this tradition appears to us after 25 centuries of development. In order to do this, we will use a traditional Tibetan mode of presentation that distinguishes a succession of three historical steps or *yanas* in the evolution of this thought and its practices. Let us point out, however, from the start, that this *successive* mode of exposition is of a pedagogical order and does not account for the circulation, the comings-and-goings between these three *yanas*, essential from the point of view of the meditator's practice.

The first of these three steps is what is called the consolidation of the tradition established by Sakyamuni. It is still found today, incarnated with great constancy in *Theravadin* Buddhism, which means the School of the "elders". These schools are primarily to be found in Burma, Vietnam, Thailand, and Ceylon, where large communities are very active. These traditions take the gesture of the Buddha very seriously and very literally, essentially by creating monastic orders. For the *Theravadins*, going down the path is a slow and difficult task. It requires taking away anything that distracts him from his capacity for active presence. According to this logic one ends up by establishing monastic rules or *vinaya*.

The work of development of Buddhism during the first centuries after Buddha allowed the establishment of this corpus of rules or *vinaya* – still alive in the *Theravadin* schools – which consist in setting down Sakyamuni's teachings, the *sutras*. In the end, they systematized the accumulated observations and commentaries in a corpus of knowledge analogous to a psycho-phenomenology, the *abbidharma*. The basic corpus of the Buddhist tradition (the *sutras*, the *vinaya*, and the *Abbidharma*) was thus well established from the 3rd Century BCE on.

The Mahayanist turn

Towards the 5th Century of the Christian Era, although there was already a Buddhist tradition started sometime between 150 BCE and 100 CE, in the North of India there took place what is called the "great turn" or the "turning of the Great School", *mahayana* in Sanscrit, which signifies literally "great vehicle". The *Mahayana* interpretation brought with it a veritable schism that persists in a weakened manner up to the present. The *Maha*-yanists call the Elders the *Hina*-yanists, that is, the people of the "small vehicle", a devalorizing appellation, to be sure, contrasted with their preferred designation, the *Theravadins*, the Elders. In fact, the Theravada is only one school of the so-called Hinayana schools: it is the only one still in existence today, hence today the only so-called Hinayana Buddhists left are the Theravadins. But this was not true during the time of the rise of the Mahayana. In short, one could say that the strict *Theravadins* regard the *Mahayanists* in the same way as Catholics, in times past viewed the Protestants.

The key person of the Mahayanist "turn" is Nagarjuna (150–250 CE). Historians disagree as to whether he is a single person, or an amalgam of several. We will pass on this historiographical problem and focus on his radiating influence in the 5th Century in the North of India, as well as on his corpus of writings. Here, Nagarjuna carried out *two* great gestures that are at the heart of the *Mahayana* School (Streng 1967; Garfield 1995).

The first gesture is that of noting that, in order to be faithful to what the Buddha proposed in terms of the way of developing existential possibilities, the exclusive practice of mindfulness – as it was established inside the monasteries – is not completely efficacious. It lacks the *intersubjective* dimension, that which can only be learned with the practice of mindfulness in society, in the world of ordinary life. Here intersubjectivity is made central to the way: it relativizes the monastic ideal, making the active life a way of practice, if one can free oneself of the natural attitude through cultivating the capacity for mindfulness.

The Mahayanist turn thus places the accent on compassionate empathy in the wide sense, that is, on the capacity each person has to enter into resonance, into affinity with the disposition of the mind of another person, in short, to put onself in the place of the other. This type of approach to practice has interesting echos with the (late) discovery of the importance of intersubjectivity, *Einfühlung* and alterity as key-themes in Phenomenology, as we have already seen in Chapter VI and as we shall see later at the end of this Chapter. The Mahayanist turn affirms the possibility that human experience is much more powerful as a *means of transformation* than mindfulness alone. To mobilize this dimension of *Einfühlung* as a means of transformation has a pragmatic meaning. It is not at all a matter of a gesture of morality or of pity. It is the affirmation that if one does not invest this wider dimension of empathy, there cannot be an interior transformation, a veritable apprenticeship.

The second Mahayanist gesture has to be situated on the conceptual plane, where a new development that will be absolutely determinant for the Buddhist tradition that follows sees the light of day. This development is the reconceptualization of the notion of non-substantiality, of impermanence *lato sensu*, or even the impossibility of finding solid and apodictic fixed points, either in the world or in human knowledge. The *Theravadins* had already shown this, but Nagarjuna bestows a remarkable rigor on the thinking through *emptiness* (*sunyata*). Building on the Mahayana Perfection of Wisdom (*prajnaparamita*) literature, Nagarjuna founded the middle way or Madhyamaka school, whose central teaching is emptiness (*sunyata*). The Madhyamaka school grew and developed from Nagarjuna's time onwards.

Just as for the translation of *dukkha*, that of the term *sunyata* cannot account for the richness of this concept, whose meaning greatly exceeds what we designate by *emptiness*. For example, one might also translate *sunya* as *fullness*. *Sunyata* designates the fact that things are *too* interdependent, and this prevents us from uncovering whatever substantial character they might have. *Sunyata* is not, therefore, to be understood as an absence in the sense of a deprivation, but rather as an overdetermination of all events, including psychical and experiential life. More precisely, emptiness is defined by Nagarjuna as the absence of inherent being (*svabhava*) (and also the absence of intrinsic identity (*svalaksana*) by the Prasangika Madhyamaka who follow Candrakirti's commentary on Nagarjuna. But this absence is none other than the dependent co-origination of all dharmas, i.e., the interdependency of everything. Things are empty of inherent being (inherent being is absent in them) precisely because they are dependently originated. What characterizes the Mahayanist turn on the intellectual plane is that it makes of this notion of vacuity or emptiness, *sunyata*, the keystone of a fundamental ontology. This ontological thought of non-substantiality forms the heart of the Buddhist tradition.

From 750 CE the mostly Pala dynasty ruled in the north-east. Its rule weakened in the 11th century. From around 986 CE the Muslin Turks started raiding north-west India from Afghanistan, and they plundered India in the 11th century, establishing rule over it by 1192. The great Buddhist university Nalanda was sacked in 1198. The Persian Empire's invasion was thus progressing in all of the south of India and the South Asia. During this entire period, the Musulman Empire had effectively wiped out the Buddhist tradition, which it considered as the worst of its enemies, not leaving a stone standing. Since these events, Buddhist activity has nearly completely vanished from India. Buddhism massively emigrated towards the lands to the North: China, Tibet, later Japan. The great Mahayanist Schools, dominant today in numbers and influence, are situated in these three countries where they find their historical origin. Today India is divided between Muslims and Hindus; Buddhism is followed by a very small minority. Of all the historical sites of Buddhism, whether they be the places of the principal events of the Buddha's life (his birth-place, the place where he gave his first teaching), the places where the first Schools were founded, as well as the great Nalanda University where Nagarjuna taught, only the historical traces later reconstructed remain.

Tibet and the Vajrayanist turn

In this respect, Tibetan Buddhism has a completely exceptional character. Buddhism came to be established in a stable manner in Tibet from the 9th Century on. What is unique is that Buddhism became the true center of life for ten centuries. It is, so to speak, a sort of laboratory of the practice of mindfulness. There is still today a great gap between the remarkable sophistication of this tradition of thought and practice and the low level of economic and cultural life.

It is in the heart of this laboratory that the third turn, so characteristic of Tibet, was developed. We have already spoken of the small and great vehicle: this time, it is a matter of what one traditionally calls the indestructible vehicle, the ultimate vehicle, the *Vajrayana*. *Vajra* means "adamantine", that which has the quality of diamond. We know the *Vajrayana* particularly through contemporaries such as the Dalai Lama and, consequently, Europeans often call it Lamaism, an erroneous designation.

The most subtle Vajrayanist thought and practice, that which is distinct from the Mahayanist tradition and the popular form of Tibetan Buddhism, is in the minority in Tibet. It exists under the form of the three great Schools, the School of the elders (*Nyigmapa* school), the School of the new translators (*Kagyupa* school), and finally a reformist tradition called *Gelugpa*. They are today equally known under the names of the *Dzogchen* (Nyigmapa), *Mahamudra* (Kagyupa), two minor schools that have coexisted (more or less peaceably) in Tibet with the dominant *Gelugpa* tradition, represented by the Dalai Lama.

What essentially constitutes the teaching of these schools is not easy to express and leads us rapidly to the unspeakable. In order to say these things in a simple way, there is something new to be noted: one can go further than these two previous steps – *Hinayana* and *Mahayana* – and find a more radical way of introducing practice into the heart of daily life. At its very base the Vajrayana vehicle introduces a new level of work founded on basic constitutional aspects of the human psycho-physical complex. Some of these are expressed as symbolic iconography visualized by the practitioner in ritual setting (*sadhana*) until he is thoroughly familiar with them. As well, a number of very precise exercises operate on subtle bodily levels so that the practitioner's experience is quite dramatically transformed.

These efficient skills in Vajrayana coincide with a change in the overall view of the path that comes with the practices themselves. One gets to the point of questioning the attitude that consists in seeking a way. Actually, there is *nothing* to accomplish in practice, but at the same time, one must practice in order to arrive at this particular knowing that there is nothing to do. For the West, this is a bewildering thought since it is completely paradoxical. The *Dzogchen* and *Mahamudra* schools are particularly interesting to us since, not only do they share with the other Vajrayana schools a fine culture of philosophical analysis and literary expression of this movement, but they also have great experience of the practice of their teaching. In this respect, the *Kagyupa* describe themselves as "the offspring of practice".

The three turnings in question are less – we remarked this at the beginning – historical turns than *qualitative changes* that, with the appearance of a school, bring about a mode of practice and thought that constitutes an important transition. Assuredly, there is in the West an entire spectrum of exchanges where these schools coexist. But this does not go to say that one can assimilate them all, mix them all up together: these traditions are often quite different, even contradictory.

7.3. Sitting practice and the phenomenology of experience

After having provided the context, it is time now to approach the key point of this chapter: what the tradition of mindfulness brings to us from the point of view of practical life, that is, from the point of view of a phenomenology of experience that would be a phenomenological pragmatics (Laycock 1994). In order to uncover this, we limit ourselves exclusively to *questions of practical method* in structural relation with the three previously indicated turnings:

1. The *Hinayanist* foundational turn, which corresponds to the basis of the *shamatha/vipashyana* practices.
2. The *Mahayanist* turn, which develops the methods of meditation in action, notably *tong-len* and *lojong*.
3. The *Vajrayanist* turn (*sensu dzogchen* and *mahamudra*), which deploys the radical methods of suspension.

Such a correlation will allow us to illustrate concretely – even at the level of practical methodology – the non-successive and non-linear character of these three paths, that is, their mode of constant inter-action and circulation in the experience of the meditator.

The point of practice no.1: The shamatha method

The point of departure of this tradition of mindfulness, shared in one way or another with all of the schools, namely the great revolution of the Buddha, rests on the discovery of a gesture, of an apprenticeship, of a practice. In other terms, it is not a matter only of understanding, but also of *doing*.

The Buddha characterized what must be done using the Sanscrit word *shamatha*, whose translation, like those of all the Sanscrit or Tibetan terms expressing fundamental Buddhist concepts, is difficult. The traditional translation is "mental stability" and its literal meaning "quiescence". It is so named, since *shamatha*, in its developed form, gives rise to a serene attentional state in which the hindrances of excitation and laxity have been thoroughly calmed. The discipline of *shamatha* is not bound to any religious or philosophical creed. In the Tibetan tradition, one uses the term *shiné*, which means "to hold oneself well upright". In English an excellent translation is "mindfulness", which one can translate in French by "être complètement présent", and which we abbreviate by the expression "présence attentive", or by the word "attention". However, this last term should not be retained because it is not a matter of attention in the habitual meaning of concentration or fixation, but of a lighter *attentive* presence, completely open to the environing space and holding to it with tact. In that respect, the translation of *mindfulness/awareness* by *shamatha/vipashyana* is attributed to the genius of Trungpa, notably in 1972. (The translation by "présence attentive" is introduced in Varela et al. 1991; French translation: 1993: 53–58.)

The heart of *shamatha* is a gesture that unfolds in two phases: (1) *what* to do and (2) *how* to do it. *What* to do resembles a gesture of suspension of all belief, of bracketing prejudices. It is a gesture that engages me personally in suspending everything habitual, everything that is automatic in my way of interpreting and of looking at the world; (2) *how* to do it: this "reduction" of the natural attitude is accompanied by a suspension of *action*. It is a suspension that touches not only the interior attitude but also concrete behavior. This non-action is as follows: one sits quite simply on the ground or on a seat, expressing thus the attitude of suspension *through one's body*. This gesture that has manifestly become emblematic is to put one's buttocks on the ground in an attitude of silence and equanimity. Once in this posture, one keeps a straight back and a gaze that expresses a certain dignity, precisely the dignity that accompanies the gesture of placing the *habitus* in suspense, this gesture by which I leave the natural attitude and situate myself on the plane of a reflecting attitude. It is what one can see for example in the most beautiful images of Japanese, Thai, or Chinese Buddhist iconography.

The method of sitting practice can be described according to three major axes. We have already indicated the axis of *interior attitude*, which corresponds to the gaze reflecting on experience that takes its point of departure in the suspension of habitual associations, of the automatic following of thoughts proper to the natural attitude. The second axis refers to the bodily posture, which is extremely important in this tradition. The accent is placed here on the indissociability between good position and the capacity to maintain this internal gesture of suspension. Finally, what is very original and what we will detail now is the use of *breathing* as a means of uniting the two axes, the interior attitude and the bodily posture.

Breathing is thus the key-mediation between the two first axes. This is one of those things that it is easier to do and to note for onself than to explain. One could say that breathing is used as a sort of sufficiently non-referential, non-corporeal marker to be a general support for attention and, at the same time, it is concrete enough to allow us to notice when we have lost the thread. Of course, it is equally corporeal and mental, immediately affected by one's mental state and a basic life process of the body. The basic instructions for starting practice could be formulated as follows: "just sit on the ground, and do nothing but maintain this state of suspension focussing on your breathing." But the question that immediately comes to mind is this: how to know when one has left this attitude? When I notice that I am no longer following the course of my breathing. This takes place spontaneously: there is nothing to do, since I breathe anyway, I do nothing other than breathe. Actually, I engage myself in the attitude of *doing nothing other than "being there"*. Breathing serves as a point of reference, a little like a compass that I use to orient myself on a mountain expedition. As soon as I find myself "somewhere else", in the process of doing what I do habitually, namely, producing associations of ideas – holding a conversation with myself, reifying emotional states – I use the moment when I suddenly note that I have lost sight of my breathing as a marking point. It is surprising to see how breathing, which is apparently a minor element, of a physiological kind, is not minor at all: it ensures the mediation between corporeality and the interior stabilization of the gesture of mindfulness.

It is a technique of *genuine* attentiveness and not just of simple attention. For example, if I am capable of having a "quality of mindfulness" with regard to a text that I am reading, of being present to myself at the same time as I am attentive to my reading, and if a person drops a glass behind me, this does not make me start, for my attention is not only focalized on the reading but embraces, with a certain panoramic vision, all of the space that surrounds me. Sometimes, waiters in a café give us superb demonstrations of mindfulness. They are attentive to not tipping over platters of dishes, but they never forget the feet of the tables. In the Kagyupa schools, they say that one must give about 40% of attention to breathing and 60% to the periphery. We can express this equilibrium by speaking of "the correct tension", which is that of posture, with muscles neither too tight nor too relaxed.

By contrast with the phenomenological philosophical tradition and with the gesture of reduction as Husserl thematized it, the tie with corporeality is particularly interesting here. The genuine attitude of the body is not an ideal posture, for an ideal posture does not exist. It is not a question of bodily technique either. The search for stabilization of attention is accompanied by a dialogue with the body. There is a progressive synchronization between the field of the mental and that of the lived body. When we try to grasp the specific quality of the reductive gesture, such a synchronization is not apparent. We quite simply do not have the habit of taking it as a point of reference.

This kind of stability is the foundation for a first-hand examination of mind. The initial problem is to train the attention so that it is more reliable. With no such training, it is certainly possible to direct one's awareness inwards, but the undisciplined mind is fragile, it rapidly succumbs to attentional excitation, or scattering; and when the mind eventually calms down, it tends to drift into an attentional laxity in which vividness is sacrificed. A mind that is alternately prone to excitation and laxity has little capacity for attentiveness, and the Buddhist tradition considers such a mind as being out of synchrony.

Thus, the first step toward mindfulness is to refine the attention so that the mind is made properly synchronous, not so prone to the extremes of wildness and drowsiness (Trungpa 1995; Wallace 1998). To do so, those two hindrances must be clearly identified in terms of one's own experience. Wildness, the first obvious interference to observing the mind, is an agitated, intentional mental process that follows after attractive objects; it is a derivative of a compulsive desire to step out of non-action. Compulsive desire is understood here as a mental tendency that superimposes a categorization and judgement upon its object and yearns for it (Guenther & Kawamura 1975). Drowsiness, on the other hand, is an intentional mental process that occurs when attention becomes slack and the meditative object is not apprehended with vividness and forcefulness. It is said to be a derivative of delusion.

Stages in mindfulness

Progress in the gradual cultivation of *shamatha* is assessed in terms of stages or techniques for resting the mind (Trungpa 1979; Wallace 1999). The initial challenge in this training is to develop a continuity of sustained, voluntary attention, but in the first state called *resting or placing the mind*, the mind is strongly dominated by excitement, so one enhances the focus on the breath. Because one is now consciously trying to sustain attention unwaveringly on a single object instead of allowing it to roam about freely, it seems as if the mind were more overwhelmed by compulsive ideation than usual. Although it is very difficult to attend continuously to an object that does not change, that ability can be enhanced by means of recurrent motivation and effort.

At the outset of this training, one is encouraged to practice for short sessions each day – say, half hours sessions – with as few distractions between sessions as possible. As a result of persevering in this practice, one moves to the second *shamatha* stage called *continuously resting/placing*. During this phase, the mind is still subject to so much excitation that attention is more often away from breathing than on it, but at times one experiences brief periods of continuity in mindfulness, for up to a minute or so. Thus only a gross level of attentional stability has been achieved by this extension of practice.

As one continues in the training, one gradually reduces the number of sessions per day, while increasing the duration of each one. The next attentional stage in this development is called *literally resting*, at which point mindfulness is mostly on breathing, but it needs to be brought constantly back, in a recurrent manner. When one accomplishes the fourth attention state, called *thoroughly resting*, mindfulness is stabilized to the point that one does not entirely wander off for the full duration of each session, having overcome subtle thoughts.

At this point in the training particularly, it is very easy to fall into complacency, feeling that one has already achieved the aim of *shamatha*. Thus, the fifth stage of mindfulness called *taming*, and the sixth, called *pacifying*, are achieved with the force of suspension, with which one closely monitors the meditative process, watching for the occurrence of drowsiness and subtle agitation. By that time, an increasing sense of joy and satisfaction arises while meditating, so that the seventh and eighth attentional states of *thoroughly pacifying* and *one-pointedness* are carried out by the force of enthusiasm. In the seventh stage, even subtle laxity is eliminated; and at the point of one-pointedness the mind can dwell with utter stability and vividness for long periods of time.

With the attainment of the ninth stage called *resting evenly*, accomplished through long familiarization with practice, only an initial impulse of effort is needed at the beginning of each meditation session ; uninterrupted, sustained mindfulness occurs effortlessly, letting the mind be as it is. Moreover, the engagement of the will, of effort and intervention at this point is actually a hindrance. It is now possible to let the natural balance of the mind maintain itself without interference.

Practice and ordinary life

The assiduous practice of this technique, we have just said, leads to a *stabilization* of suspension, that is, of the capacity of mindfulness. The preceding description indicates that the capacity to look at things in this attitude of suspension without constantly allowing oneself to proceed to evaluations and habitual judgements is an extremely fragile gesture. There are exceptional cases, but most often, one cannot maintain this state beyond a few seconds. One of the questions that is posed with respect to the phenomenological reduction as *epoche* as we detailed it in Part I, is exactly that of its ephemerality. Such a practice requires cultivation and much time, typically at least an hour per day for years, if not more.

Further, what we have sketched is only a small glimpse of the technique of *shamatha*; it clearly has to be adapted according to practitioners, in such a way that the capacity for suspension is manifested in ordinary life in a more and more stable manner. Actually, what is essential is that there be a circulation between sitting meditation, the practice of *shamatha*, and post-meditation.

The consequences of *shamatha* meditation must therefore manifest themselves in ordinary life. In this context mindfulness becomes linked to any activity we are currently carrying out, not merely breathing as during the formal exercise. In fact, every specific, lived circumstance in our lives always corresponds to the background of a very basic sensori-motor embodiment, which can always provide an analogous role as breathing. Thus, if I sit in a café and order coffee, there is the smell steaming from the cup, the hot sensation on my hands as I pick it up and the sensations of thirst and pleasure the taste of the beverage provides. This bodily field furnishes the anchoring point for mindfulness and the synchronization between where I am here and now, and the rest of my inner life: thoughts, emotions and phantasies. This is why it is often said that a seasoned practitioner can be detected easily by a certain precision in his daily activities: he avoids "living in the head", as it is popularly said.

In every moment of life, our senses are there, just as we are in constant relation with the world. We actually use our lived body as a reference point in order to maintain a dialogue between the *shamatha* exercise as such and ordinary life, the post-meditation. Since practice is directed towards ordinary life, mindfulness must be cultivated in each of the gestures of daily life, in the field of immediate perception. The objective is to cultivate stability, "stabilize *shamatha*" as is traditionally expressed, or better, "to succeed" *shamatha*. It is by no means a matter of meditative acrobatics, but rather of apperceiving the capacity of mindfulness in ordinary life.

So, the practice of meditation does not require extraordinary bodily capacities. After all, one submits to the same kind of *apprenticeship* with respect to other aptitudes. For example, musical aptitudes are not given from the start. Expertise implies repetitive technical sessions, where one learns fingering etc. By regular practice, one can come to play expressively and with mastery. This obviously does not happen in a day, but it is not miraculous: it remains within the scope of every human being.

A possible transformation of the existential position results, from the development of this capacity that we acquire, to insert ourselves into life without the automatic dimension of the natural attitude. Thus a way is cleared towards a state of rest or peace, which corresponds to another possible translation of *shamatha*. Such an interior pacification should not be taken in the sense of a passive state but rather of a quieting that opens onto the possibility of a constant suspension regarding the flux of immediate events.

Point of practice no.2: Vispashyana

The Mahayanist turn is embodied very clearly on the level of practice. As we already said, one of the fundamental discoveries of the Mahayanist tradition consists in accounting for the pragmatic efficacy of intersubjectivity. Here, we discover the importance of practice as description or test of completely immediate experience, and move into a description from within active life; in the course of this we evoke the capacity for benevolence, sympathy and empathy, in short, the ability to abandon a self-centered point of reference and cultivate a more vast and more encompassing non-referentiality. But let us be clear from the outset that here the practices proper to the Mahayana level are described in a more encapsulated form than *shamatha*. *Shamatha*, defined as quiescence or calm and stable attention, is not unique to Buddhism. Indeed, *shamatha* so defined is a basic practice of yoga pre-dating the Buddha. So both *shamatha* and its suspension of action are not original to Shakyamuni. Rather, it is *vipashyana* that is the most original step proposed by the Buddha, that is, it is the analytic and panoramic insight into the moment-to-moment arising of mental states, with *shamatha* as its foundation. It is this form of meditation – *shamatha* combined with *vipashyana* – that the Buddha takes up after abandoning asceticism and that leads to his enlightenment.

It is perhaps easier to examine how this change of perspective is reflected at the level of sitting practice itself. It can be stated thus: the gradual transformation of *shamatha* into the closely connected practice of *vipashyana* or awareness so that one often speaks about the entire technique as *shamatha/vispashyana* (mindfulness/awareness) practice (Namgyal 1986), encompassing both the meditation and post-meditation experience. *Vipashyana* is customarily translated in English by "insight meditation", which one can render in French by the expression "conscience panoramique". In Tibetan, the term is *laktong*, which means literally "superior seeing" and which can also be expressed as "spacious gaze".

Vipashyana as practice is based on relaxing the relatively tight grip of the *shamatha* technique into a more free or floating awareness, which is accompanied by a sharpened vividness. The larger field of view makes it possible to examine all of our experience in minute detail. It is important to notice that space is a central notion in *vipashyana*, since the entire exercise is predicated on a de-centering of one's position, an expansion of one's attentional scope. This spaciousness is inseparable from its quality of sharper intellectual acuity or clarity. Thus space and clarity are two of the main experiential correlates of the *Mahayana* path in all its stages.

Point of practice no.3: Tonglen *and empathy*

The main consequence of *vipashyana* is during post-meditation periods, in ordinary life. The opportunity here is the following: in the same way that one can cultivate a quality of mindfulness, one can also *cultivate* a capacity for identification with the other. Assuredly, such empathy (*Einfühlung*) is not foreign to us. All the same, the accent here is placed on the fact that one can cultivate it in a way that is analogous to the exercise of mindfulness. Still, the stabilization of mindfulness is an absolutely necessary but not sufficient condition for acquiring this capacity of empathic identification. On the contrary, unless one mobilizes the interpersonal dimension beyond one's boundaries, the expansiveness of *vipashyana* is not possible. In some basic sense, the Mahayanic motivation for working with others is also a pragmatic part of the exercise, not an uncontextualized aspiration.

To this effect, at least two techniques have been added to *shamatha* practice. On the one hand, there is this type of practice called *tonglen*, which consists, as we just said, in cultivating the capacity for empathy by *putting oneself in the place of the other,* by means of visualization exercises. This can take a completely literal form of a phenomenological exercise of "imaginary variation": how would I feel, what feelings would I have, if I was in the place of X? *Tonglen* presents itself then as a method for maintaining a capacity of active identification. But *tonglen* can also take a much more abstract form that consists, beginning with the attitude of suspension, in making emerge, or better, surge forth, this capacity of empathy in a much less structured manner. As this is quite difficult, one always maintains, in the techniques of *tonglen* a circulation between the abstract level of *Einfühlung* as the field of experience and the more concrete level where the life of others in quite precise situations is evoked, for example, motivated by singular events, lived by the people surrounding us (Shantideva 1996; Trungpa 1993).

The second technique, which accompanies *tonglen,* is the practice of a guide of behavior, an ethical guide, called *lojong* or "moral behavior". It is not a matter of morality in the sense of imperative and arbitrary *a priori* principles, but rather of an ethical behavior allowing certain values to be cultivated; these are typically the values of altruism, of solidarity, by which one puts oneself in service of others. In other words, it is an ethic that serves as a guide by profiting from maxims. In all of the Mahayanist training, the apprenticeship of these rules of ethical behavior is essential.

The conceptual foundation of *Mahayana* consists in giving expression to the *expansivity* met with in *vipashyana* and *tonglen* practice. Such an expansivity is crystallized in the concept of emptiness or *sunyata,* which is *the* theme in the Buddhist tradition (Varela 2000). There is an enormous literature on this subject, and it would be impossible to claim to offer a summary of these extremely rich works. Let us be content to emphasize that *sunya* should not be understood as a solely intellectual way. It is above all something noted experientially that leads us to the fact that *the field of experience in suspension does not have a finite horizon.* Actually, this field can always go further: it is endowed with a potential of space, or expansion. One notes it by the fact that the horizon of the experiential field is never fettered, never limited. The metaphor of space does not lead back to space in the literal, objective, physical sense of the term, but to a space interior to the possible radiating of experience, which irradiates from the intimate consciousness of each person. Such is the firsthand, personal, and intersubjective experience of persons that have long practiced assiduously, or who have a gift for this: the space of experience, inextricably interior and exterior, does not stop enlarging itself in amplitude and intensity and such an enlargement is inexhaustible.

Point of practice no.4: Natural spontaneity as second spontaneity

In the Vajrayanist framework, *sunyata* undergoes a transformation of meaning, which consists in examining such an emptiness inside-out, that is, as the *origin* of all possible experience. The matrix of experience harbors an indefinite and non-masterable generativity, an inexhaustible causal density. By inverting things, this space is in reality the basis from which everything surges outward. Thus it is said in this tradition that *sunyata* contains a pouring out of the void and a pouring of spontaneous manifestation or generation. In Tibetan, one uses the term *lundrup*, which actually designates what appears completely alone, spontaneously (Dudjom Rinpoche 1986; Namgyal 1986).

When one considers things in this way, every appearance, every experience has a somewhat magical side. It always appears accompanied by the surprise that is part of its mode of appearance. Such is the inexhaustible dimension of the generativity of the origin of all experience, which emphasizes the link that exists between this aspect of *sunyata* and the capacity for creativity, namely, the aptitude of cultivating an intuition beginning with given situations. This last aspect of *sunyata*, as origin of the genesis of experience, is very developed in the *dzogchen-mahamudra* school. Since experience in expansion manifests itself spontaneously, one can abandon all method and cultivate this "letting-go" in every way. One remains quite simply in a fundamental rest, without nonetheless losing the suspensive gaze born from *shamatha*, doubled from the Mahayanist attitude. What then is cultivated is *the accomplishment* of the way, namely the enjoyment of rest and of relaxation.

With the schools of Vajrayanist practice – whose technical procedures we have not detailed here – one rapidly approaches what the practice of transformation and exploration of experience harbors of the ineffable. One reaches the limit of what can be said, namely, the heart of experience in its apophantic dimension (Sells 1994). Exactly because there is no longer any possible determination, no more seeking, no more descriptions of invariants, no longer the way of practice. One is at the edge of the unsayable, a recurring term in certain Western spiritual traditions (in particular, in the negative mystical theology). The practitioners who teach this kind of practice always pay extreme attention that the basis of the practice, *shamatha*, be firm, and that the numerous years of Mahayanist practice equally contribute to stabilizing the relation to the others. These two periods are indispensable before one can adventure, without risk, into this more radical, but at the same time more attractive, strongly aesthetic gesture of letting-go.

7.4. Relating back to other motivations

Having made this (too) quick survey of some essential points of the disciplined exploration of experience in the Buddhist tradition, it is now necessary to make some remarks in connection to our two previous motivations: research (in Cognitive Neuroscience and Introspective Psychology) and Phenomenology.

Practice of shamatha sitting meditation and introspective psychology

It could be said that a seasoned *shamatha* practitioner is a trained observer. Although his natural habitat is not the laboratory, nothing goes against the possibility of transforming his first-hand account into a corpus of phenomenal data. In this sense the limits and possibility of a corpus of knowledge based on first-hand access finds in *Abbhidharma* a high standard, which is one of the reasons we felt it was necessary to include this chapter here. No other human tradition has for so long, so explicitly, and so clearly accumulated a body of first-hand descriptions.

Aside from the opportunity of transformation given to all practitioners, we also find in this tradition an intellectual test that accompanies suspension. Such a test of experience "under reduction" unveils or expresses the discovery of certain essential structures of experience. These structural invariants have been formulated in a corpus called *Abbidharma*, which is presented as a descriptive phenomenological psychology accumulated by the tradition. The basic manual, the *Abbhidharmakosa* of Vasubandhu (literally, the *Treasury of Abbhidharma*) is of great complexity (Vasubandhu 1980). Without an oral commentary that gives meaning to its multiple categories, it remains very dry (Trungpa 1989). Among the most important established descriptions three should be mentioned here:

First, the constitution of a mental moment in the present through the so-called five *skandas*, or heaps. These heaps of events arise from a formless background into a basic dual form, followed by feeling tone, perception-action, discursive and conceptual constitution to culminate in a unified space of mind or consciousness.

Next is the very important analysis of the manner in which the mental events deployed in time lead normally to a solidification of the self-other distinction and to a craving of the object, which is the source of the wildness and drowsiness encountered in practicing *shamatha*. This process of intentional identification starts with any encounter ("contact") and proceeds through a causal chain of cognitive events known as the chain of *nidanas*, which recur cyclically (Varela et al. 1991). In this sense it is interesting to see that the Buddhist meditators discovered the vector of intentionality in conscious temporality at the very core of the human mind, as would be the case, starting with Brentano and Husserl, centuries later in the West.

Finally, another discovery is described in the Abbhidharma under the form of mental factors that are the universal invariants accompanying *all* acts of consciousness. The permanent mental factors include "contact", attention, and feeling-tone. Given the extensive development in the cultivation of attention, for example, it is quite clear that seasoned practitioners are ideal subjects for experiments seeking neuro-cognitive correlates. In fact, the extensive use of permanent "mental factors" such as attention are more and more frequently used in third-person studies to study their difference from sensory and motor events, as we mentioned it in Chapter 4. The study of both mental states and traits acquired through practice by means of empirical correlates is an open research program, with few results so far, but which holds an enormous promise (Lutz et al. 2002).

Meditative practice of the three yanas and the phenomenological ways of the reduction

We have sketched out the links between the first-person descriptions proposed in the *Abbhidharma*, which are grounded on *shamatha* meditative practice, and the constitution of an empirical psycho-phenomenology of an introspective type, completely intentional (distinguishing between the act and the content of consciousness) and eidetic (proceeding to a categorization of experience by extracting the invariants). It is striking to note that Husserl distinguished – we detailed this in Chapter 6 – three principal ways of the experience of the reduction, which correspond astonishingly well to the three *yanas* (*Hina-*, *Maha-*, *Vajra-*) of Tibetan Buddhism. Bringing out the homologies between these culturally distinct ways or paths implies leaving the phenomenological plane of a first-person psychology, whether it be intentional or eidetic; as we have shown in the second part of Chapter 6, we must take into account the transcendental dimension of experience by situating the phenomenological reduction on this level of radicality. It is there that the dynamic of the act of becoming aware receives its maximal amplitude, that is, its own proper, non-dual and plastic ontology, by which the dualizing traps of reflexivity are definitively eliminated; these traps always lead, in the last instance, to a unilateral ontology opposing subject and object.

Convergences

The ways of the reduction and the Tibetan *yanas* thus have a double common base. 1) A radical suspension of the natural attitude, which is both the first phase of the practice of *shamatha* and the inaugural gesture of the *epoche* in Phenomenology; 2) the structural categorization of experience by means of a series of invariants; this, in the Abbhidharma is completely within the framework of the *eidetic* reduction.

In both cases there are differentiated methods, made up of phases in which we have to stay for the time necessary for the assimilation and apprenticeship of this knowledge of self that is working on the self (Bugault 1968/1982). The phenomenologist, like the Buddhist, carries out paths (*Wege/yanas*) that are just as much progressive accesses to detachment as they are cultivated practices of calm. To each *yana* thus corresponds a form of phenomenological reduction, which presents a consciousness intensified by degrees, both more dense and more irradiant.

1. The egological path and Hinayana. To the practice of stabilization of the mind (*shamatha*) corresponds the conversion of attitude by which the natural ego, naively immersed in an activity, makes a return to itself in order to consider itself as ego, center, pole, or axis of what it has experienced. Egoic consciousness rendered thematic in this way is nonetheless not cut off from its natural environment: it is more receptive as it is discovered as "put back on an axis": it has (re)found its point of reference by re-centering itself on itself. But there is a certain price to pay for this re-centering of consciousness on its egoic axis: a radical methodological solitude, a solipsism that fills the same function as the life-long engagement of the monks of the "little vehicle" (*Hina-yana*).

Still, such a centered consciousness is necessary for the deepening of the practice of calm and of presence to self. Neither in Buddhism nor in Husserlian phenomenology is the ego denied or rejected (*a fortiori* deconstructed) in favor of a totally disintegrated consciousness, made of states or lived experiences without internal connection. The ego has its place, but a relativized place. The polarization of consciousness is thus irreducible. It is precisely such a non-negational relativization that these two other *yanas* use as do the two other forms of reduction.

2. The intersubjective path and Mahayana. In Mahayana Buddhism, as in Husserlian phenomenology, intersubjectivity plays an essential role by virtue of the decentering of the ego: whether it is a matter of empathy (*Einfühlung*) or of compassion (*tonglen*), in both cases there is the same movement of consciousness which consists in putting oneself in the place of the other by developing a form of active identification with the other. In the Husserlian context, empathy takes place by what is called an analogical transfer experienced in others: I directly perceive the body of the other and I maintain an immediate interior relation to my own psychical experiences. The direct perception that others have of my body leads me to apprehend the other – according to a lived analogy experienced by myself – as depository of this same organic "body-mind" totality that I experience in myself. Such an empathy originates in the immediate resemblance of our two bodies and is deployed in parallel on the mode of a transposition in imagination (*Hineinphantasieren*) in the other's psychic lived experience. Just as Mahayana appeals, in order to develop the propensity to compassion, to exercises of imaginative visualization of others, in Husserl's work imagination contributes in a decisive way to favoring this sensory inscription into the other: empathy is only possible on the basis of this imaginative transference (Depraz 1995: Chapter III; Varela & Depraz 2001; Depraz & Varela 2002a).

But this empathy is not solely unilateral, founded on the a-symetical connection of an ego-*princeps* and an alter-ego made a satellite to the ego. If every egoic consciousness constitutes itself seemingly *via* this relation of empathetic resemblance with each consciousness, it is because there is an inter-empathetic intersubjectivity through which each situated person puts him- or herself in the place of an other. In order to designate this expansive space of mutual empathy, Husserl speaks of an "intersubjective reduction" which contributes *a fortiori* to decentering the ego from itself, since it thus enlarges its interior space to that of each other person. Why an "intersubjective *reduction*"? Because, even if there is a necessary solitude in the performance of the suspension and conversion, it is admittedly essential to share the intuitive evidence acquired while alone in the framework of a community of subjects (Depraz 1995: Chapter IV). Such an inter-empathetic multiplication of the subjective space of the reductive act is not without evoking the panoramic consciousness that one acquires by yoking together *vipashyana* and *tonglen* in *Mahayana*.

3. *The ontological path of the life-world and Vajrayana.* Such an intimate space in expansion is embodied in the sensory everyday world where we act and are affected. This world, which is the practical world of our life, deploys and engenders an embodied spatiality whose horizon is indefinitely extended, to the extent that the interlacing of my home-world (*Heimwelt*) and the alien-worlds (*fremde Welten*) that border on my world become interlaced (Husserl 1973a: n.27, n.35, Appendix XLVIII; 1993: n.4, 2), n.6, 1)). In this sense, we as

egoic consciousnesses coincide with the sensory world in which we live; we marry it to the degree of our action in it.

But such a coincidence is not the immersion or imprisonment in the world that corresponds to the natural attitude. There we might speak of a "second coincidence" or of a "second spontaneity", by which I am closer to the world at the very moment when I am absolutely disinterested (*unbeteiligt*) with respect to it. Or better: the more I am detached *vis-à-vis* the actions that I pursue in the heart of the world (from their finality), the more I marry them in their own dynamic. From this point of view, we can say that the path of the life-world corresponds completely to the inscription of *shamatha* practice in post-meditative everyday life and contains the accents – disinterest, detachment – that are not without resemblance in structure to the attitude of letting-go proper to *Vajra-yana*.

The limits of the homology
After having indicated these remarkable points of convergence between the Husserlian and Tibetan progressive ways, we cannot fail to perceive also what differentiates them. The major line of demarcation resides in the finality that is proposed: while Buddhism gives primacy to a *soteriological* end of freeing from suffering and engages, in order to do this, an attention to the body, an ethics and a practice, the phenomenological movement, at least the Husserlian one, has an essentially *gnoseological* goal which culminates in a consciousness of self, others, and the world. Such a difference, without forbidding bridges – we saw this in the first Part of the work – explains certain accents, or omissions.

1. The status of the body. We begin with the phenomenological non-thematization of the corporeal posture required in order to accomplish the reduction: would this non-thematization be an index of an absence of the practice of this? Certainly the ego serves as an axis of re-centering structuring consciousness: but it appears that only the interior attitude of suspension and of conversion is shared with the practice of *shamatha*: neither the bodily posture, nor the mediation of respiration, which serves in the meditative practice as a concrete re-centering on oneself, are thematized.

One could respond by saying that this practice, being actually practiced, is not thematized in Phenomenology, but that only the theorized exposition of different levels of experience is. It is true that the body is disposed in such a way that it accompanies and serves as support for a disposition of the mind, which one stays with alone in the Husserlian formalization. Is this to say that the body is denied? It would be more exact to say that it is neutralized: the bodily "technique" is not to be thematized for its own sake if this does not open onto a complete transformation of self of which the mind alone forms the vector. If the practical (technical) incline of the reduction is set aside here, it is to the advantage of its discursive explicitation. In Merleau-Ponty's works, of course, we can find the mooring in corporeality thematized, but it is astonishing to note that such a bodily accent is then carried to the detriment of any thematization of the reduction, including in its practical and empirical procedurality (Depraz 1998b, 2002).

2. Empathy and compassion. In the same way, the Husserlian conception of intersubjectivity remains essentially situated on a cognitive level, an inter-cognitive level of sharing of acts of consciousness and, notably, of the reductive act; it does not thematize an ethic of compassion or the affective disposition of a type of sympathy. In this respect, we find developments in more greater affinity with the ethico-practical content of the Mahayanist descriptions in the material ethics of M. Scheler, who gives primacy to the feeling of sym-pathy; regarding this, we can speak of an "emotional intuitionalism" (Scheler 1986), parallel to Husserl's gnoseological intuitionism, specifically in the immemorial exposition of the Other in Levinas' work, which corresponds to a sort of radical ethics of compassion (Levinas 1978; Pitkin 2001), or better, in the affective immanence of Henryian "pathos-with" (Henry 1990).

Still, here as well, even with respect to the body, the insistence placed in these authors' works on an affective and pathic intersubjectivity automatically leaves in the cloud the *interaffective reduction itself as a concrete operation.* Could it be that the concrete embodiment of the reduction cannot be described in any way? In any case, it seems that all of the post-Husserlians we have mentioned have seen there an impossibility, and have tied the fortunes of the reduction to that of theorization. Even Heidegger inscribes himself in this exclusionary logic: it requires the hermeneutic perspicuity of eminent commentators to reveal in the *Stimmungen* of anxiety or of boredom the thematized places in the text where the reduction is at work. In each case, as with corporeity, the reduction is never described by the abovementioned phenomenologists in its affective, ethical, or inter-pathetic pragmatics. Truly, Husserl sometimes describes an inter-affective intersubjectivity, thus making of empathy a compassion of an ethical type:

> In this world, human beings exercise on each other 'spiritual influences', they enter into contact on the mental plane, they act on each other (...) By having compassion, by rejoicing with another, I do not suffer simply as myself, but it is the suffering of the other that lives in my suffering or, even better put,

inversely, I am absorbed in the other and I live in his life and, in particular, I suffer his suffering (Husserl 1973b: n.13, §9).

However, he himself falls under the blow of this critique, in the sense that, when he thematized the intersubjective reduction, he treated it as a particular case of cognitive act, namely, as a sort of inter-cognitive act and does not reconnect it to the singular reductive dimension that it still manifestly contains (Depraz 1999a).

3. Non-dualist ontology of letting-go and the disinterest of the spectator: The danger of methodism. The ontological path of the life-world doubtlessly allows one to develop a *second-order* spontaneity of each daily gesture, which explains why our attitude at the heart of the sensory world resembles the natural attitude while distinguishing itself finely by a specific, non-reflexive *epoche* situated in the bloom of the world, an *epoche* well named as by A. Schutz a "natural *epoche*", or a "counter *epoche*". In so doing one is very close to the spontaneity naturally cultivated in the framework of *Vajrayana*, and also to the abandonment of all method, which always leads, in the last analysis, to the subject-object distinction or to a duality between the one who has access to and the thing to which one has access. Certainly one finds the beginnings of such a movement in the non-dual correlation of the aprioris that are subjectivity and world in the *Crisis*. Such a path, radically freed of the duality of spectator and of spectacle, could correspond to the Tibetan diamond path, which does not deny the other but leads the spectator (like the spectacle) back to themselves, that is to say as relative phases. This is true, then, of a non-dual ontology undamaged by any reflexive temptation. In this respect, Fink's *Sixth Cartesian Meditation* is doubtless the one that went furthest along such a path. This includes what he proposed in a later manuscript of 1934 (Ms. Z-XIV V/3a: Bruzina 1992: 286–287, n.19), that is, a structural comparison between phenomenology and Buddism: "Das System des sich vollendenden Geistes, I. Teil: Kosmologie (Demonstration); II. Teil: Phänomenologie des Geistes (Reduktion); III. Teil: Meontische Kosmogonie (Spekulation). In der Sprache der alten Metaphysik, I. Kosmologie, II. Psychologie, III. Theologie; in der Sprache des Buddhismus: I. Lehre vom Samsâra; II. Der siebenfache Weg; III. Lehre vom Nirvâna." It goes to the point of perceiving the ineffable character, the mutism (*Sprachlosikeit*) of the spectator (Fink 2000: §10), despite all of the dualist – hyperreflexive – ambiguities that allow the revindication of a "phenomenologizing spectator", radicalizing the Husserlian disinterested spectator (Depraz 1997: 113–135). In this regard, one would need the dexterity of the Merleau-Ponty of the *Phe-*

nomenology of Perception in order to re-capture what he calls hyper-reflection as the very genesis of the unreflected.

Where are we?

We have come to the end of this fourth and last dimension of our survey of the different motivations for the study of human experience with a method. This has been an amazing Chapter in that we have introduced an important set of traditions: the human wisdom tradition and the practices of human transformation they have bequeathed us. Furthermore, among those we have chosen to formulate in detail, only the Buddhist tradition of *shamatha/vispashyana* is exemplary. Since this tradition is still quite alien to most western readers, an extra effort had to be made to provide the historical context, describe in detail the relevant practices, and make attempts to link them back to both introspection and philosophy. We hope the reader has borne with us in what might have seemed, at points, foreign material. However, the vocation of Part I was to provide a universal structural analysis of reduction as a *praxis*, and these wisdom traditions could not therefore have been absent as background.

Open conclusion

The "finality" of the act of becoming aware and the stakes of our venture

The difficulty of executing a work with several authors shows up here not only in the precarious and fragile unity of the discourse and its form. It also comes from the confrontation of distinct fields or disciplines whose problem-spaces and stakes are clearly heterogeneous.

The wager taken by a work like this one is to try to preserve the differences, even the disagreements, (which are obvious in the second Section), and to see the encounter as a mutual intensification. In the first section we elaborate a description of an act, that of becoming aware, that is apparently irreducible to the specific fields we represent, in short, that transcends them, but that draws its potentiality from each of them.

In this respect it is interesting to note that none of the authors can claim to dominate completely the fundamental stakes, or better, the multiple partial stakes of our enterprise. This means that this work is truly the integral non-summative resultant of multiple interactions between individual abilities; its scope goes beyond that of each individual author.

The thesis of this book, the unified description of the structural dynamics of the act of becoming aware in its procedural, (i.e., both operative and performative), dimension, may be pertinent to our readers in itself. Yet the work nevertheless opens up multiple trajectories because of the plurality of fields mobilized in order to produce it. The authors share these trajectories, although each of us is implicated by them in differing ways and to varying degrees.

We can list at least three types of ends that refer both to fields or disciplines and to distinct intellectual communities to which our readers might belong:

1. Empirical stakes, which concern the possibility of using this description of the act of becoming aware in the fields of neurobiology and cognitive psychology. In this case the application re-articulates the relation between epistemological model and laboratory experimentation. It argues for the fecundity of first-person accounts or descriptions, sustained by internal intuitive criteria that function as a necessary dimension correlative to an objectifying third-person description. How is the mode of objectivity of neurobiological or psychological data modified when we also take into account the way in which the subject grasps, in the first person, the subjective phenomenal experience of the experimental task?

In this first case the end is clearly of an epistemological nature. The subjective dimension of experience has a role to play in the re-evaluation of scientific objectivity. On these grounds the requirements of expression and validation of the act of becoming aware are not optional, but necessary.

2. Practical stakes, that concern both practitioners of cognition as well as religious or spiritual practitioners. In this case the end of the act of becoming aware is not external, but strictly internal. It is the accomplishment of the act itself, with its different stages, that constitutes the inner goal of the description in question.

In respect to this, one might ask the question of the self-sufficiency of the practice itself. To what extent does a practitioner need a dynamical model for becoming aware when he experiences it intensely in everyday life activities and is nourished by the experience? There are two types of response to this question: either one considers that living is sufficient and that one is not required to question one's experience epistemologically or philosophically since it is complete unto itself; or one thinks that any embodied practice, whatever its content may be, *is always improved on* by being captured by thought, that it becomes richer as it becomes more intelligible to the person experiencing it. From this perspective the model we propose can act as a trigger for a better comprehension of our experience, and this doubtless leads to changes in how we live.

3. Philosophical stakes, which benefit tremendously from the re-innervation of experience afforded by the dialogue with the positive or empirical realms and from the resources provided by a praxis of experience. Whether he is interested in the fine and immanent description of lived experience, or in its categorial formalization in the framework of an eidetic comprehension, the philosopher gains by the confrontation with the empirical world and by the test of *praxis*. Could there be a better way to give concepts their fullest intelligibility, their true effectiveness, and to guard against speculative extravagance? Philosophers are concept-inventors: this descriptive model of the act of becoming aware presents them with a challenging new space for reflection and food for thought on a renewed conceptualization of experience.

In this third possible context for our model, the end is both descriptive, if one is centered in the phenomenological tradition of philosophy, and, more generally, categorial.

Nonetheless, even if the stakes of each discipline may be specified, each of these ends will be fertile and propulsive for a specific field of research if, and only if, it enters into resonance with another field that allows it to develop new questions from its own perspective. Thus, the renewal of objectivity in the framework of the empirical sciences *via* the recognition of internal or subjective experience comes from an interplay with phenomenology viewed as psycho-phenomenology; an improved understanding of a practice comes from taking into consideration the philosophical and epistemological reconceptualization of this immanent activity; the re-mooring of philosophical speculation to experience that gives the concepts their full validity comes from the fruitful confrontation of practical and empirical fields.

The different stakes we have mentioned, reviewed in the light of this interdisciplinary methodology of mutual or co-intensification, are thus constrained, i.e., inevitably potentialized by the formulations coming from other realms.

Thus, our view of the interaction between disciplines is not one of instrumentalization. Rather, each field functions in relation to the others, generating fresh questions for itself. Or better, if there is instrumentalization it is reciprocal (co-instrumentalization), to the degree that the means/end relation is neutralized in favor of a mutual circulation or co-genesis of questions and concepts.

Postface

While this work was in gestation one of its authors was seriously ill: his decline in health was slow and expected, yet at the same time brutal and shocking. This gives the book its specific emotional tone: through long periods of discussion and then at the different stages of writing, we shared the imminence of the possible disappearance, at any moment, of one of our group. This gave each of our meetings an unparalleled intensity: the quality of our exchanges was intensified to a degree that is rare in theoretical discussions. Between us there was a complicity, a tacit, but often explicit sharing of the approaching loss. This resulted, surprisingly, in an infinite lightness, a grace and plasticity in our interactions that, in my opinion, is never attained in ordinary moments. For here, we had the gift of sharing this extraordinary time, a time whose density was equal to the gravity of the experience one of us was going through: the radical state of expectation, between life and death, when awaiting a liver transplant; the absolute expectation of the end, between death and life. One question haunted me: would we be able to finish this shared exploration before Francisco gave "death back its rights", as he wrote a year before his death in a magnificent and troubling account of his experience of the transplant, entitled "Intimate distances. Fragments for a Phenomenology of Organ Transplantation" (Thompson 2001)?

Francisco died at home in Paris on May 28th, 2001, at dawn. He was born on the 7th of September 1946 in Chile. He received his M.Sc. in Biology in 1967 from the University of Chile in Santiago, where he studied with the neurobiologist Humberto R. Maturana. In 1968 he undertook graduate work at Harvard University, and returned to Chile with his doctorate in 1970. There he resumed work with Maturana, and between 1970–1973 they developed the theory of *autopoiesis*. After the military coup he fled to the United States where he taught and did research for 5 years at the University of Colorado, before returning to Chili from 1980–1985. In 1986 he came to France to join the CREA (Centre de Recherche en Epistémologie Appliquée), and from there became a Director of Research at the CNRS (Centre National de Recherche Scientifique) in 1988.

From its very roots his project was one of a re-vision of the living in terms of what he called "*auto-poiesis*": the organism as a self-regulating identity coupled with the surrounding world as it is laid out in *The Tree of Knowledge: The Biological Roots of Human Understanding* (1987). This initial intuition is developed in *Principles of Biological Autonomy* (1979), and in the context of cognitive neuroscientific theories of the dynamics of emergence. Francisco refuted the validity of the computationalist hypothesis upheld by reductive cognitivist perspectives, which claims that the mind may be reduced to an ensemble of sub-personal and disembodied symbolic processes. As a theoretician of biological phenomena, he devoted himself to the study of dynamical or emergent properties, elaborating a theory of consciousness that links the emergence of the conscious mind to the body as organism, and that asserts the irreducibility of mind to any organic substrate. His search for a theory of embodied cognition leads him to take emergence on an even more radical path, giving precedence to action, know-how and to praxis as what define us as living beings in the world. This is the paradigm of enaction as it is developped in *The Embodied Mind: Cognitive Science and Human Experience*, co-written with Evan Thompson and Eleanor Rosch (1991), an alternative view to cognition based on minds as symbolic or representational systems. The *action* of enaction is both the active coupling of the embodied cognitive agent with the world, as well as its autonomous functioning as an autopoietic or self-producing identity. It is thus with enaction that Francisco recast the theory of mind and living phenomena.

This emergent dynamical perspective finds a natural partner for dialogue with the phenomenology of Husserl and Merleau-Ponty on the status of consciousness. A deep affinity with the immanentist paradigm developed by Merleau-Ponty in *The Phenomenology of Perception* and *The Visible and the Invisible* precedes a profound confrontation with Husserl's later work in genetic phenomenology.

Convinced of the irreducibility of consciousness to causal explanations (neural correlates), Varela's neurophenomenological approach to consciousness gives first-person methodologies a central role. Here the experimental subject's first-person account of his experience is integrated with the "objective" data on his neural functioning: his article "Neuro-phenomenology of consciousness: A remedy for the hard problem" (1996b) provides a first framework, whereas the Special Issue of the *Journal of Consciousness Studies: The view from within. First person methodologies*, co-edited by Francisco J. Varela and Jonathan Shear (1999) lays out the whole research project.

What characterizes neurophenomenology are the "*generative* mutual constraints" that regulate the interaction between phenomenology and empirical neurobiology. This idea is best developed in his article "The Naturalization of Phenomenology as the Transcendence of Nature. Searching for generative mutual constraints"(1997). Instead of maintaining a static and isomorphic parallelism between subjective or experiential data and empirical neurobiological correlates, the idea is to see how they are interwoven, and how this interrelation benefits both the experiential and the empirical approaches. Francisco puts this co-generative methodology to the test in articles devoted to the experience of time: "Present Time-consciousness" (1999) and in "The Specious present: A neuro-phenomenology of time-consciousness" (1999b), published in the volume he co-edited with Jean Petitot, Jean-Michel Roy and Bernard Pachoud, *Naturalizing Phenomenology*. In this article he meticulously confronts Husserl's phenomenology of time-consciousness with recent experimental results on non-linear dynamics of time. His study confirms Husserl's intuition on the genetics of the living present and at the same time actualizes its formulation, radically recasting the static diagram of time originally proposed by the founder of phenomenology. Another group of articles takes up the question of affective and emotional experience, and its specific, i.e. self-anticipatory temporality, either in Francisco J. Varela and Natalie Depraz "At the source of time: valence and the constitutional dynamics of affect" (1999) or in Natalie Depraz and Francisco J. Varela "Au cœur du temps: l'auto-antécédance", in three parts, respectively submitted to *Etudes phénoménologiques*, *Intellektika* and *Raisons pratiques.*

But Francisco's philosophical project is not exclusively epistemological. The restyled epistemology he is searching for is diametrically opposed to objectivist or reductionist positivism. It is rooted in a particular ontology, the one offered by Buddhist thought, which gives primacy to non-substantiality, or, in more equivocal terms, to "emptiness", viewed as the dense interdependence of all things in the universe. "Pour une phénoménologie de la *sunyata* I" (2000), published in: *La gnose, une question philosophique* co-edited by N. Depraz and J.-Fr. Marquet, develops such a radical view at a refined pragmatic level. This radically non-substantialist ontology finds echos in the Heideggerian quest for being as nothing (*Nichts*). One may also say that the primacy of non-duality in Buddhist metaphysics is in affinity with the refusal of any nature/mind dualism expressed explicitly at the origin of Hussel's phenomenological project. It is therefore clear how Francisco's epistemological research finds its natural (non)-grounding in an ontology of nothing as understood and practiced in Buddhist thought. Moreover, in his latest work "Radical Embodiment. Neural Dynamics and Conscious Experience" (2001), co-written with Evan Thompson, he attempts an epistemological reformulation of this natural spontaneous gener-

ativity, elaborating the notion of a double causality which involves both up-
ward (emergent or local to global), and downward (global to local) causation.
This double movement accounts not only for the irreducibility of consciousness to neural substrates, but also for the effective capacity of consciousness to
constrain the functioning of the neural dynamic itself.

Finally, Buddhism, before being an ontology or a metaphysics, is seen primarily as a practice or a pragmatics. This is certainly an innovative aspect
of Francisco's work: the experience of the non-duality of mind and nature
as delineated in the phenomenology of Husserl and Merleau-Ponty, the co-
generativity of consciousness and neural substrates as revealed experimentally,
are radically put to the test of the practical phenomenology for examining
consciousness that is Buddhist sitting practice.

The rootedness in experiential pragmatics offered by Buddhist meditation
makes both the phenomenological as well as the scientific approach more concrete, furnishing an experiential base that both approaches lack. Francisco and
I interweave these three threads of investigation in the context of our essay on
imagination, "Imagining: Embodiment, Phenomenology and transformation"
(2002), published by A. Wallace in a volume called *Breaking the ground: Essays
on Tibetan Buddhism and the Natural Sciences*. Our intention is for *On Becoming Aware* to provide the synthetic platform for this type of inter-disciplinary
integration.

Francisco will never see this book *published*. He will never hold it in his
hands; but he is so intensely present in every line that its publication perpetu-
ates the extraordinarily attentive presence he embodied for his friends and that
he will no doubt instill in his readers.

N. D.

References

Althusser, Louis (1963). *Pour Marx*. Paris: Maspero.
Argyris, Chris & A. Donald Schön (1976). *Theory in practice*. San Francisco: Jossey-Bass Publishers.
Aubenque, Pierre (1963). *La prudence chez Aristote*. Paris: PUF.
Avanzini, Guy (1974). *A. Binet: écrits psychologiques et pédagogiques*. Toulouse: Privat.
Bachelard, Gaston (1931/1970). *Etude sur l'évolution d'un problème de physique*. Paris: Vrin.
Batchelor Stephen (1983). *Alone with Others: An Existential Approach to Buddhism*. New York: Grove Press.
Berger, Gaston (1939). Husserl et Hume. *Revue internationale de philosophie, 2*, 342–353.
Bergson, Henry (1927/1985). *Essai sur les données immédiates de la conscience*. Paris: PUF.
Bergson, Henry (1934). *La Pensée et le Mouvant*. Paris: PUF.
Bergson, Henry (1939/1997). *Matière et Mémoire*. Paris: PUF.
Bermudes, José Luis (1998). *The Paradox of Self-Consciousness*. Cambridge: MIT Press.
Bernet, Rudolf (1994). *La vie du sujet*. Paris: PUF.
Binet, Alfred (1894). *Introduction à la psychologie expérimentale*. Paris: Alcan.
Binet, Alfred (1903). *L'étude expérimentale de l'intelligence*. Paris: Costes.
Blankenburg, Wolfgang (1991). *La perte de l'évidence naturelle*. Paris: PUF.
Block, Ned (1996). How can we find the neural correlate of consciousness? *Trends in Neuroscience, 19* (11), 456–459.
Boring, Edwin Garrigues (1953). A History of Introspection. *Psychological Bulletin, 50*, 3, 159-189.
Bourgine, Paul & Francisco Varela (Eds.). (1992). *Towards a Practice of Autonomous Systems: Proceedings of the First European Conference on Artificial Life*. Cambridge: MIT Press.
Brand, Gerd (1955). *Ich, Welt und Zeit*. The Hague: Martinus Nijhoff.
Brentano, Franz (1874). *Die Psychologie vom empirischen Standpunkt*. Leipzig: Duncker & Humblot.
Bruzina, Ronald (1992). Last Philosophy: Ideas for a Transcendental Phenomenological Metaphysics – Eugen Fink with Edmund Husserl, 1928–1938. In *Phenomenology and Indian Philosophy*. New Delhi: Shri Jainendra Press.
Bugault, Guy (1968/1982). *La notion de prajna ou de sapience selon les perspectives du Mahayana: part de la connaissance et de l'inconnaissance dans l'anagogie bouddhique*. Paris: De Boccard.
Burloud, Albert (1927). *La pensée d'après les recherches expérimentales de Watt, Messer, Bühler*. Paris: Alcan.
Burloud, Albert (1938). *Principes d'une psychologie des tendances*. Paris: PUF.

Casey, Edward (1977). Imagination and phenomenological method. In F. Elliston & P. McCormick (Eds.), *Edmund Husserl: Expositions and Appraisals*. South Bend: Notre Dame Press.

Chalmers, David (1995). Facing up to the problem of consciousness. *Journal of Consciousness Studies, 2* (3), 200–219.

Churchland, Patricia S. & Terrence J. Sejnowski (1992). *The Computational Brain*. Cambridge: MIT Press.

Claesges, Ulrich (1972). Epochè. In J. Ritter & K. Gründer (Eds.), *Historisches Wörterbuch der Philosophie*, vol. 2 (pp. 595–596). Basel: Schawbe.

Claparède, Edouard (1934). Genèse de l'hypothèse. *Archives de Psychologie, 24*, 1–155.

Clément, Olivier (Ed.) (1995). *La Philocalie: Les écrits fondamentaux des pères du désert aux pères de l'Eglise (IVème-XIVème siècle)*. Paris: Desclée de Brouwer/J.-Cl. Lattès, 2 volumes.

Cobb-Stevens, Richard (1974). *James and Husserl: The Foundations of Meaning*. The Hague: Martinus Nijhoff.

Cohen, Gillan (1989). *Memory in the Real World*. Hove: Lawrence Erlbaum.

Comte, Auguste (1830/1975). *Philosophie première. Cours de philosophie positive*. Paris: Hermann.

Courtine, Jean-François (1990). L'idée de la phénoménologie et la problématique de la réduction. In: *Heidegger et la phénoménologie*. Paris: Vrin.

Crick, Francis (1994). *The Astonishing Hypothesis*. New York: Scribners.

Crick, Francis (1996). Visual perception: Rivalry and consciousness. *Nature, 379*.

Crick, Francis & Christof Koch (1990). Towards a neurobiological theory of consciousness. *Seminar in Neurosciences, 2*, 263–275.

Damasio, Antonio (1995). *Descartes' Error*. New York: Scribner.

Dantziger, Karl (1990). *Constructing the subject*. Cambridge: CUP.

Dastur, Françoise (1992). De la phénoménologie transcendantale à la phénoménologie herméneutique. In *Paul Ricoeur, les métamorphoses de la raison herméneutique*. Paris: Cerf.

Davidson Richard & Steven Sutton (1994). Affective neuroscience: The emergence of a discipline. *Currrent Opinion in Neurobiology, 5*, 217–224.

De la Garanderie, Antoine (1965). *Comprendre et imaginer*. Paris: Le Centurion.

De la Garanderie, Antoine (1969). *Schématisme et thématisme*. Louvain: Nauwalaerts.

De la Garanderie, Antoine (1989). *Défense et illustration de l'introspection*. Paris: Centurion.

De la Garanderie, Antoine (1990). *Pour une pédagogie de l'intelligence*. Paris: Centurion.

De Muralt, André (1958). *Idée de la phénoménologie: L'exemplarisme husserlien*. Paris: PUF.

Dennett, Daniel (1991). *Consciousness Explained*. Boston: Little, Brown.

Dennett, Daniel & Marcel Kinsbourne (1992). Time and the observer: The where and when of consciousness in the brain. *Behavior and Brain Sciences, 15*, 183–247.

Depraz, Natalie (1993). Naître à soi-même. *Alter, 1*.

Depraz, Natalie & Jean-Marc Mouillie (1993). Se "donner" la mort". *Alter, 1*. Paris.

Depraz, Natalie (1994). De l'altérité dans l'apperception comme structure fondamentale de la conscience: accéder à autrui par son apperception. *Etudes phénoménologiques, 19*, 11–38.

Depraz, Natalie (1995a). Phénoménologie et non-phénoménologie. *Recherches husserliennes, 4*, 3–27.

Depraz, Natalie (1995b). *Transcendance et Incarnation. Le statut de l'intersubjectivité comme altérité à soi chez Edmund Husserl*. Paris: Vrin.

Depraz, Natalie (1996a). La logique génétique husserlienne, quelle logophanie? In J.-Fr. Courtine (Ed.), *Phénoménologie et logique*. Paris: P.E.N.S.

Depraz, Natalie (1996b). Puissance individuante de l'imagination et métamorphose du logique dans *Expérience et jugement*. *Phänomenologische Forschungen*.

Depraz, Natalie (1997). Le spectateur phénoménologisant: au seuil du non-agir et du non-être. In N. Depraz & M. Richir (Eds.), *Eugen Fink, Actes du Colloque de Cerisy-la-Salle 23–30 juillet 1994* (pp. 113-135). Amsterdam: Rodopi.

Depraz, Natalie (1998a). Can I anticipate myself? Temporality and self-affection. In: D. Zahavi (Ed.), *Time, alterity and self-awareness*. Dordrecht: Kluwer.

Depraz, Natalie (1998b). Das Ethos der Reduktion als leibliche Einstellung. In B. Waldenfels & I. Därmann (Eds.), *Der Anspruch des Anderen*. München: Fink Verlag.

Depraz, Natalie (1999a). Phenomenological Reduction as a Praxis. In F. Varela & J. Shear (Eds.). *The View from within: First-person approaches to the study of consciousness*. London: Imprint Academic.

Depraz, Natalie (1999b). *Ecrire en phénoménologue: "une autre époque de l'écriture"*. Fougères: Encre Marine.

Depraz, Natalie (1999c). *Husserl*. Paris: A. Colin.

Depraz, Natalie (2000). Entre Husserl et Derrida: de l'empirisme transcendantal. *Alter, 8*. Paris.

Depraz, Natalie (2001a). *La conscience. Approches croisées: des Classiques aux sciences cognitives*. Paris: A. Colin.

Depraz, Natalie (2001b). *Lucidité du corps. De l'empirisme transcendantal en phénoménologie*. Kluwer: Dordrecht.

Depraz, Natalie (2002), What about the praxis of reduction: Husserl and Merleau-Ponty, L. Embree (Ed.), *Merleau-Ponty's reading of Husserl*. Dordrecht: Kluwer.

Depraz, Natalie & Francisco Varela (2002a). Empathy and Compassion as experiential praxis. Confronting phenomenological analysis and buddhist teachings". In Chang-Fai Cheung & D. Carr (Eds.), forthcoming in the proceedings from the Hong Kong Conference *Space, Time, Culture* (Nov. 2000).

Depraz, Natalie & Francisco Varela (2002b). Au coeur du temps: l'auto-antécédance I, II, III. Respectively submitted to *Etudes phénoménologiques, Intellektica* and *Raisons pratiques*.

Derrida, Jacques (1967). *L'écriture et la différence*. Paris: Seuil.

Derrida, Jacques (1973). *Speech and Phenomena*. Evanston: Northwestern University Press.

Desanti, Jean-Toussaint (1975). *La Philosophie Silencieuse*. Paris: Seuil.

Dewey, John (1922). *Human Nature and Conduct. An Introduction to social psychology*. London: G. Allen and Unwin.

Dilts, Robert (1990). *Spelling Strategy for NLP Practitioners*. Ben Lomond: Dynamic Learning Publications.

Dudjom Rinpoche (1986). *The Nyigma School of Tibetan Buddhism*. London: Wisdom Publishing House.

Dumas, Georges (1923/1924). *Traité de psychologie*. Paris: Alcan.

Dupuy, Jean-Pierre (1993). *Aux Sources des Sciences Cognitives*. Paris: La Découverte.

Ebbinghaus, Hans (1885/1913/1964). *Memory: a Contribution to Experimental Psychology*. Mineola: Dover Publication.

English, Horace Bidwell (1921). In Aid of Introspection. *American Journal of Psychology, 32*, 404–414.

Epstein, Mark (1994). *Thoughts without a Thinker*. New York: Harper.

Ericsson, K. Anders & Herbert Alexander Simon (1984/1993). *Protocol Analysis: Verbal Protocols as Data*. Cambridge: MIT Press.

Fields, Rick (1984). *Crystal Mirror, Volume VII, A Survey of Buddhist History*. Berkeley: Dharma Publishing.

Fields, Rick (1993). *How the Swans came to the Lake: The history of buddhism*. Boston: Shambala.

Fink, Eugen (1974). *De la phénoménologie*. Paris: Minuit.

Fink, Eugen (1994/2000). *Sixth Cartesian Meditation*. Bloomington: Indiana University Press.

Flannagan, Owen (1992). *Consciousness Reconsidered*. Cambridge: Bradford/MIT Press.

Fraisse, Paul & Jean Piaget (1963). *Traité de psychologie expérimentale*, tome 1: *Histoire et méthode*.

Freud, Sigmund (1912). Recommendations to Physicians Practising Psycho-analysis. In: *Complete Works Standard Edition*, vol. 12.

Gallagher, Shaun (1997). Mutual enlightenment: Recent phenomenology and cognitive science. *Journal of Consciousness Studies, 4* (3).

Gallagher, Shaun (1998). *The Inordinance of Time*. Evanston: Northwestern University Press.

Garfield, Jay (1995). *The Fundamental Wisdom of the Middle Way: Nagarjuna's Madhyamikakarika*. New York: Oxford University Press.

Gazzaniga, Michael (Ed.). (1997). *A Handbook of Cognitive Neurosciences*. Cambridge: MIT Press.

Gendlin, Eugene (1962/1997). *Experiencing and the Creation of Meaning: A philosophical and psychological approach to the subjective*. Evanston: Northwestern University Press.

Gil, Fernando (1993). *Traité de l'Evidence*. Grenoble: J. Millon.

Giorgi, Amadeus (1985). The Phenomenological Psychology of Learning and the Verbal Learning Tradition. In A. Giorgi (Ed.), *Phenomenology and Psychological Research*. Pittsburg: Duquesne University Press.

Guenther, Herbert V. & Leslie S. Kawamura (1975). *Mind in Buddhist Psychology*. Emeryville: Dharma Publishing.

Guillaume, Paul (1942). *Manuel de psychologie*. Paris: PUF.

Gupta Bina (1998). *The Disinterested Witness. A Fragment of Advaita Vedanta Phenomenology*. Evanston: Northwestern.

Gusdorf, Georges (1951). *Mémoire et personne*. 2 vols. Paris: PUF.

Hameroff, Stuart, Alfred Kazniak & Alwyn Scott (Eds.). (1996, 1997, 1998, 1999). *Towards a Science of Consciousness* (Tucson I, II, III, IV). Bradford: MIT Press. (http://www.phil.vt.edu/ASSC/).

Heidegger, Martin (1927/1975). *Die Grundprobleme der Phänomenologie*. Frankfurt: Klostermann, GA 24.

Heidegger, Martin (1949). *Holzwege*. Frankfurt/am Main: Klostermann.

Heidegger, Martin (1929-30/1983). *Die Grundbegriffe der Metaphysik, Welt, Endlichkeit, Einsamkeit.* Frankfurt: Klostermann, GA 29/30.

Heidegger, Martin (1927/1984). *Sein und Zeit.* Tübingen: M. Niemeyer.

Henry, Michel (1963). *L'essence de la manifestation.* Paris: PUF.

Henry, Michel (1976). *Marx, I. Une philosophie de la réalité, II. Une philosophie de l'économie.* Paris: Gallimard.

Henry, Michel (1990). *Phénoménologie matérielle.* Paris: PUF.

Henry, Michel (1991). Quatre principes de la phénoménologie. *Revue de Métaphysique et de Morale, 96.1,* 3–26.

Holton, Gerald (1981). *L'imagination scientifique.* Paris: Gallimard.

Howe, Reed B. K. 1991). Introspection: a Reassessment. *New Ideas in Psychology, 9,* 1, 25–44.

Hume, David (1739-40/1962). *Treatise of Human Nature.* Paris: Aubier-Montaigne.

Hume, David (1748/1947). *An Enquiry Concerning Human Understanding.* Paris: Aubier-Montaigne.

Humphrey, George (1951). *Thinking, an introduction to its experimental psychology.* London: Methuen.

Husserl (1925). Über die Reden Gotamo Buddhos. *Husserliana* XXVII. Dordrecht: Kluwer.

Husserl, Edmund (1939/1973). *Experience and Judgment.* Evanston: Northwestern University Press.

Husserl, Edmund (1954). *Die Krisis der europäischen Wissenschaften und die transzendentale Phänomenologie.* The Hague: Martinus Nijhoff.

Husserl, Edmund (1956–1959). *Erste Philosophie I.* The Hague: Martinus Nijhoff.

Husserl, Edmund (1956–1959). *Erste Philosophie II.* The Hague: Martinus Nijhoff.

Husserl, Edmund (1960). *Cartesian Meditations.* The Hague: Martinus Nijhoff.

Husserl, Edmund (1962). *Phänomenologische Psychologie.* The Hague: Nijhoff.

Husserl, Edmud (1964). *The Phenomenology of Internal Time-Consciousness.* Bloomington: Indiana University Press.

Husserl, Edmund (1966). *Analysen zur passiven synthesis.* The Hague: Martinus Nijhoff.

Husserl, Edmund (1970). *Logical Investigations.* New York: Routledge.

Husserl, Edmund (1973a/b/c). *Zur Intersubjektivität.* Den Haag: Martinus Nijhoff.

Husserl, Edmund (1974). *Formale und transcendentale Logik.* Den Haag: Martinus Nijhoff.

Husserl, Edmund (1982). *Ideas* I. The Hague: Martinus Nijhoff.

Husserl, Edmund (1991). Lettre à Hofmannsthal. *La part de l'œil: Art et phénoménologie, 7,* Brussels, 13–19.

Husserl, Edmund (1993). *Die Krisis der europäischen Wissenschaften und die transzendentale Phänomenologie. Ergänzungsband. Texte aus dem Nachlaß (1934–1937).* Dordrecht: Kluwer.

Husserl, Edmund (1997). *Thing and Space.* Boston: Kluwer.

Jackendoff, Ray (1987). *Consciousness and the Computational Mind.* Cambridge: MIT Press.

James, William (1890). *The Principles of Psychology.* New York: MacMillan.

Jeannerod, Marc (1994). The representing brain: Neural correlates of motor intention and imagery. *Behavior and Brain Science, 17,* 187–245.

Julezs, Bela (1971). *Foundation of Cyclopean Perception.* Chicago: Chicago University Press.

Kelkel, Arion Lothar (1957). Réflexions husserliennes. *Revue de Métaphysique et de Morale.*

Kern, Iso (1962/1977). Die drei Wege zur transcendental-phänomenologischen Reduktion in der Philosophie Edmund Husserls. *Tidjschrift voor Filosophie* (English translation in Elliston Frederick & Peter Mc Cormick. *Husserl. Expositions and Apprasails*). London: Notre Dame Press.

Kern, Iso (1988). The Structure of Consciousness according to Xuanzang. *Journal of the British Society for Phenomenology, 19*, 282–295.

Kosslyn, Stephen M. (1994). *Image and Brain, The Resolution of the Imagery Debate.* Cambridge: MIT Press.

Laloy, Jean (Ed.). (1978). *Récits d'un pélerin russe à son père spirituel.* Paris: Seuil.

Landgrebe, Ludwig (1963). *Der Weg der Phänomenologie.* Gütersloh: Gerd Mohn.

Landgrebe, Ludwig (1982). Der phänomenologische Begriff der Erfahrung. *Faktizität und Individuation* (pp. 58–70). Hamburg: F. Meiner.

Latour, Bruno (1987/1995). *Science in Action: How to Follow Scientists and Engineers through Society.* Cambridge: Harvard University Press.

Latour, Bruno (1995). *We Have Never Been Modern.* Cambridge: Harvard University Press.

Laycok, Stephen (1994). *Mind as Mirror and the Mirroring of Mind: Buddhist Reflections on Western Phenomenology.* New York: SUNY.

Leahey, Thomas Hardy (1987). *A History of Psychology.* Prentice-Hall: Englewood Cliffs.

Leder, Drew (1991). *The Absent Body.* Chicago: Chicago Univ. Press.

Lee, Nam-In (1993). *Edmund Husserls Phänomenologie der Instinkte.* Dordrecht: Kluwer.

Levinas, Emmanuel (1930/1973). *The Theory of Intuition in Husserl's Phenomenology.* Evanston: Northwestern University Press.

Levinas, Emmanuel (1978). *Autrement qu'être ou au delà de l'essence.* Den Haag: Martinus Nijhoff.

Levinas, Emmanuel (1988). *En découvrant l'existence avec Husserl et Heidegger.* Paris: Vrin.

Libet, Benjamin (1985). Unconscious cerebral initiative and the role of conscious will in voluntary action. *Behavior and Brain Sciences, 8*, 529–566.

Livet, Pierre (1997). *Penser le pratique.* Paris: Klinsieck.

Lobo, Carlos (2000). *Le phénoménologue et ses exemples.* Paris: Kimé.

Loy, David (1991). *Non-Duality.* Yale UP.

Lutz, Antoine, Jean-Philippe Lachaux, Jacques Martinerie & Francisco J. Varela (2002). Guiding the study of brain dynamics using first-person data: Synchrony Patterns correlate with on-going conscious states during a simple visual task. *Proceedings of National Academy of Sciences.*

Lutz, Antoine (2002). Prelude to a neurophenomenological study of stereoscopic vision. *Theoria Scientiarum* [Special Issue "Embodiment", Shaun Gallagher & Natalie Depraz (Eds.)].

Lyons, William E. (1986). *The Disappearance of Introspection.* Cambridge: MIT Press.

Maine de Biran (1807/1932). *Essai sur les fondements de la psychologie et sur les rapports avec l'étude de la nature.* Paris: Alcan.

Mandler, Jean-Matter et George Mandler (1964). *Thinking from Association to Gestalt.* New York: John Wiley & sons.

Mangan, Bruce (1993). Taking phenomenology seriously: The "fringe" and its implications for cognitive research. *Consciousness and Cognition, 2*, 89–108.

Marion, Jean-Luc (1989). *Réduction et donation, Recherches sur Husserl, Heidegger et la phénoménologie.* Paris: PUF.

Maturana, Humberto & Francisco Varela (1992). *The Tree of Knowledge.* Boston: New Science Library/Shambhala.

Mazis, Glen (1993). *Emotion and Embodiment: A fragile ontology.* Evanston: Northwestern University Press.

McInerney, Peter (1991). *Time and Experience.* Philadelphia: Temple University Press.

Marquer, Josette (1995). Variabilité intra- et inter-individuelle dans les stratégies cognitives: l'exemple du traitement des couples de letters. In J. Lautrey (Ed.), *Universel et différentiel en psychologie* (pp. 107–130). Paris: PUF.

Merleau-Ponty, Maurice (1945/1962). *Phenomenology of Perception.* New York: Humanities Press.

Merleau-Ponty, Maurice (1968). *The Visible and the Invisible.* Evanston: Northwestern University Press.

Merleau-Ponty Maurice (1977). *Les sciences de l'homme et la phénoménologie* (pp. 1–77). Paris: Centre de Documentation Universitaire.

Mipham, Sakyong (1999). *The Nine Stages of Shamatha.* Transcript. Shambhala.

Mishrahi, Robert (1996). *La jouissance de l'être: le sujet et son désir. Essai d'anthropologie philosophique.* La Versanne: Encre Marine.

Moore, Francisc Charles Timothy (1970). *The Psychology of Maine de Biran.* Oxford: Clarendon.

Montaigne, Michel Eyquem de (1906). *Essais.* Bordeaux: Fortunat Strowski.

Montavont, Anne (1994). Le phénomène de l'affection dans les analyses sur la synthèse passive. *Alter, 2.*

Montebello, Pierre (1994). *La décomposition de la pensée.* Grenoble: Millon.

Moustakas, Clark (1994), *Phenomenological Research Methods.* Sage Publications.

Murphy, Ronald T. (1980). *Hume and Husserl.* Den Haag: Martinus Nijhoff.

Nagaï, Shin (1993). *Edmund Husserls Phänomenologie der Instinkte.* Review of Nam-In Lee. *Alter, 3,* Paris.

Nagel, Thomas (1974). What is it like to be a bat? *The Philosophical Review.*

Namgyal, Tashi (1984). *Mahamudra: The Quintessence of Mind and Meditation.* Boston: Shambhala.

Neisser, Ulrich (Ed.). (1982). *Memory Observed: remembring in natural contexts.* New York: Freeman and Company.

Nisbett, Richard E. & Timothy DeCamp Wilson (1977). Telling More than we can Know: Verbal reports on mental processes. *Psychological Review, 84,* 3, 231–259.

Nishitani, Keiji (1983). *Religion and Nothingness.* California: UP.

Patocka, Jan (1992). *Introduction à la phénoménologie.* Grenoble: J. Millon.

Pessoa, Luis, Evan Thompson, & Alva Noë (1998). Finding Out About Filling In: A Guide to Perceptual Completion for Visual Science and the Philosophy of Perception. *Behavior and Brain Sciences, 21,* 723–802.

Pitkin, Anabella (2001). Scandalous Ethics: Infinite Presence with Suffering. In Evan Thompson (Ed.), *Between Ourselves: Second Person Issues in the Study of consciousness.* London: Imprint Academic.

Philips, Michael (1981). Is Kant's practical reason practical? *Journal of Value Inquiry, 15,* 95–108.

Piaget, Jean (1937/1974). *La construction du réel chez l'enfant.* Neuchâtel: Delachaux et Niestlé.

Piaget, Jean (1950). *Introduction à l'épistémologie génétique,* 3 vols. Paris: PUF.

Piaget, Jean (1968). *Sagesse et illusion de la philosophie.* Paris: PUF.

Piaget, Jean (1977). Recherches sur l'abstraction réfléchissante. In: *L'abstraction de l'ordre des relations spatiales EEG,* Tome XXXV. Paris: PUF.

Picton Terence W. & Stuss Donald T. (1994). Neurobiology of conscious experience. *Current Biology, 4,* 256–265.

Piguet, Jean-Claude (1975). *La connaissance de l'individuel et la logique du réalisme.* Neuchâtel: La Baconnière.

Posner Michael I. (1994). Attention: The mechanisms of consciousness. *Proceedings of National Academy of Sciences (USA), 91,* 7398–7403.

Posner, Michal I. & Marcus E. Raichle (1994). *Images of the Mind.* New York: Scientific American Library, Freeman.

Radford, John (1974). Reflections on Introspection. *American Psychologist, 29,* 245–250.

Richir, Marc (1984). *Phénoménologie et institution symbolique.* Grenoble: Millon.

Ricoeur, Paul (1950/1988). *Philosophie de la volonté I. Le volontaire et l'involontaire.* Paris: Aubier.

Ricoeur, Paul (1996). *Le conflit des interprétations, Essais d'herméneutique.* Paris: Seuil.

Ricoeur, Paul (1997). Le "questionnement à rebours" (*die Rückfrage*) et la réduction des idéalités dans la *Krisis* de Husserl et *l'Idéologie allemande* de Marx. *Alter, 5,* Paris.

Rizzolatti, Giacomo, Luciano, Fadiga, Leonardo Gogassi & Vittorio Gallese (1997). The space around us. *Science, 277.*

Rorty, Richard (1970). Incorrigibility as the mark of the mental. *Journal of Philosophy, 67,* 399–424.

Rorty, Richard (1971/1979). *Philosophy and the Mirror of Nature.* Princeton University Press.

Rorty, Richard (1982). *The Consequences of Pragmatism.* Brighton: The Harvester Press.

Rotman, Brian (1993). *Ad Infinitum: The Ghost in Turing's Machine.* Stanford: Stanford University Press.

Sartre, Jean-Paul (1940). *L'imaginaire.* Paris: Gallimard.

Scheler, Max (1986). *Gesammelte Werke.* Bonn: Bouvier.

Schön, A. Donald (1983). *The reflective practitioner.* New York: Basic book.

Schön, A. Donald (1990). *Educating the reflexive practitioners.* San Francisco: Jossey-Bass Publishers.

Schotte, Jean-Claude (1997). *La raison éclatée, Pour une dissection de la connaissance.* Brussels: DeBoeck University.

Schuhman, Karl (1988). *Husserls Staatsphilosophie.* Freiburg/München: K. Alber Verlag.

Searle, John (1992). *The Rediscovery of the Mind.* Cambridge: MIT Press.

Sells, Michael (1994). *Mystical Languages of Unsaying.* Chicago: Chicago UP.

Sextus Empiricus (1997). *Esquisses pyrrhoniennes.* Paris: Seuil.

Shantideva (1996). *The Bodhisattva's Way of Life,* Boston: Shambhala.

Shapin, Steven (1994). *Leviathan and the Air Pump.* Princeton: Princeton University Press.

Shapin, Steven (1995). *A Social History of Truth.* Chicago: University of Chicago Press.

Shepard, Roger N. (1990). *Mind's Sight*. New York: Freeman & Company.

Shepard, Roger N. & Lynn A. Cooper (1992). *Mental Images and their Transformation*. Cambridge: MIT Press.

Shoemaker, Sydney (1975). Functionalism and qualia. *Philosophical Studies, 27*, 291–315.

Singer, Wolf (1993). Synchronization of cortical activity and its putative role in information processing and learning. *Annual Review of Physiology, 55*, 349–374.

Spiegelberg, Herbert (1975). *Doing Phenomenology*. The Hague: Martinus Nijhoff.

Steels Luc & Rodney Brooks (Eds.). (1993). *The Artificial Life route to Artificial Intelligence: Situatedness, emergent functionality and symbol grounding*. New Jersey: LEA.

Steinbock, Anthony and Natalie Depraz (Eds.). (2002). *The Phenomenon of Attention between Theory and Practice*. Proceedings from Conferences at The Touch of Nature and at the Collège International de Philosophie (Southern Illinois University, April 2001/Paris, May 2002, co-organized by N. Depraz and A. Steinbock). Forthcoming.

Stengers, Isabelle (1994). *L'invention des sciences modernes*. Paris: La Découverte.

Streng, Frederick J. (1967). *Emptiness: A Study in Religious Meaning*. Nashville: Abingdon Press.

Szilasi, Wilhelm (1959). *Einführung in die Phänomenologie Husserls*. Tübingen.

Thich Nhat Hanh (1991). *Old Path, White Clouds*. Berkeley: Parallax Press.

Thompson, Evan (Ed.) (2001). *Between Ourselves: Second Person Issues in the Study of consciousness*. London: Imprint Academic.

Thompson, Evan & Francisco Varela (2001). Radical Embodiment: Neural dynamics and conscious experience. *Trends in Cognitive Science, 5* (10), 418–425.

Tilliette, Xavier (1995). *L'Intuition Intellectuelle de Kant à Hegel*. Paris: Vrin.

Titchener, Edouard Bradford (1909). *Lectures on the Experimental psychology of Thought Processes*. New York: Macmillan.

Titchener, Edouard Bradford (1912). The Schema of Introspection. *American Journal of Psychology, 23*, 485-508.

Trungpa, Chögyam (1972). *Meditation in action*. Boulder: Shambhala.

Trungpa, Chögyam (1979). *1979 Hinayana-Mahayana Seminary*. Boulder.

Trungpa, Chögyam (1989). *Glimpses of Abhidharma*. Boston: Shambala.

Trungpa, Chögyam (1993). *Training the Mind and cultivating Loving-kindness*. Boston: Shambhala.

Trungpa, Chögyam (1995). *The Heart of Meditation*. Boston: Shambhala.

Varela, Francisco (1979). *Principles of Biological Autonomy*. New York: Elsevier North Holland.

Varela, Francisco (1987). *The Tree of Knowledge: The Biological Roots of Human Understanding*. Boston: New Science Library.

Varela, Francisco (1988). *Cognitive Science. A Cartography of Current Ideas*.

Varela, Francisco, Evan Thompson & Eleonor Rosch (1991). *The embodied mind*. Cambridge: MIT Press.

Varela, Francisco (1995). Resonant Cell Assemblies: A new approach to cognitive functions and neuronal synchrony. *Biological Research, 28*, 81–95.

Varela, Francisco (1996a). *Invitation aux Sciences Cognitives*. Paris: Seuil.

Varela, Francisco (1996b). Neurophenomenology: a Methodological remedy for the hard problem. *Journal of Consciousness Studies, 3*, 330–350.

Varela, Francisco (1997). The naturalization of phenomenology as the transcendence of nature. *Alter, 5.* Paris.

Varela, Francisco (1999a). *Ethical Know-how.* Stanford: Stanford University Press.

Varela, Francisco (1999b). The Specious Present: The neurophenomenology of present time consciousness. In *Naturalizing Phenomenology: Contemporary Issues on Phenomenology and Cognitive Science.* Stanford: Stanford University Press.

Varela, Francisco & Natalie Depraz (1999). At the source of time: Valence and the constitutional dynamics of affect. *Ar@base.* Electronic Journal: http://www.arobase. In hard copy in Presses Universitaires de Rouen, S. Gallagher (Ed.), (2002).

Varela, Francisco & Jonathan Shear (Eds.). (1999). *The View from Within: First-person approaches to the study of consciousness.* London: Imprint Academic.

Varela, Francisco (2000). Pour une phénoménologie de la Sunyata. I. In N. Depraz, & J.-Fr. Marquet (Eds.), *La gnose, une question philosophique. Actes du Colloque de la Sorbonne-Paris-IV (16-17-18 octobre 1997).* Paris: Cerf.

Varela, Francisco (2001), Jean-Philippe Lachaux, Eugenio Rodriguez & Jacques Martinerie. The brainweb: Phase synchronization and large-scale integration. *Nature Reviews Neuroscience, 2,* 229–239.

Varela, Francisco & Natalie Depraz (2002). Imagining. Embodiment, phenomenology and transformation. In A. B. Wallace (Ed.), *Buddhism and Science: Breaking the Ground.* Columbia University Press.

Vasubhandhu (1980). *Abhidharmakosa* (1923–1931). French translation by L. de La Vallée Poussin, Nouv. Éd. anastatique, prés. by E. Lamotte. Bruxelles: Institut belge des Hautes études chinoises.

Vermersch, Pierre (1993). Pensée privée et représentation pour l'action. In Weill A., P. Rabardel & D. Dubois (Eds.), *Représentation pour l'action* (pp. 209–232). Toulouse: Octarès.

Vermersch, Pierre (1994). *L'entretien d'explicitation, en formulation initiale et en formation continue.* Paris: ESF.

Vermersch, Pierre & Delphine Arbeau (1996). La mémorisation des oeuvres musicales chez les pianistes. *Médecine des Arts, 18,* 24–30.

Vermersch, Pierre (1997). Se référer. Questions de méthode. *Alter, 5.* Paris.

Vermersch, Pierre (1999). Introspection as practice. In F. Varela & J. Shear (Eds.), *The view from within. First-person approaches to the study of consciousness.* London: Imprint Academic.

Voutsinas, Dimitri (1964). *La psychologie de Maine de Biran.* Paris: S.I.E.P.

Waldenfels, Bernhardt (1980). *Der Spielraum des Verhaltens.* Frankfurt: Suhrkamp.

Waldenfels, Bernhardt (1998). L'auto-référence de la phénoménologie. In N. Depraz, & M. Richir (Eds.), *Eugen Fink. Actes du Colloque Eugen Fink de Cerisy-la-Salle.* Amsterdam: Rodopi.

Wallace, Alan B. (1998). *The Bridge of Quiescence: Experiencing Tibetan Buddhist Meditation.* Chicago: Open Court.

Wallace, Alan B. (1999). The Buddhist Tradition of samatha. In F. Varela & J. Shear (Eds.), *The view from within. First-person approaches to the study of consciousness.* London: Imprint Academic.

Watt, Henry J. (1905). Experimentelle Beiträge zu einer Theorie des Denkens. *Archiv für die gesamte psychologie, 4,* 289–436.

Wundt, Wilhelm (1874/1904). *The Principles of Empirical Psychology.* New York: Macmillan.

Zahavi, Dan (1999). *Self-Awareness and Alterity.* Evanston: Northwestern University Press.

Glossary of terms

With this glossary of selected key-terms, we wish to help the reader to become familiar with the different research fields we relied on in this integrative attempt at describing the act of becoming aware. Our hope is that it may contribute to invent readers open to all these fields and able to access them. In short, we want not only to reach phenomenologists, cognitive scientists, applied psychologists, and practitioners of spiritual disciplines, considered as separate classes of readers, but also give birth to a new kind of reader, one who, from wherever he/she starts from, naturally finds him/herself led into foreign areas, but in such a way that a higher ("eidetic") unity becomes visible: that of becoming aware.

We wish to thank E. Thompson and A. Lutz for their inspiring comments and their help in re-writing some of the following definitions.

N. D.

Phenomenology

apodicticity: *apodeiksis* is Greek for "a proof that is necessary and absolutely founded". It is the highest and most constraining level of truth. A synonym for it is undoubtedness.

constitution: the activity of a subject through which an external object or a lived inner experience is given to me and acquires a meaning for me.

givenness: the very process through which an external object or a lived inner experience imposes itself on me so as to become conscious for me, which leads me to endow it with a meaning, to constitute it as a unity of meaning. When the constitution is a willful, active appropriation of the object by the subject, the giveness combines the passivity of the coming of the object to my consciousness and my active welcoming of it.

eidetic: from *eidos*, essence in Greek. It is a modality of intuition and characterizes the process of variation, which is a specific method in phenomenology, belonging to the different forms of "reduction". The eidetics is the theory of the essences, not as abstracted entities separated from our sensory lived experience, but as embodied in our common spatio-temporal intuition as concrete singularities. Through of the activity of variation, I observe the different features of an external object or of a lived inner experience and discriminate what intrinsically belongs to it and what remains acccidental to its definition. According to its originally mathematical meaning, I vary the features, that is I change them or substitute one for another, using first my perceptual knowledge but also extending it to imaginary features in order to broaden the scope of the possibilities inherently contained in the object. While changing the features, I gradually set aside the contingent ones, opening the way for the invariant structure of the object.

epoche: the inaugural gesture of the phenomenological method called the "reduction", which consists in a general suspension of every belief and prejudices and is completed through an interruption of the flow of our unexamined thoughts and emotions. This gesture of breaching the taken-for-granted attitude is both definitive and unceasing. It is both complete and has to be reaccomplished again and again. It is the absolute pre-requisit of the reduction, the generic name for the phenomenological method.

evidence: the name of truth in phenomenology, which has a strong intuitive meaning. In its genuine meaning, it is linked to "vision" (*intueri* in Latin means "to see", and *Evidenz* in German, like "évidence" in French, contains the Latin root *videre*: to see). Nonetheless, it is not an organic sensory vision, but a formalized or inner one, a capacity of feeling and living the events while embodying them.

horizon: the very dimension of the our experience of any object, basically perceptual, but also remembered and imaginative. The world itself is given to us through the structure of its horizons. The object is given to me through one of its profiles at a time, which corresponds to its "inner horizon", and as such, I can identify it as being a whole: I don't need to walk around it to apprehend it as a complete unity. The horizons of the object are also external, and designate the immediate spatial, temporal, affective and meaning context of the object.

intentionality: the very structure of consciousness, by which it is not a closed up polar unity but is constitutively open to the objects of the world. It qualifies every act of consciousness (perceptual, remembering, imaginative, empathetic, predicative, volitional), and corresponds to the process through which we direct our attention to an object and provide it with a first meaning. Thus intentionality combines directedness and openness, and leads to question the dichotomy between object and subject. Its technical name is the noetico-noematical correlation, noetic meaning the subjective of the lived experience while noematic means the objective side of the world.

life-world: the unique embodied anchorage of all our experiences as subjects. It has a sensory but also a practical, historical, sedimented and communitarian meaning.

living present: contrary to the present as it is usually understood as a punctual unity or as an instantaneous moment, the living present is a dynamical extended presence including what has just occured as past (called retention) and what is just about to happen as an anticipation (called protention).

reduction: the generic name for the phenomenological method, through which my relation and my attitude towards the world (objects and others) is radically changed. We can distinguish three main gestures of the reduction, which equally modify or alter my subjective identity as ego: first and most basically, the reflective conversion is the process through which I don't get stuck to objects but look at them through the way I am accessing them, that is, through my perceptual activity; I thus modify my attitude and observe the intentional act and not the object in itself; second and more locally, the eidetic reduction, through which I modify my attitude and don't get stuck to the facts but attempt to reach their essence; finally and radically, the transcendental epoche, which leads me to suspend the immediate, pre-given reality of the world and of objects and to question their meaning for me.

static/genetic phenomenology: the key methodology in phenomenology. Static phenomenology corresponds to an experiential logic of stratification of the different acts of consciousness, starting from perception and giving way to remembering, imagination and empathy. The genetic method was developed a bit later by Husserl, in the twenties, in order to account for the process through which the objects and the lived experiences of a subject are produced, or born. Whereas the focus of the static method is the object or the lived experience as a leading thread of our intentional activity, the genetic approach concentrates on the very process of emergence of the object or the lived experience in my consciousness.

transcendental: it designates the ego, the subjectivity, but also the experience as such. Contrary to the Kantian meaning, which identifies transcendental with formal conditions of possibility of our experience, thereby seeing *a contradictio in adjecto* in the very idea of a "transcendental experience", Husserl understands the transcendental as a genuine level of our possible experience as subjects. It corresponds to the attitude I am able to reach as soon as I accomplish the gesture of the reductive method. My experience is transcendental when I radically change my attitude towards the world, the objects and the others, that is, whan I become able to observe them at a distance without being dellusioned by them.

Cognitive sciences

coupling: whenever the conduct of two or more unities is such that the conduct of each one is a function of the conduct of the others. (Spec. structural coupling: whenever there is a history of recurrent interactions leading to the structural congruence between two (or more) systems.)

emergence: the name is derived from the idea that many cognitive tasks (such as vision and memory) seem to be handled best by systems made up of many simple components, which, when connected to appropriate rules, give rise to global behavior corresponding to the desired task. For connectionists a representation consists in the correspondence between such an emergent global state and properties of the world, it is not a function of particular symbols.

enaction: the enactive approach is born from a deeper dissatisfaction than the connectionist search for alternatives to symbolic processing. It questions the centrality of the notion that cognition is fundamentally representation of a pregiven world by a pregiven mind but is rather the enactment of a world and a mind on the basis of a history of the variety of actions that a being in the world performs. The enactive approach takes seriously, then, the philosophical critique of the idea that the mind is a mirror of nature but goes further by addressing this issue from within the heartland of science.

qualia: qualitative data which refer to the conscious first hand experience of a subject.

nonlinear dynamical system: defines a dynamical system, that is a set of variables evolving through time, governed by a nonlinear differential equation (a differential equation has the form of $dz/dt = F(z,t)$ and a linear equation has the form of $F(ax + by) = a\,f(x) + b\,f(y)$). The study of such systems encompasses several recent disciplines such as the theory of chaos, theory of complexity or theory of self-organization. These disciplines provide formal tools to study how complex behaviors can emerge in systems like the brain or the heart. In such systems, the dynamics is shifting constantly like the flow of a river in which eddies or vortices are transiently formed and then disappear. Three concepts are central in this field to characterize, in a deterministic way, the dynamical properties of such systems: *bifurcations, limit-cycle oscillations and chaos.* Bifurcations are changes in the qualitative behaviors of the dynamics. For instance, a change in one parameter can make a steady state become unstable and lead then to new oscillations. Variations in the temperature, for instance, can lead a fluid through a variety of possible states or patterns. Limit-cycle oscillations describe the ability to re-establish a stable oscillation following an external perturbation. For instance, electrical shocks on the heart modify transiently its dynamic which, then, can re-establish itself within a few seconds into its former frequency. Chaos, finally, refers to a sensitivity to initial conditions. Two initial states, extremely similar, can lead to two radically different behaviors. Bifurcation and chaos are important notions to account for the flexibility and adaptability of the living system. More generally, nonlinear dynamical systems have been proposed as a relevant framework to investigate how brain, behavior and human experience can be related.

phenomenal consciousness: the subjective experience associated with cognitive or mental events.

reduction/reductionism: in strict opposition with the phenomenological reduction, scientific reduction consists in explaining the multifarious components and dimensions of a phenomenon at one unique level, primarily material or neuronal. Reductionism therefore corresponds to a scientific stance which eliminates the variations of a given phenomenon and imposes on it a pre-given structure which is supposed to explain it completely.

synchrony: synchrony is defined mathematically as a stationary relation between the temporal structures (i.e. the phase) of two signals regardless of their amplitude. For example, a couple dancing the waltz expresses a form of synchrony. In neurophysiology, synchronization describes the temporal coordination of oscillating neuronal discharges in a large range of frequencies (from 4 to 80 Hz). This phenomenon is similar to spectators in a stadium doing the 'wave'. Neural synchrony has been proposed to act as an integrative mechanism selecting and transiently coordinating subsets of neurons. Integration can be either local, in a specific brain area, or large-scale, between a distributed networks of areas. This latter could underline the unity of a cognitive act.

third-person/first-person/second-person: the objective stance in contrast to the experiential, subjective stance. However, the former is a specific form of a socially distributed mediation, and the latter, although singular and unique, is far from a solipsistic private attitude forming the opposite of a external objective validation. The first-person accounts are also examined, expressed, thus opened up to an intersubjective validation. The second-person therefore is not so much a third pole than the mediating plastic continuity between first- and third persons, in its turn modulating and altering both through social accounts and intersubjective validation.

Tibetan Buddhism

Bodhicitta [Sanscrit]: *Bodhi* means "enlightenment," "awakening," and is cognate with the term *Buddha* (one who is enlightened or awakened). *Citta* means "mind." Thus *bodhicitta* means "mind of enlightenment" or "awakening mind," the attitude of mind that tends toward enlightenment, and hence buddhahood. *Bodhicitta* is said to have two aspects, absolute *bodhicitta* and relative *bodhicitta*. Absolute *bodhicitta* is the direct nondual realization of emptiness (*shunyata**). Relative *bodhicitta* is the aspiration to attain buddhahood and the attitude of loving-kindness and compassion toward all sentient beings. The classic text of Mahayana* Buddhism that discusses absolute and relative *bodhicitta* is *The Way of the Bodhisattva* (*Bodhisattvacaryavatara*) by the 8th century CE Indian philosopher Shantideva. For a translation based on the Tibetan text, see *Shantideva, The Way of the Bodhisattva,* translated by the Padmakara Translation Group (Boston: Shambala Press, 1997).

Bodhisattva [Sanscrit]: one who strives to attain enlightenment for the sake of all sentient beings. The activity of the bodhisattva is to develop *bodhicitta**. The term *bodhisattva* refers to individuals at many levels of realization – from those who have generated for the first time the aspiration to attain enlightenment, to those who have entered the bodhisattva path, which develops through ten stages and culminates in enlightenment, the attainment of buddhahood.

Dzogchen [Tibetan]: "The Great Perfection." A system of meditation practice and philosophy belonging to the Tibetan Nyingma* school of the Vajrayana* tradition of Indo-Tibetan Buddhism. In the Nyingma tradition, Dzogchen is considered the pinnacle of nonconceptual and nondual insight or gnosis. The great eighth century Indian Buddhist, Padmasambhava, revered in Tibet as the founding father of Tibetan Buddhism, stated the core of the Dzogchen practice of investigating the mind as follows:

> While steadily maintaining the gaze, place the awareness unwaveringly, steadily, clearly, nakedly and fixedly without having anything on which to meditate in the sphere of space. When stability increases, examine the con-

sciousness that is stable. Then gently release and relax. Again place it steadily and steadfastly observe the consciousness of that moment. What is the nature of that mind? Let it steadfastly observe itself. Is it something clear and steady or is it an emptiness that is nothing? Is there something there to recognize? Look again and report your experience to me! (Padmasambhava 1998:116).

Hinayana [Sanscrit]: one of the three vehicles of Buddhist teaching (the other two being Mahayana* and Vajrayana*). Literally it means "Lesser Vehicle." This term was originally a derogatory term introduced by the proponents of the Mahayana* (literally "Greater Vehicle) to differentiate their teachings, which emphasized the figure of the bodhisattva*, from those of other Buddhist schools, which emphasized individual liberation. Today the only surviving school of Hinayana Buddhism is the Theravada or "School of the Elders." To avoid the derogatory connotations, some scholars today prefer to translate "Hinayana" as "Individual Vehicle" and "Mahayana" as "Universal Vehicle." In Tibetan Buddhist presentations of the path of liberation, the Hinayana is called the "Path of Discipline," the Mahayana the "Path of Opening and Compassion," and the Vajrayana* the "Path of Transmutation" (see Kalu Rinpoche 1997).

Kagyu [Tibetan]: one of the four principal schools or lineages of Tibetan Buddhism. The Kagyu is known as "the tradition of practice" because of its emphasis on meditative discipline. The other three schools are the Nyingma*, the Gelug, and the Sakya.

Lojong [Tibetan]: mental training. The practice of cultivating bodhicitta.*

Mahayana [Sanscrit]: one of the three vehicles of Buddhist teaching (the other two being Hinayana* and Vajrayana*). Literally it means "Greater Vehicle." The term was originally introduced by its proponents to contrast with other Buddhists whom the Mahayanists derogatorily labeled Hinayana* (literally "Lesser Vehicle"). Whereas proponents of the Hinayana emphasized individual liberation, Mahayana proponents emphasized the bodhisattva* vow of dedicating oneself to the enlightenment of all sentient beings. To avoid the derogatory connotations, some scholars today prefer to translate "Mahayana" as "Universal Vehicle" and "Hinayana" as "Individual Vehicle." In Tibetan Buddhist presentations of the path of liberation, the Hinayana is called the "Path of Discipline," the Mahayana the "Path of Opening and Compassion," and the Vajrayana* the "Path of Transmutation" (see Kalu Rinpoche 1997).

Mahamudra [Tibetan]: "Great Seal." A system of meditation practice and philosophy belonging to the Tibetan Kagyu* school of the Vajrayana* tradition of Indo-Tibetan Buddhism. It is considered to be the culmination of all practices and essentially one with Dzogchen* of the Nyingma* lineage. The "sign" or "seal" referred to is the emptiness (*shunyata**) of all phenomena, and to the state that never departs from the primordial wisdom of emptiness.

Nyingma [Tibetan]: "The Old School." The oldest of the four principal schools or lineages of Tibetan Buddhism (the other three being the Kagyu*, Gelug, and Sakya).

Shamatha [Sanscrit]: meditative quiescence or "calm abiding." A basic meditation practice common to Buddhist and non-Buddhist traditions, in which one calms the mind and enhances the stability of attention. In Tibetan Buddhism, shamatha is considered to be an indispensible prerequisite for the cultivation of contemplative insight (*vipashyana**).

Shunyata [Sanscrit]: "Emptiness." The ultimate nature of all phenomena, their lack of inherent existence. It is one of the central notions of Mahayana* Buddhism. According to the Madhyamaka ("Middle Way") school of Indo-Tibetan philosophy founded by the Indian philosopher Nagarjuna (c. second century CE), all phenomena lack (are empty of) inherent existence, i.e., existence independent of causes, parts, and conceptual imputation. Nothing exists that does not depend upon causes, components, and mental or conceptual imputation upon those causes and components.

Tonglen [Tibetan]: "Giving and taking." A meditative practice in which one gives all of one's virtue and well-being to another and accepts in exchange all of that person's pain and suffering.

Vajrayana: "Diamond Vehicle" or "Adamantine Vehicle." One of the three vehicles of Buddhist teaching (the other two being Hinayana* and Mahayana*). The Vajrayana can be seen as a branch of the Mahayana. Whereas the main teachings of the Mahayana are based on texts called sutras (discourses of the Buddha), the Vajrayana teachings are based on texts called tantras. Its essential teachings are transmitted orally, however, and emphasize directly realizing the nature of the mind and removing afflictions generated in the mind.

Vipashyana [Sanscrit]: "Insight" or "clear seeing." A meditative practice belonging to Buddhism, in which one cultivates awareness of the moment-to-moment arising and passing of experiences.

Sources

Depraz, N. (1995). *Transcendance et incarnation. Le statut de l'intersubjectivité comme altérité à soi.* Paris: Vrin.

Depraz, N. (1999). *Husserl.* Paris: A. Colin, coll. "Synthèses".

Kalu, Rinpoche (1997). *Luminous Mind: The Way of the Buddha.* Boston: Wisdom Publications.

Maturana, H. R. & Varela, F. J. (1998). *The Tree of Knowledge. The Biological Roots of Human Understanding* (1987). Boston & London: Shambhala.

Padmasambhava (1998). *Natural Liberation: Padmasambava's Teachings on the Six Bardos.* (Commentary by Gyatrul Rinpoche, translated by B. Alan Wallace). Boston: Wisdom Publications.

Trungpa, Chögyam (1998). *Training the Mind and Cultivating Loving-Kindness.* Boston & London: Shambhala.

Varela, F. J., Thompson, E. & Rosch, E. (1991). *The Embodied Mind. Cognitive Science and Human Experience.* Cambridge: MIT Press.

Index

Advances in Consciousness Research

A complete list of titles in this series can be found on the publishers' website, *www.benjamins.com*

12   STAMENOV, Maxim I. (ed.): Language Structure, Discourse and the Access to Consciousness. 1997. xii, 364 pp.

11   PYLKKÖ, Pauli: The Aconceptual Mind. Heideggerian themes in holistic naturalism. 1998. xxvi, 297 pp.

10   NEWTON, Natika: Foundations of Understanding. 1996. x, 211 pp.

9   Ó NUALLÁIN, Seán, Paul Mc KEVITT and Eoghan Mac AOGÁIN (eds.): Two Sciences of Mind. Readings in cognitive science and consciousness. 1997. xii, 490 pp.

8   GROSSENBACHER, Peter G. (ed.): Finding Consciousness in the Brain. A neurocognitive approach. 2001. xvi, 326 pp.

7   MAC CORMAC, Earl and Maxim I. STAMENOV (eds.): Fractals of Brain, Fractals of Mind. In search of a symmetry bond. 1996. x, 359 pp.

6   GENNARO, Rocco J.: Consciousness and Self-Consciousness. A defense of the higher-order thought theory of consciousness. 1996. x, 220 pp.

5   STUBENBERG, Leopold: Consciousness and Qualia. 1998. x, 368 pp.

4   HARDCASTLE, Valerie Gray: Locating Consciousness. 1995. xviii, 266 pp.

3   JIBU, Mari and Kunio YASUE: Quantum Brain Dynamics and Consciousness. An introduction. 1995. xvi, 244 pp.

2   ELLIS, Ralph D.: Questioning Consciousness. The interplay of imagery, cognition, and emotion in the human brain. 1995. viii, 262 pp.

1   GLOBUS, Gordon G.: The Postmodern Brain. 1995. xii, 188 pp.